The Civil Rights Movement

PROBLEMS IN AMERICAN CIVILIZATION

The Civil Rights Movement

Edited and with an introduction by

Jeffrey O. G. Ogbar
University of Connecticut

Houghton Mifflin Company   Boston   New York

For the Ancestors

Editor-in-Chief: Jean L. Woy
Sponsoring Editor: Jeff Greene
Editorial Assistant: Noria Morales
Project Editor: Jane Lee
Editorial Assistant: Talia Kingsbury
Associate Production/Design Coordinator: Christine Gervais
Manufacturing Manager: Florence Cadran
Senior Marketing Manager: Sandra McGuire

Cover Image: Flip Schulke/CORBIS

Printed in the U.S.A.

Library of Congress Control Number: 2001133323

ISBN: 0-618-07737-5

23456789-CRS-06 05 04 03

The Editor

Jeffrey Ogbonna Green Ogbar was born in Chicago, Illinois, a grandchild of those who traveled in the Great Migration from the South. He was raised in Los Angeles, California. Jeffrey graduated with honors and received his B.A. in History and a minor in African studies from Morehouse College in Atlanta (1991). He earned his M.A. (1993) and Ph.D. (1997) in U.S. History with a minor in African studies from Indiana University in Bloomington. In 1993, the National Council on Black Studies awarded Jeffrey the Ella Baker–W. E. B. Du Bois Essay Award for its graduate division contest. In 1996–1997 he was named a Jeffrey Campbell dissertation fellow at St. Lawrence University in New York, while he completed his dissertation. Since 1997, he has taught at the University of Connecticut's Department of History.

Jeffrey O. G. Ogbar's research interests include the twentieth-century United States with a focus in African American history. From 1999 to 2000, Professor Ogbar worked as a research fellow at Harvard University's W. E. B. Du Bois Institute for Afro-American Research while completing his book manuscript, *Black Power: The Nation of Islam, the Black Panther Party, and African American Identity, 1960–1981*. In the fall of 2001, Professor Ogbar was a scholar-in-residence at the Schomburg Center for Research in Black Culture in New York City while working on his second book manuscript, which focuses on the culture and politics of hip hop.

Contents

Preface

The civil rights movement is one of the most significant events in modern American history. America, long resistant to granting full citizenship rights and privileges to all of its citizens, experienced significant cultural and political shifts in the years following World War II. Since the 1960s, historians and others have attempted to explain what brought about these changes. How far back into history does the civil rights movement extend? Who were its major proponents? What roles did region, class, and gender play in the unfolding of civil rights activities? These and other questions are answered in this volume.

The introduction provides a general overview of the civil rights movement and contextualizes the scholarship in addition to placing the movement in a historical framework. Part I provides a foundation for the study of the struggle for civil rights by examining the origins of racial segregation in the nineteenth century and the methods used to maintain it. Part II offers essays on the social, political, and economic dynamics that gave rise to the civil rights movement. Part III examines the various ways in which activists mobilized to resist racial oppression in America. These essays reflect the tactical and philosophical diversity of the movement. Part IV provides essays that study the decline of the civil rights movement and the rise of the Black Power movement. The introductory notes help to clarify the thematic thrust of each essay and place each in context. The chronology provides the reader with a timeline of significant events in the rise and fall of legal codes that supported racial discrimination. The suggested reading offers a comprehensive bibliography of scholarship on the subject.

I wish to thank the authors and publishers of the works reprinted in this book for their cooperation. I would also like to thank the many helpful people at Houghton Mifflin who made this project happen, including Noria Morales who cut her teeth on it. Thanks to Lyn Holian for the great work with permissions. I also would like to extend great thanks to my editor Jeffrey Greene, who identified the need for this book and carefully carried it through to fruition.

J. O.

Introduction

Called the Second American Revolution by some, the modern civil rights movement is one of the most significant events in the development of American society. It ushered in a new era of race relations that had substantive effects beyond the borders of the United States. To echo the words of its most celebrated icon, Dr. Martin Luther King, Jr., the civil rights movement's mission was not solely the concern of freeing the oppressed; it also aimed to uplift the oppressor by encouraging him to transcend the inherent limitations of bigotry and prejudice. The struggle against racial discrimination is as old as the practices that circumscribed black freedom in the United States. In the colonial era, both free and enslaved Africans resisted white supremacy in its explicit and *de jure* forms. Though the activities to realize rights for blacks were largely met with white resistance and indifference, there was some white sympathy. Still, it was not until the Fourteenth and Fifteenth Amendments to the U.S. Constitution were passed in 1868 and 1870 (guaranteeing citizenship and voting rights, respectively) that African Americans received constitutional protection of their civil rights. These postbellum laws, however, were met with concerted activities to curtail new black freedoms.

Reconstruction laws, such as the Civil Rights Act of 1875, granted African Americans new access to the perquisites of American citizenship. Black men voted (women did not receive the right to vote until the Nineteenth Amendment was ratified in 1920), served on juries, and held office. In fact, African Americans were the majority of the lower houses in the state assemblies of South Carolina and Mississippi. There were black mayors, U.S. representatives, and senators. Despite this progress, resistance to legally recognized racial equality was immediate, with various white supremacist groups organizing during Reconstruction. The largest and most effective of these groups was the Ku Klux Klan (KKK), founded in 1866 in Pulaski, Tennessee by former Confederate soldiers. The KKK would become the most enduring and most destructive terrorist organization in the United States. It engaged in arson, bombing, rape, kidnapping, beating, and murder. As white resistance to equality intensified in the South, northern lawmakers in Congress grew less concerned with the extension and protection of civil rights. In 1877, following a disputed presidential election, the Republican Party agreed with the Democrats to withdraw federal troops from the South in return for the presidency. A Republican, Rutherford B. Hayes, took office and Reconstruction ended with a compromise that pulled federal troops from the South. Called the "Betrayal Compromise" by many African Americans, the Compromise of 1877 ushered in a new era of white supremacy across the South. Historian Rayford Logan calls the years after Reconstruction the nadir, or low point, in African American history.

After slavery was outlawed, a new ritualistic violence began to grow in the country. Lynching, a form of vigilante mob violence, erupted across the South and in very limited cases in the North and West. Between 1884 and 1900, over 2,500 people were victims of lynchings; the great majority were black. Though most victims of lynchings were black men, black children and black women, even visibly pregnant black women, were also victims. Typically, a black person was accused of a crime—real or imagined—against a white person. Infractions ranged from murder and rape to looking at or speaking to a white person "the wrong way."

In 1896, the U.S. Supreme Court heard the case of Homer Plessy, a black man, who challenged a Louisiana law requiring segregation on railroad cars. In *Plessy v. Ferguson,* the Supreme Court upheld the state law and provided federal sanction for racial segregation that lasted for nearly sixty years. The Court affirmed that "separate but equal" accommodations were constitutional. Accommodations, particularly in areas such as education and public parks, were never equal. Moreover, blacks were still denied employment, voting, and other civil rights. So despite federal, state, and local sanction of discrimination, resistance to white supremacy continued, as did violent repression in response.

The National Association for the Advancement of Colored People (NAACP), formed in 1909, and other organizations challenged these racist policies in the courts. Black resistance was manifested in other ways as well. The Universal Negro Improvement Association, a massive international black nationalist movement, and the Harlem Renaissance precipitated a new resilience and determination among black people who increasingly challenged discrimination. But it was not until after World War II that various efforts to guarantee full citizenship rights for all Americans achieved very visible, widespread levels of participation.

From the legal successes of the NAACP to the grassroots mobilization of the Montgomery Improvement Association and the philosophical development of nonviolence, the postwar era witnessed a profound shift in the way that racial politics played out. Women's organizations, such as the Women's Political Council in Montgomery, Alabama, and various religious organizations were essential to the early mobilization efforts of the civil rights movement. African Americans faced police dogs, high-pressure water hoses from firefighters, beatings and jail terms in their quest for rights due them as American citizens. Images of men, women, and children brutalized by law enforcement officials were embarrassing for the U.S. in the age of global media and cold war politics. Though slow to respond, the federal government eventually passed major legislation with the Civil Rights Act of 1964 and the 1965 Voting Rights Act. Despite these new laws, which fundamentally undermined codified white supremacy, a new more militant movement emerged from the civil rights struggle by 1966. The Black Power movement crystallized as African Americans increasingly demanded more access to education, jobs, and an end to police brutality. Some civil rights organizations, like the Student Nonviolent Coordinating Committee, embraced a more militant emphasis in their efforts. Also, new organizations, such as the Black Panther Party, formed and demanded revolutionary change.

The scholarship on the civil rights movement emerged as the events were taking place. Social scientists and journalists wrote dozens of books and scholarly articles on the civil rights movement between 1960 and 1970. Some of the earliest work done by historians, such as Howard Zinn's *The New Abolitionists* (1965), admittedly valorized the activists for their bravery and commitment to freedom against horrific obstacles. Though most books, such as Anthony Lewis's *The Second American Revolution* (1964), placed particular emphasis on the South, scholarship began to give more attention to the institutionalized barriers against black people in the North and West. Louis Lomax's *The Negro Revolt* (1962) touched on black nationalism. Historians August Meier and Elliot Rudwick's *Black Protest in the Sixties* (1970) provided a common narrative that placed civil rights activities firmly in the control of male-dominated spheres, secular and religious. Moreover, the movement was ostensibly about integration and thoroughly committed to the philosophy of non-violence. Harvard Sitkoff in *The Struggle for Black Equality* (1981, 1993) continued this approach.

William H. Chafe in *Civilities and Civil Rights: Greensboro, North Carolina and the Black Struggle for Freedom* (1980) provided an early major study by a historian that examined a specific local organizing effort. Chafe expanded his scope by giving more than terse attention to Black Power efforts as well as civil rights activity. Clayborne Carson's *In Struggle: SNCC and the Black Awakening of the 1960s* (1981) similarly highlighted how black nationalist radicalism developed out of the civil rights movement. Carson's work also gave more attention to the role of women in the movement. Many books, such as Deborah Gray White's *Too Heavy a Load* (1999) and Paul Giddings' *When and Where I Enter* (1984) examined women in the civil rights movement in the context of the large historical narrative of African American women. However, more research and work on women in the movement is needed.

Generally, scholarship, whether by a historian or not, characterizes African Americans as petitioning white America for full inclusion into the fabric of society. In *From Exclusion to Inclusion* (1992), an edited collection of articles on black political struggle, the struggle for political power is studied from the integrationist perspective without any consideration of the challenges offered by the black nationalist community. Dianne M. Pinderhughes's study (in that volume) of black political activity from the eighteenth century to the 1990s does not mention any nationalist organization, even in a peripheral context. Other articles are similar in their approach. To be fair, leaders of the civil rights struggle lauded integration. In fact, Martin Luther King, Jr. once called integration the "promised land" for black people. In the 1990s, however, scholarship moved away from this thesis.

While national leaders such as Roy Wilkins, executive secretary of the NAACP, and Whitney Young, head of the National Urban League, promoted integration and more cautious rhetoric, local members often had different objectives. Historians have begun to examine the dynamics of civil rights activity on the local level, considering the ideological chasms that sometimes erupted between local and national leaders. Integration was only one such issue. While all leaders in the movement—local and national—wanted desegregation, integration was not always at the forefront of activity. For example, some local people preferred better funded schools and control of the school board rather than sending black children to white schools. These local people did, however, believe that a child should have the right to attend any school in his/her area. Moreover, as scholars such as John Dittmer in *Local People* (1994) and Charles M. Payne in *I've Got the Light of Freedom* (1995) document, African Americans were also concerned with ending the vast human rights abuses that occurred under the system of white supremacy known as Jim Crow. Dittmer and Payne argue that the efforts of many local civil rights activists were not centered solely on integrating with whites. In fact, blacks were chiefly concerned with suffrage, desegregation (not necessarily integration), economic and legal justice. Black people organized to end terror campaigns and abuses from rape to lynching. As Dittmer explains, black people found a degree of self-determination in the creation of cooperatives and other black-controlled autonomous institutions. Local chapters of national organizations were often given considerable independence, thereby granting them the opportunity to create chapters that were more radical than the national leadership could tolerate, as David R. Colburn explains in *Racial Change and Community Crisis* (1985). Timothy Tyson examines this phenomenon in *Radio Free Dixie: Robert F. Williams and the Roots of Black Power* (1999). Many local chapters of moderate national organizations embraced a bold militancy and defiance that is generally associated with Black Power. Such staples of Black Power as the advocation of armed self-defense and the creation of independent black institutions can be found in the local activities of many civil rights organizations. These studies add new understanding to the influence that the civil rights movement had on the militant fervor of Black Power advocates outside of the South.

The historiography on the civil rights movement, as evident in this cursory overview, offers contrasting views of the same event and process. This, of course, is not unique. Historians often disagree on the interpretation of historical events, as the selections in this book illustrate. Part I of this text examines the development of legalized white supremacy in the nineteenth century and the practices used to maintain America's de facto caste system. C. Vann Woodward's essay explores the expansion of segregation from the North to the South in the antebellum years. As Woodward notes, the South was not the place of origin for the system known as Jim Crow, further reflecting the generally hostile world in which African Americans lived in the late nineteenth and early twentieth centuries. While migration north might provide a respite from the most virulent forms of white supremacy, blacks were confronted with it everywhere. Donald G. Neiman's book excerpt is a narrative about the process by which newly legislated black citizenship rights were eradicated by "redeemers"—Southern whites who sought to reestablish white supremacy after the Civil War. Charles Payne's essay studies the campaigns of violence used to subjugate and instill fear in African Americans. With the support of Southern law enforcement, terrorists operated as fundamental extensions of the state in the maintenance of white supremacy.

Part II explores the early years of the civil rights struggle, beginning in the 1940s. Waldo E. Martin's essay on the *Brown v. Board of Education* case examines the complexity of the ruling and its role, beyond education, in dismantling legalized racial discrimination. Adam Fairclough's study of Louisiana is a fascinating look at the local politics that surrounded the activities of the NAACP and other black activist organizations. Fairclough provides a look into the relations between class, race, and ideology in the black communities of the state.

The Birmingham campaign, explored by Harvard Sitkoff, extends the study of local efforts in the civil rights struggle in Part III. Leaders who led the desegregation effort in Birmingham considered the city to be "the most segregated city this side of Johannesburg, South Africa." As Sitkoff notes, the campaign gave immense attention to the larger struggle. It also underscored the pressing moral issues regarding the repression of American citizens who simply wanted to realize the rights guaranteed them by the Constitution. Donna Langston's essay on the Highlander Folk School focuses on the actions of women in the movement. The school trained many for civil rights activism, including women such as Rosa Parks and Septima Clark, who would become central to the struggle's success.

As Jack Bloom explains, African Americans encountered major cultural changes during the movement. These changes ensured a rejection of accommodationist politics, forcing tepid black leaders to either reassess their politics or risk losing prominence. Bloom demonstrates that the grassroots efforts significantly determined the larger perspectives of the struggle. Charles Payne elaborates on this idea (see Part I). But as August Meier and Elliot Rudwick show in their study of the Congress of Racial Equality, national leadership was not without agency. Ultimately, however, national leaders and local people were inextricably connected by the larger social and political impulses of their era.

Part IV explores the ideological shifts and tactical changes that emerged within the movement. Timothy Tyson's essay on Robert F. Williams reveals the early militant impulse of civil rights activism. William H. Chafe's study shows how a local southern community adapts to the militant thrust of Black Power. And Clayborne Carson's examination of SNCC uncovers internal conflict over ideological transformations in the movement. He describes how some leaders opted to leave the organization rather than continue along an ideological trajectory that had strayed from the organization's original aim.

In the final analysis, these essays provide a broad sweep of the civil rights movement and offer classic as well as new interpretations on a significant era in the history of America. As historians continue to explore the history of the civil rights movement, new ideas and perspectives will be presented that further enrich the scholarship and, hopefully, enhance our understanding of America's Second Revolution.

Chronology

1941 A. Philip Randolph, head of the Brotherhood of Sleeping Car Porters, founds the March on Washington Movement to protest discriminatory hiring practices in the war industry.

1942 Congress of Racial Equality (CORE) founded by pacifists.

1947 Journey for Reconciliation initiated by CORE, sending integrated activists into the South to resist segregation on interstate travel. Activists are arrested and beaten.

1948 President Harry S Truman desegregates the U.S. armed forces by executive order.

1950 The NAACP's Legal Defense team continues its legal victories when the Supreme Court rules against Texas law barring blacks access to law school in *Sweatt v. Painter.*

1951 A terrorist bomb murders Henry Tyson Moore, President of Florida NAACP, on Christmas day. Days later, his wife dies from injuries from the bombing.

1953 Blacks boycott buses in Baton Rouge, Louisiana.

1954 Supreme Court rules "separate but equal" educational facilities unconstitutional in *Brown v. Board of Education* case.

1955 Roy Wilkins named executive secretary of NAACP. Fourteen-year-old Emmett Till murdered in Mississippi. George W. Lee and Lamar Smith, both NAACP activists murdered in Mississippi in two different incidents. Montgomery Bus Boycott begins.

1956 Supreme Court rules that segregation in public transportation is unconstitutional; Montgomery Bus Boycott ends. White Citizens Council, a largely middle-class group, is formed to resist desegregation and equal rights for African Americans.

1957 Southern Christian Leadership Conference (SCLC) founded. U.S. Commission on Civil Rights founded as part of the Civil Rights Act of 1957. Little Rock Nine desegregates Central High School in Arkansas.

1959 Ella Baker becomes executive director of SCLC.

1960 The Student Nonviolent Coordinating Committee (SNCC) founded.

1961 CORE initiates Freedom Rides into Deep South to test ban on interstate segregation. CORE members are beaten, buses are bombed.

1962 SNCC and SCLC begin civil rights campaign in Albany, Georgia. Activists are met with violent and fierce resistance from local authorities and other whites.

1963 SCLC begins highly visible civil rights campaign in Birmingham, Alabama. Over two hundred thousand assemble in Washington, D.C. for historic March on Washington. Weeks after the March, the 16th Street Baptist Church is bombed in Birmingham, killing four young girls and injuring twenty. Medgar Evers, Mississippi NAACP leader, assassinated in his driveway.

1964 After considerable Congressional resistance, the sweeping Civil Rights Act of 1964 passed, barring discrimination in hiring and public accommodations. Mississippi Freedom Summer initiates a grassroots campaign to expand civil rights.

1965 Selma voting rights march. Voting Rights Act of 1965 passed, ending policies such as poll taxes, literacy tests, and other methods used to prevent black suffrage. Civil unrest erupts in South Central Los Angeles, popularly known as Watts Riot.

1966 SNCC and CORE call for Black Power. Lowndes County Freedom Organization formed in Alabama. Black Panther Party for Self-Defense formed in Oakland, California. NAACP and Urban League denounce Black Power.

1968 Martin Luther King, Jr. assassinated; urban unrest in over 100 American cities.

I

The Birth of Jim Crow

The Ku Klux Klan, originally founded in 1866 for the purpose of terrorizing black people, experienced a rebirth in the early 20th century. Here an estimated 40,000 Klanspeople march in the nation's capital in 1925, proudly celebrating white supremacy. Throughout the United States, the Klan intimidated black people, immigrants, and others through beatings, arson, rape, bombings, and murder. Despite such blatant violence, the KKK continued to enjoy popular white support, even counting public officials such as mayors, sheriffs, and governors among its ranks. (Corbis)

2239

CIVIL RIGHTS MOVE...

Paper

BOSTON, ...SS.: HOUGHTON MIFFLIN, 2002
SER: PROB... IN AMERICAN CIVILIZATION.

LIST	26.76
DISC	5.0%
NET	25.42

ISBN 0618077375   LIB PO# FIRM ORD...

8395 NATIONAL UNIVERSI... LIBRAR   8214-08
DATE   8/17/05   COLS-SDC
YBP - CONTOOCOOK, N.H. 03229

SUBJ: 1. CIVIL RIGHTS MOVEMENTS—UNITED STATES. 2.
AFRICAN AMERICANS—CIVIL

DEWEY# 323.1

C. Vann Woodward

OF OLD REGIMES AND RECONSTRUCTION

Though the civil rights movement would take root in the South, segregation and the legal oppression of black people was not unique to the South. Known as "Jim Crow" by the late nineteenth century, legalized racial segregation was born in the North and migrated South after the Civil War. C. Vann Woodward's essay discusses the frightfully hostile world in which free blacks found themselves in the antebellum era. Race riots, legalized subjugation, and social marginalization greeted free blacks in the North and West. As Woodward notes, it was impractical for the type of racial segregation that existed in the North to be practiced in the South during slavery. "The mere policing of slaves required that they be kept under more or less constant scrutiny." By the end of Reconstruction in 1877, however, the system of Jim Crow was in the process of becoming deeply entrenched in the South.

C. Vann Woodward taught for many years at Yale University before he died in 1999. He published his most famous book, *The Strange Career of Jim Crow* in 1955 and later won the Pulitzer Prize for history in 1982 for *Mary Chesnut's Civil War,* an account of the conflict drawn from the letters of a Southern woman.

The long experience of slavery in America left its mark on the posterity of both slave and master and influenced relations between them more than a century after the end of the old regime. Slavery was only one of several ways by which the white man has sought to define the Negro's status, his "place," and assure his subordination. Exploitation of the Negro by the white man goes back to the beginning of relations between the races in modern times, and so do the injustices and brutalities that accompany exploitation. Along with these practices and in justification and defense of them, were developed the old assumptions of Anglo-Saxon superiority and innate African inferiority, white supremacy and Negro subordination. In so far as segregation is based on these assumptions, therefore, it is based on the old pro-slavery argument and has its remote ideological roots in the slavery period.

1

. . . The mere policing of slaves required that they be kept under more or less constant scrutiny, and so did the exaction of involuntary labor. The supervision, maintenance of order, and physical and medical care of slaves necessitated many contacts and encouraged a degree of intimacy between the races unequaled, and often held distasteful, in other parts of the country. The system imposed its own type of interracial contact, unwelcome as it might be on both sides.

With house servants the old type of intimacy was further enhanced. "Before and directly after the [Civil] war," W. E. B. Du Bois has written (with some exaggeration, to be sure), "when all the best of the Negroes were domestic servants in the best of the white families, there were bonds of intimacy, affection, and sometimes blood relationship, between the races. They lived in the same home, shared in the family life, often attended the same church, and talked and conversed with each other." It is doubtful, however, that much personal association of this type extended beyond the household servants, and this class constituted a very small proportion of the slaves. The great bulk of the bondsmen, the field hands, shared little but the harsher aspects of contact with white people. There is not much in the record that supports the legend of racial harmony in slavery times, but there is much evidence of contact.

In so far as the Negro's status was fixed by enslavement there was little occasion or need for segregation. But within the slavery regime itself there were Negroes whose status was not established by slavery. These were the few hundred thousand free, or quasi-free, Negroes. It was in the treatment accorded these people that the slave states came nearest to foreshadowing segregation. Denied full rights and privileges of citizens, deprived of equality in the courts, and restricted in their freedom of assembly and freedom of movement, the so-called free Negro shared many of the deprivations of the slave. In addition, measures of ostracism were leveled at members of this class to emphasize their status. Free Negroes tended to concentrate in cities, and the urban slaves were subjected to some of the same measures of ostracism and separation to which their free brothers were prone.

Urban life was a small and untypical aspect of the culture of the Old South, and urban slavery was an even more untypical aspect of the Peculiar Institution. In a history of segregation, however, the urban experience requires special attention. Richard C. Wade in *Slavery in the Cities,* has produced evidence of a rudimentary pattern of segregation in some of the larger cities of the slave states. The pattern was not uniform, and segregation was never complete. It did not always have the force of law, and enforcement was not rigid. But segregation in some of its modern aspects unmistakably appeared in ante-bellum Southern cities. Hotels and restaurants were generally off limits for all Negroes, free or slave, and Negroes were usually discriminated against in public conveyances, though the races were mixed in some towns and Negroes were entirely excluded in others. Hospitals, jails, and public buildings regularly separated the Negroes when they were accommodated at all. As racially mixed as New Orleans was, the Opera House confined Negro patrons to the upper tiers of boxes. Charleston, Richmond, and Savannah excluded them from certain public grounds and gardens or limited them to certain hours.

The very appearance of segregation in the cities, however, was a reaction to an opposite condition of racial mixing. For in the cities of the slave states the races lived in closer physical proximity and greater intimacy of contact and association than they did in any other part of America. "In every city in Dixie," writes Wade, "blacks and whites lived side by side, sharing the same premises if not equal facilities and living constantly in each other's presence." The typical dwelling of a slave-owning family was a walled compound shared by both master and slave families. Neither non-slaveholding whites nor free Negroes escaped this intimacy, for they were "sprinkled through most parts of town and surrounded by people of both races." In spite of changes in the ratio of races which resulted in some racial concentration by 1860, the pattern of residential intermixture prevailed to the end of slavery—and did not disappear quickly thereafter. The pattern was the same in all cities. "In no case did anything like full residential segregation emerge," concludes Wade. "Few streets, much less blocks, were solidly black." Nothing quite comparable existed in Northern cities at that time or since.

The purpose, of course, was the convenience of the masters and the control of the subject race. But the result of this and other conditions of urban living was an overlapping of freedom and bond-age that menaced the institution of slavery and promoted a familiar-ity and association between black and white that challenged caste taboos. The celebrated masked balls and other casual relations be-tween races in New Orleans were popularly attributed to exotic Latin influences. "Actually," says Wade, "what visitors noticed about New Orleans was true of urban life throughout the South." Every South-ern city had its demimonde, and regardless of the law and the pillars of society, the two races on that level foregathered more or less openly in grog shops, mixed balls, and religious meetings. Less visibly there thrived "a world of greater conviviality and equality." Under cover of night, "in this nether world blacks and whites mingled freely, the conventions of slavery were discarded," and "not only did men find fellowship without regard to color in the tippling shops, back rooms, and secluded sheds, but the women of both races joined in." The police blotters of the period are cluttered with evidence of this, but they bear witness only of the sinners who were caught.

In addition to urban factors of proximity there are important demographic data that help account for intimate interracial associa-tion at various levels. In all the Southern cities during the four decades prior to 1860 there was a striking imbalance of the sexes in both races. The significant fact is that the imbalance in one race was the reverse of that in the other. Among whites, especially in the cities west of the seaboard states, there was a great preponderance of men over women, always a phenomenon of rapid urban growth. Among blacks, on the other hand, there was a great preponderance of women over men, occasioned by the practice of selling off young males to the country. Among both races the shortage was always greatest among young adults. This situation helps to account for a considerable amount of cohabitation between white men and Negro women and a growing population of mulattoes. While the census of 1860 listed 12 per cent of all the colored people in the South as "mulattoes," the percentage of them in the cities was much larger, often three or four times as large.

On balance, then, the urban contribution to racial segregation in the South would seem to be less impressive than the encour-agement that city conditions gave to interracial contact, familiar association, and intimacy. In any case, it would be a mistake to place too much emphasis on the urban experience, either as evidence of segregation or the opposite tendency. For the civilization of the Old South was overwhelmingly rural, and urban life was quite untypical of it. Five Southern states did not have a town with as much as 10,000 population in 1860, and only 7.8 of the total population, and an even smaller percentage of the Negroes, lived in towns as large as 4000.

City life proved to be clearly hostile to slavery. It corroded the master's authority, diminished his control, and blurred the line between freedom and bondage. Slavery was declining rapidly in vitality and numbers in all the cities during the last forty years of its existence. . . . The proportion of both white and slave population involved in the urban experience was . . . quite small. The great mass of both races was completely untouched by it, and relations between them were shaped by another environment, to which segregation had little relevance.

2

Segregation in complete and fully developed form did grow up contemporaneously with slavery, but not in its midst. One of the strangest things about the career of Jim Crow was that the system was born in the North and reached an advanced age before moving South in force. Without forgetting evils peculiar to the South, one might consider Northern conditions with profit.

By 1830 slavery was virtually abolished by one means or another throughout the North, with only about 3500 Negroes remaining in bondage in the nominally free states. No sectional comparison of race relations should be made without full regard for this difference. The Northern free Negro enjoyed obvious advantages over the Southern slave. His freedom was circumscribed in many ways, as we shall see, but he could not be bought or sold, or separated from his family, or legally made to work without compensation. He was also to some extent free to agitate, organize, and petition to advance his cause and improve his lot. . . .

Leon F. Litwack, in his authoritative account, *North of Slavery,* describes the system in full development. "In virtually every phase of existence," he writes, "Negroes found themselves systematically separated from whites. They were either excluded from railway cars, omnibuses, stagecoaches, and steamboats or assigned to special "Jim

Crow" sections; they sat, when permitted, in secluded and remote corners of theaters and lecture halls; they could not enter most hotels, restaurants, and resorts, except as servants; they prayed in "Negro pews" in the white churches, and if partaking of the sacrament of the Lord's Supper, they waited until the whites had been served the bread and wine. Moreover, they were often educated in segregated schools, punished in segregated prisons, nursed in segregated hospitals, and buried in segregated cemeteries."

In very few instances were Negroes and other opponents of segregation able to make any progress against the system. Railroads in Massachusetts and schools in Boston eliminated Jim Crow before the Civil War. But there and elsewhere Negroes were often segregated in public accommodations and severely segregated in housing. Whites of South Boston boasted in 1847 that "not a single colored family" lived among them. Boston had her "Nigger Hill" and her "New Guinea," Cincinnati her "Little Africa," and New York and Philadelphia their comparable ghettoes—for which Richmond, Charleston, New Orleans, and St. Louis had no counterparts. A Negro leader in Boston observed in 1860 that "it is five times as hard to get a house in a good location in Boston as in Philadelphia, and it is ten times as difficult for a colored mechanic to get work here as in Charleston." . . .

Alexis de Tocqueville was amazed at the depth of racial bias he encountered in the North. "The prejudice of race," he wrote, "appears to be stronger in the states that have abolished slavery than in those where it still exists; and nowhere is it so intolerant as in those states where servitude has never been known."

Racial discrimination in political and civil rights was the rule in the free states and any relaxation the exception. . . . Only 6 per cent of the Northern Negroes lived in the five states—Massachusetts, New Hampshire, Vermont, Maine, and Rhode Island—that by 1860 permitted them to vote. The Negro's rights were curtailed in the courts as well as at the polls. By custom or by law Negroes were excluded from jury service throughout the North. Only in Massachusetts, and there not until 1855, were they admitted as jurors. Five Western states prohibited Negro testimony in cases where a white man was a party. The ban against Negro jurors, witnesses, and judges, as well as the economic degradation of the race, help to explain the disproportionate numbers of Negroes in Northern prisons and the heavy limitations on the protection of Negro life, liberty, and property.

By the eve of the Civil War the North had sharply defined its position on white supremacy, Negro subordination, and racial segregation. The political party that took control of the federal government at that time was in accord with this position, and Abraham Lincoln as its foremost spokesman was on record with repeated endorsements. He knew the feelings of "the great mass of white people" on Negroes. "A universal feeling, whether well or ill-founded, can not be safely disregarded. We can not, then, make them equals." In 1858 he had elaborated this view. "I will say then I am not, nor ever have been in favor of bringing about in any way the social and political equality of the white and black races [applause]—that I am not nor ever have been in favor of making voters or jurors of negroes, nor of qualifying them to hold office, nor to intermarry with white people, and I will say in addition to this that there is a physical difference between the black and white races which I believe will for ever forbid the two races living together on terms of social and political equality. And inasmuch as they cannot so live, while they do remain together there must be the position of superior and inferior, and I as much as any other man am in favor of having the superior position assigned to the white race."

It is clear that when its victory was complete and the time came, the North was not in the best possible position to instruct the South, either by precedent and example, or by force of conviction, on the implementation of what eventually became one of the professed war aims of the Union cause—racial equality.

3

In the South the traumatic experiences of Civil War, invasion, defeat, emancipation, occupation, and reconstruction had profound and complex—sometimes contradictory—effects on racial relations. The immediate response to the collapse of slavery was often a simultaneous withdrawal of both races from the enforced intimacy and the more burdensome obligation imposed by the old regime on each. Denied the benefits of slavery, whites shook off its responsibilities— excess hands, dependents too old or ill or too young to work, tenants too poor to pay rent. Freedmen for their part often fled old masters and put behind them old grievances, hatreds, and the scene of old humiliations. One of the most momentous of racial separations was the voluntary withdrawal of the Negroes from the white-dominated Protestant churches, often over white protest, in order to establish and control their own separate religious institutions. In these and other ways the new order added physical distance to social distance between the races.

The separations were not all voluntary. Whites clung unwaveringly to the old doctrine of white supremacy and innate Negro inferiority that had been sustained by the old regime. It still remained to be seen what institutions or laws or customs would be necessary to maintain white control now that slavery was gone. Under slavery, control was best maintained by a large degree of physical contact and association. Under the strange new order the old methods were not always available or applicable, though the contacts and associations they produced did not all disappear at once. To the dominant whites it began to appear that the new order required a certain amount of compulsory separation of the races.

The temporary anarchy that followed the collapse of the old discipline produced a state of mind bordering on hysteria among Southern white people. The first year a great fear of black insurrection and revenge seized many minds, and for a longer time the conviction prevailed that Negroes could not be induced to work without compulsion. Large numbers of temporarily uprooted freedmen roamed the highways, congested in towns and cities, or joined the federal militia. In the presence of these conditions the provisional legislatures established by President Johnson in 1865 adopted the notorious Black Codes. Some of them were intended to establish systems of peonage or apprenticeship resembling slavery. Three states at this time adopted laws that made racial discrimination of various kinds on railroads. Mississippi gave the force of law to practices already adopted by railroads by forbidding "any freedman, negro, or mulatto to ride in any first-class passenger cars, set apart, or used by and for white persons." Nothing was said about the mixing of the races in second-class cars, and no car was required for exclusive use of Negroes. The Florida legislature went a step further the same year by forbidding whites to use cars set apart for use of Negroes, as well as excluding Negroes from cars reserved for whites, but it did not require the railroads to provide separate cars for either race, nor did it prohibit mixing of the races in smoking cars. Texas carried the development further in 1866 with a law that required all railroad companies to "attach to passenger trains one car for the special accommodation of freedmen." Theses three laws, as well as local ordinances of this character, were on the books only a short while, however, for they were either disallowed by military government or repealed by subsequent legislatures. Regardless of the law, the discriminatory practice of denying Negroes the use of first-class accommodations nevertheless continued on many railroads throughout Reconstruction and beyond. Not until the arrival of the full Jim Crow system much later, however, was the separation of the races required in second-class coaches or universal in first-class cars.

Other aspects of segregation appeared early and widely and were sanctioned by Reconstruction authorities. The most conspicuous of these was the segregation of the public schools. While the law might not provide for it and individuals might deplore it, segregation of the schools nevertheless took place promptly and prevailed continuously. There were very few exceptions. The only notable one was the public schools of New Orleans, which were thoroughly and successfully integrated until 1877. Attempts elsewhere were probably restrained by the knowledge that the whites would withdraw if integration were attempted. This in fact did occur at times when desegregation of colleges and other institutions was attempted. This situation prevailed generally throughout major government-supported services and facilities. The law sometimes provided for separate facilities for the races during Reconstruction. But even when this was not the case, and when both races were housed in the same jails, hospitals, or asylums, they were usually quartered in separate cells, floors, or wings. All these practices, legal or extra-legal, had the consent or at least the acquiescence of the Reconstruction governments. . . .

What happened in North Carolina was a revelation to conservative whites. "It is amazing," wrote Kemp Battle of Raleigh, "how quietly our people take negro juries, or rather negroes on juries." Randolph Shotwell of Rutherfordton was dismayed on seeing "long processions of countrymen entering the village by the various roads mounted and afoot, whites and blacks marching together, and in frequent instances arm-in-arm, a sight to disgust even a decent negro." It was disturbing even to native white radicals, as one of them admitted in the Raleigh *Standard,* to find at times "the two races now eat together at the same table, sit together in the same room, work together, visit and hold debating societies together." It is not that such occurrences were typical or very common, but that they could happen at all that was important.

Southern Negroes responded to news of the Reconstruction Act of March 1867 with numerous demonstrations against incipient Jim Crowism. In New Orleans they demonstrated so vigorously and persistently against the Jim Crow "Star Cars" established in 1864 that General Phil Sheridan ordered an end to racial discrimination on street cars in May 1867. Similar demonstrations and what would now be called "sit-ins" brought an end about the same time to segregated street cars in Richmond, Charleston, and other cities. One of the strongest demands of the freedmen upon the new radical state legislatures of 1868 in South Carolina and Mississippi was for civil rights laws that would protect their rights on common carriers and public accommodations. The law makers of those states and others responded with comprehensive anti-discrimination statutes. Their impact was noted in South Carolina in 1868 by Elizabeth H. Botume, a Northern teacher, on a previously segregated river steamer from Charleston to Beaufort. She witnessed "a decided change" among Negro passengers, previously excluded from the upper deck. "They were everywhere," she wrote, "choosing the best staterooms and best seats at the table. Two prominent colored members of the State Legislature were on board with their families. There were also several well-known Southerners, still uncompromising rebels. It was a curious scene and full of significance." In North Carolina shortly after the adoption of the Federal Civil Rights Act of 1875 Negroes in various parts of the state successfully tested their rights in railroads, steamboats, hotels, theaters, and other public accommodations. One Negro took the railroad from Raleigh to Savannah and reported no difficulty riding and dining unsegregated. Future Congressman James E. O'Hara, a Negro, successfully integrated a steamer from Greenville to Tarboro.

As a rule, however, Negroes were not aggressive in pressing their rights, even after they were assured them by law and protected in exercising them by the federal presence. It was easier to avoid the painful rebuff or insult by refraining from the test of rights. Negroes rarely intruded upon hotels or restaurants where they were unwelcome. Whites often withdrew from desegregated facilities or cut down their patronage. . . .

It would be wrong to exaggerate the amount of interracial association and intimacy produced during Reconstruction or to misconstrue its character and meaning. If the intimacy of the old regime had its unhappy and painful aspects, so did that of the new order. Unlike the quality of mercy, it was strained. It was also temporary, and it was usually self-conscious. It was a product of contrived circumstances, and neither race had time to become fully accustomed to the change or feel natural in the relationship. Nevertheless, it would be a mistaken effort to equate this period in racial relations with either the old regime of slavery or with the future rule of Jim Crow. It was too exceptional. It is impossible to conceive of innumerable events and interracial experiments and contacts of the 1860's taking place in the 1900's. To attempt that would be to do violence to the nuances of history.

Donald G. Neiman

EQUALITY DEFERRED, 1870–1900

In the early twentieth century, the popular historical interpretation of Reconstruction tended to view it as a dismal failure fraught with corrupt and inept black publicly-elected officials who victimized white southerners. Historians such as U. B. Phillips and William Dunning, who were proponents of this school of thought, rejected W. E. B. Du Bois' *Black Reconstruction* (1935), which examined the rise of virulent forces of white supremacist terror that undermined Reconstruction (which had never been dominated by blacks). Donald G. Neiman's essay is an extension of Du Bois' thesis. Here, Neiman considers the waning years of Reconstruction, which were a promising period of black political participation. By the 1880s, however, southern "redeemers" were able to secure the subjugation of African Americans through terrorist organizations like the Ku Klux Klan and legal maneuvers which received little substantive resistance from the federal government. By the dawn of the twentieth century, white supremacy had been firmly reestablished in the region.

Donald G. Neiman was a professor of history at Clemson University for several years and is the author of *To Set the Law in Motion: The Freedmen's Bureau and the Legal Rights of Blacks, 1865–1868*.

From *Promise to Keep: African-Americans and the Constitutional Order, 1776 to the Present* by Donald G. Neiman, copyright © 1991 by Oxford University Press, Inc. Used by permission of Oxford University Press, Inc.

Located in the rich Brazos River Valley some eighty miles northwest of Houston, Washington County, Texas, was part of the nineteenth-century South's cotton kingdom. Although fall usually focused the attention of the county's residents on the harvest and the price of the fleecy staple, the fall of 1886 was different. Politics displaced cotton as the prime subject of discussion at the Barrel House, a popular black bar in Brenham, the county seat; at Routt's bustling cotton gin in nearby Chappell Hill; and at dozens of other gathering spots throughout the county. With the support of the county's slight black majority, Republicans had controlled local government from 1869 until 1884, when Democrats had reclaimed the county courthouse in a closely contested election. For Democrats, the victory had been sweet, bringing to an end fifteen years in which black men and their white allies had governed the county. But Democrats were worried as the 1886 canvass approached. Republican leaders were formidable opponents, and the county's blacks remained politically active and determined to return the county to Republican control. Republicans were equally apprehensive. They recalled that two years earlier their opponents had used violence to reduce the black turnout and believed that local Democrats would resort to whatever means were necessary to guarantee white rule.

Republicans' fears were not misplaced. In three heavily Republican precincts located in the predominantly black eastern portion of the county, masked men clad in yellow slickers seized ballot boxes from election officials at gunpoint. The raids accomplished their purpose, destroying enough Republican ballots to give Democrats a narrow victory in the closely contested canvass. Yet all did not go according to plan for the Democrats. Anticipating foul play, a group of black Republicans in the Flewellen precinct remained at the polling station as election officials tallied the ballots. When masked intruders burst into the room to seize the ballot box, Polk Hill, one of the black observers, opened fire with his shotgun, instantly killing one of the bandits, Dewees Bolton, the son of the Democratic candidate for county commission.

Although Hill fled, local officials arrested eight black men who had been present at the shooting and charged them with murder. In jailing the blacks, they did more than satisfy whites' demands that Bolton's killing be avenged. Democratic leaders, including the county judge, Lafayette Kirk, had orchestrated the election-day fraud and feared that Hill's companions had seen too much. By identifying young Bolton's comrades, they might provide evidence that would enable Republicans to contest the election and put the Democratic conspirators behind bars. On the night of December 1, after Republican lawyer F. D. Jodon had initiated habeas corpus proceedings on behalf of the imprisoned blacks, a band of disguised men broke into the county jail in Brenham. Easily overpowering the jailer, they went to the cells where the black men were being held and asked for Shad Felder, Alfred Jones, and Stewart Jones. After identifying the three, they dragged them out of jail, took them to the bank of nearby Sandy Creek, and hanged them. Two days after the lynching, as an angry mob of whites gathered in Brenham, prominent Democrats informed Stephen Hackworth, James Moore, and Carl Schutze, three of the county's leading white Republicans, that they must leave town. Fearing for their lives, all three quickly departed.

Hackworth and his comrades refused to accept exile, however, and turned to the national government for redress. They found ready allies among Senate Republicans, who had long advocated stronger federal criminal sanctions against election fraud and violence. In mid-February 1887, William Evarts of Massachusetts, a Republican member of the Senate Committee on Elections, initiated hearings on the Washington County affair. During the ensuing three weeks, several dozen Washington County citizens—black and white, Republican and Democrat—made the long trip to the nation's capitol and gave committee members their versions of the 1886 election and its violent aftermath. Running to almost 700 pages of small print, the testimony vividly detailed the fraud and violence that plagued southern elections, offering strong support for advocates of federal regulation of elections. Democrats now controlled the House of Representatives and the White House, however, and Republicans themselves were divided over the wisdom of more vigorous protection of their southern allies. Consequently, Republican leaders were unable to translate indignation over the highhandedness of Washington County whites into legislation providing more effective protection for beleaguered black voters.

Washington County Republicans did not pin all their hopes on congressional intervention. As the Senate hearings got under way,

United States Attorney Rudolph Kleberg won an indictment against Lafayette Kirk and eight other prominent Washington County Democrats in the United States district court in Austin. Framed under federal election laws adopted during Reconstruction, the indictment charged the defendants with conspiring to interfere with election officials and to steal ballots at an election at which a congressional representative was elected. Despite his own affiliation as a Democrat, Kleburg threw himself into the case, conducting a thorough investigation and vigorously presenting his case to the jury. Nevertheless, after a lengthy trial in August 1887, jurors were unable to agree on a verdict, and the judge declared a mistrial. Undaunted, Kleberg brought the case to trial again in April 1888, only to have the jury return a verdict of not guilty. In both trials, the government had produced strong circumstantial evidence that Washington County Democratic leaders had engineered the theft of the ballot boxes. Yet because three key Republican witnesses had been lynched and other potential black witnesses were reluctant to give testimony that might cost them their lives, the district attorney did not have a "smoking gun." Not surprisingly, therefore, he was unable to convince juries composed mainly of white Texans to return a guilty verdict against the respectable white defendants. Federal officials could harry Washington County Democrats, but they could not bring them to justice.

The April 1888 acquittal brought an end to the Washington County affair. Because murder was a state, not a federal offense, the Washington County sheriff was responsible for investigating the lynching of the three black men and bringing the guilty parties to justice. Although the identities of the lynch mob's leaders were common knowledge among local whites, community leaders showed no interest in prosecuting the guilty parties. "[M]ost good citizens regret the hanging," the *Brenham Daily Banner* piously noted, "but in the present state of public feeling it is regarded as one of those occurrences that could not well be avoided." Not surprisingly, Sheriff N. E. Dever, a white Democrat, made no effort to arrest the guilty parties. This forgive-and-forget attitude did not extend, however, to Polk Hill. Dever and his deputies conducted a manhunt that led to Hill's arrest in late 1886. Hill was transferred to the Milam County jail for safekeeping, a step that probably saved him from the fate of his late neighbors, Shad Felder, Alf Jones, and Stewart Jones.

Subsequently, he was convicted of manslaughter by an all-white jury and sentenced to twenty-five years in prison.

Events in Washington County were symptomatic of developments elsewhere in the South during the last decades of the century. Despite an unparalleled extension of federal authority during the early 1870s, by 1877 southern Democrats had reclaimed control of state government from the Republicans throughout the South. While the new regimes steadily chipped away at the rights blacks had won during Reconstruction, Democrats' counterrevolutionary designs met determined resistance. Blacks refused to abandon the dream of citizenship and equality and skillfully used the political and legal avenues opened to them during Reconstruction to defend their newly won rights. Moreover, while the national government's vigor in protecting civil rights waned after the mid-1870s, neither Congress, the Justice Department, nor the federal courts completely abandoned blacks during the late 1870s and 1880s. Yet as the demise of Washington County Republicanism suggests, southern blacks were only able to slow, not stop, the counterrevolution. By the end of the century, northern Republicans paid little more than lip service to protection of black rights, the federal courts had transformed the Reconstruction amendments into mere platitudes, and conservative Democrats had successfully employed terror and economic reprisals to overcome black resistance and reestablish white supremacy. It took three decades to accomplish, but by 1900, southern Democrats had reversed the Reconstruction revolution.

Securing the Republican Revolution

Even as Republicans celebrated ratification of the Fifteenth Amendment in February 1870, they recognized the vulnerability of the dramatic civil rights gains they had achieved in the 1860s. Across the South, the Ku Klux Klan and kindred groups had launched a campaign of terror designed to destroy the fledgling Republican regimes and reverse the Republican commitment to equality. State and local officials proved either unwilling or unable to challenge the Klan. Confronting a large, well-armed terrorist group, Republican sheriffs were reluctant to risk igniting a race war by mobilizing their supporters (most of whom were black) into posses to arrest Klansmen. Furthermore, when fearless local officials made arrests and initiated prosecutions, it was difficult to win convictions. Witnesses, fearing for their lives, frequently refused to testify against Klansmen, and many jurors were too intimidated or (in the case of whites) too sympathetic to the Klan to return guilty verdicts.

In early 1870, with Klan violence spreading and state officials unable to check it, congressional Republicans considered bold new legislation to enforce the Fourteenth and Fifteenth Amendments. As they had done during the Civil War, Republicans viewed the Constitution as a source of power, arguing that it gave Congress discretion to choose the means necessary to protect the rights of citizens. "The people know that . . . the Constitution is created for the people, and not the people for the Constitution," argued Mississippi Republican George McKee, "and I would rather trust the clear, simple judgement of the people than that of any legal quibbler who ever split a constitutional hair on either side of this House."

Some Republicans argued that the national government had an inherent right to legislate to protect its citizens, whether they were threatened by state or private action. "I desire that so broad and liberal a construction be placed upon its provision as will insure protection to the humblest citizen," explained Joseph Rainey, a black congressman from South Carolina. "Tell me nothing of a constitution which fails to shelter beneath its rightful power the people of a country."

Most Republicans, however, feared that giving Congress such open-ended authority threatened the federal system. Carried to its logical conclusion, they argued, it would empower the national government to enact a general code of laws governing crime, property, contracts, family relations, and other matters that properly lay within state jurisdiction. Consequently, theirs was a more restrictive view of federal power. They acknowledged that the Fourteenth and Fifteenth Amendments were designed to prevent states from denying individual rights rather than to give Congress primary responsibility for defining and protecting individual rights. Nevertheless, they pointed out that the amendments gave Congress authority to enact "appropriate legislation" to enforce their guarantees, thereby conferring broad discretion to choose the means best suited to that end. They also pointed out that states could, through inaction, deny the rights guaranteed by the amendments. In other words, states might just as effectively deny individuals equal protection of the laws by failing to punish murderers as by enacting blatantly discriminatory statutes. Most Republicans concluded that when states, through inaction, denied black citizens rights guaranteed by the Fourteenth and Fifteenth Amendments, Congress could provide the remedies against private action that the states failed to afford.

Acting on this theory, congressional Republicans passed the Enforcement Act in May 1870, dramatically expanding federal protection for individual rights. Designed primarily to enforce the Fifteenth Amendment, the act made it a federal crime for state officials to deny otherwise qualified voters the right to register or to vote. It also established criminal penalties for private citizens who used force, violence, intimidation, bribery, or economic coercion to deny any person the right to vote. At the behest of their black and white southern colleagues, who were particularly sensitive to the problem of violence, congressional Republicans went beyond protection of voting rights. They established stiff criminal penalties (fines of $5,000 and imprisonment for ten years) for those who conspired to deny persons rights guaranteed by the Constitution or federal laws. The act thus broke new ground, affording individuals federal remedies against private acts of violence, something that previously had been the exclusive responsibility of the states.

Less than one year later, in April 1871, congressional Republicans took even firmer action, passing a measure popularly known as the Ku Klux Klan Act. The law made it a federal crime for two or more persons to conspire to deprive any person of equal protection of the laws. Invoking Congress's authority to regulate federal elections, it also established criminal penalties for persons who used force or intimidation to prevent citizens from supporting candidates of their choice in congressional elections. More to the point, it gave the government additional tools with which to combat terrorism. When terrorist groups prevented state authorities from guaranteeing persons equal protection of the laws, the president might use the army or the militia to assist in arresting offenders. And when such organizations were "so numerous and powerful as to . . . set at defiance the constituted authorities," the chief executive might suspend habeas corpus, allowing the military to hold those whom they arrested without initiating formal charges against them.

Between 1870 and 1873, federal officials used the new legislation to mount an impressive and effective campaign against the Ku

Klux Klan. Consider the government's effort in western South Carolina, where a powerful Klan organization (in York County more than three-quarters of adult white males were members) declared war on local blacks during late 1870 and 1871, murdering several dozen black Republicans and severely beating hundreds of others. Federal officials conducted a thorough investigation of Klan violence in the region, gathering a massive amount of evidence against Klansmen. At the urging of Attorney General Amos T. Akerman, who had gone to South Carolina to consult with federal investigators and prosecutors, President Ulysses Grant invoked his broad authority under the Klan Act. In October 1871, he suspended habeas corpus in nine South Carolina counties and authorized the army to assist federal marshals in making arrests. Although many Klan members fled (some went as far as Canada), marshals made hundreds of arrests, and hundreds of other Klansmen, convinced that they could not escape the dragnet, surrendered. By year's end, 195 York County Klansmen resided in the county jail, popularly known as the "United States Hotel." After filling the Spartanburg County jail, federal officials had to rent two additional buildings to house men arrested in that county.

During late 1871 and 1872 trials began in federal courts in Columbia and Charleston. Because federal officials had carefully assembled evidence and the juries impaneled contained black majorities, prosecutors were successful in winning convictions. The trials, however, were time-consuming; the first five cases that went to trial took more than one month to complete. And the creaky federal judicial system was ill-equipped to deal with large numbers of lengthy criminal trials. With only two federal judges assigned to the state and two attorneys responsible for all of the prosecutions, federal officials soon realized that they could bring to trial only a small portion of those whom they had arrested. Consequently, they concentrated on the worst offenders, hoping that the mass arrests and the few dozen convictions they were able to win would demonstrate federal resolve and deter further terrorism. Their strategy worked. Although the government won convictions in only about 150 cases (most of which resulted from guilty pleas rather than jury trials) and ultimately dismissed more than 1,000 cases, it effectively destroyed the Klan in South Carolina. . . .

Congressional Republicans also confronted the prickly problem of segregation. Although there were wide variations in the depth and vehemence of race prejudice and legally imposed segregation was rare, the years immediately following the war witnessed white resistance to integration of public places. In the South, most hotels and restaurants denied service to blacks; public schools, asylums, and parks generally excluded blacks; and theaters, railroads, streetcars, and steamboats frequently segregated blacks or excluded them altogether. In the North, where segregation had been common in the antebellum years, there was intense prejudice against blacks, but it was neither as broad nor as deep as that which existed in the South. The result was a more confusing, complex pattern of race relations: blacks were denied service at most hotels and restaurants, while others accommodated the few well-to-do blacks who sought admission; most public school systems insisted that blacks attend separate schools that were generally inferior to those provided for whites, but schools were integrated in New England and some other places; railroads, steamboats, and streetcars frequently, but not always, segregated blacks. . . .

The Counterrevolution Gains Force

Even as Republican radicals struggled with the capstone, cracks appeared in the foundation. During the mid-1870s, with federal judges supportive and the Klan on the run, Republicans backed away from vigorous federal intervention in the South. In part this was a response to the success of the 1871–1872 campaign against the Klan and the concomitant decline in terrorism. There were deeper reasons for the party's new posture, however. Most Republicans viewed law enforcement as a state, not a federal, responsibility, considered the campaign against the Klan extraordinary, and were note prepared to continue it indefinitely. They were also concerned about the political consequences of further federal intervention. In a society that worshipped the self-reliant individual, was skeptical of active government, and had long viewed a strong central government as suspect, there was little enthusiasm for continuation of a large-scale federal enforcement program. Furthermore, Democrats charged that tales of Klan terror were nothing more than Republican propaganda, denounced the enforcement program as a ruthless effort to prop up unpopular, incompetent governments with federal bayonets, and portrayed President Grant as a latter-day Caesar. Aware that these charges effectively appealed to Americans' fear of military despotism, Republicans agreed that they must curb federal intervention in the South.

During 1873, Republican leaders began to distance themselves from the mailed-fist policies that had proved so effective in South Carolina. Under George Williams, who succeeded Akerman as attorney general in late 1871, the Justice Department became more cautious about initiating new civil rights cases. While Williams did not order district attorneys to halt new prosecutions under the Enforcement and Klan Acts, he neither encouraged them to undertake vigorous action nor allowed them the resources necessary for large-scale prosecutions. In fact, the administration became more conciliatory toward white southerners, perhaps hoping that this would moderate their opposition to the new order and bring to an end charges of bayonet rule. Beginning in 1873, President Grant pardoned many of the Klansmen who remained in prison, and the attorney general ordered federal attorneys in the South to dismiss prosecutions against thousands of Klansmen who had been indicted between 1870 and 1872.

Events of 1873–1874 reinforced Republican cautiousness. Members of Grant's inner circle and prominent Republican congressmen implicated in financial scandals were the subjects of congressional investigations during 1873. With the scent of corruption trailing it, the party was also saddled with blame for the severe economic depression that struck in September 1873. Facing a hostile electorate as the 1874 congressional races approached, Republicans were reluctant to add to their woes by undertaking potentially unpopular action in the South. When the dust settled after the election, the party had been routed and a 110-vote Republican majority in the House had become a 60-vote margin for the Democrats. Shell-shocked and fearing further losses in important state elections in 1875, party leaders became even more reluctant to renew large-scale intervention in the South.

Taking advantage of Republican cautiousness, southern Democrats launched a new offensive against their adversaries between 1874 and 1876. By making active support for the Democratic party a test of racial solidarity, they increased the white turnout significantly. They also developed new techniques of intimidation that effectively reduced Republican turnout without reviving northern support for federal intervention. Armed Democrats regularly disrupted Republican meetings, demanding equal time to expose Republican "lies" or shouting down Republican speakers. Seeking to impress on blacks the perils of political involvement, armed bands rode through the countryside at night during the weeks preceding elections, firing small arms and sometimes even canon, and patrolled polling places on election day. And when they did resort to beatings and murders, they usually defined their targets carefully and struck quickly rather than inaugurating an ongoing campaign of terror. Democrats also mastered the technique of the "race riot." They provoked altercations between their own supporters and Republicans and, under the pretext of self-defense, launched punishing attacks against their opponents. At the beginning of the 1875 election campaign in Mississippi, for example, white Democrats in Clinton precipitated a fight at a Republican rally in which several blacks and whites were killed. Alleging that the Republicans had initiated a war of the races, Democrats swept the surrounding countryside during the next two days, killing between twenty and thirty blacks and beating hundreds of others.

Despite his recent policy of conciliation and caution, Grant did not ignore the resurgence of violence. He authorized the War Department to station small squads of troops in areas where Democratic intimidation was most pronounced, hoping the presence of bluecoats would cow whites and reassure blacks. Under instructions from Washington, moreover, district attorneys, supported by troops, occasionally arrested persons charged with intimidating voters. The government's effort, however, was far too modest and ultimately proved woefully inadequate. There were too few troops available (by October 1874 only 7,000 bluecoats remained in the South) to make a show of force in more than a few trouble spots. And because the overwhelming majority were infantry, they possessed limited mobility and were not effective against mounted adversaries. Then, too, the number of prosecutions initiated under the Enforcement Act by federal attorneys was too small to serve as a deterrent. What was needed was a large-scale campaign of arrests and prosecutions patterned after the South Carolina effort of 1871–1872. Republican leaders, however, fearing that they lacked popular support for such a campaign, did not meet the Democratic challenge.

The results were disastrous for southern Republicans. Democrats were able to regain control of state government in Texas (where only one-third of the population were blacks) and Arkansas and

Florida (where bitter factional disputes doomed Republicans) without resorting to widespread violence. In the rest of the unredeemed South, however, the new techniques of terror were crucial. In 1874, Alabama Democrats carried statewide elections, in part by employing violence and intimidation in key black belt counties, while Louisiana Democrats smashed Republican organizations in many rural parishes, winning control of the state assembly. The following year white Mississippians mounted an impressive campaign of terror to carry the state legislature. With that accomplished, they swiftly impeached Republican Governor Adelbert Ames. In 1876, Democrats in Louisiana and South Carolina effectively used violence to carry state elections, completing the process of redemption. By 1877, then, the Democratic counterrevolution had recaptured the South, ending Republican control in every state in the region.

Although freedmen continued to vote in large numbers and Republicans still held office in some predominantly black counties after 1877, southern Democrats relied on fraud and intimidation of black voters to cling to power. As a prominent Mississippi Democrat admitted in 1890, "we have been stuffing the ballot boxes, committing perjury, and . . . carrying the elections by *fraud* and violence" since 1875. The consequences of Democratic hegemony were momentous. While blacks remained eligible to serve on juries, in most areas local officials manipulated jury selection procedures to exclude them. Consequently, black plaintiffs and defendants once again found justice elusive as they confronted all-white juries. Blacks also felt the economic consequences of redemption: Democratic legislatures repealed measures that the Republicans had enacted to protect agricultural laborers; state supreme courts developed legal doctrines that reinforced the authority of landowners against sharecroppers; sheriffs again used vagrancy statutes to compel reluctant black workers to accept unfavorable contracts with planters; and justices of the peace turned a deaf ear to complaints that black workers lodged against their employers. Absence of effective legal protection, combined with a steady decline in the price of cotton, left black sharecroppers and agricultural workers impoverished, reinforcing their economic dependence on whites. Black children also suffered as state legislatures cut support for public education and local officials reduced the proportion of school funds that went to black schools.

As southern Democrats moved ahead with the counterrevolution, the United States Supreme Court circumscribed national authority to protect civil rights. Most members of the Court were conservative northern Republicans who were not hostile to civil rights but had never shared the radicals' passion for equality. Like most of their contemporaries, they were committed to preserving a decentralized federal system and believed that this required strict limits on national authority and sharp delineation of state and national functions. It is difficult for Americans living in the late twentieth century to appreciate this commitment to federalism. We are the heirs of more than fifty years of steady growth of federal authority and believe that the scope of national power is virtually limitless. Nineteenth-century Americans were products of a much different world, however. The federal government played little role in their day-to-day lives, and, with the exception of the local postmaster, they rarely encountered a federal official. Moreover, as products of a political tradition that equated centralized authority and tyranny, they believed that self-government demanded that local communities enjoy substantial autonomy. It is hardly surprising, therefore, that they viewed expansion of federal authority with suspicion. . . .

When it decided *The Civil Rights Cases* in 1883, the Court used the state action theory to strike down the provisions of the Civil Rights Act of 1875 banning discrimination in hotels, restaurants, theaters, and public transportation. Justice Bradley, who wrote the Court's opinion, denied that the Fourteenth Amendment's equal protection clause sanctioned the law. It merely prohibited discrimination by state authorities, he held, not by private individuals and businesses. Bradley also denied that the Thirteenth Amendment authorized the statute. He admitted that it abolished all "badges and incidents" of slavery and decreed "universal civil and political freedom throughout the United States." He also conceded that the Thirteenth Amendment, unlike the Fourteenth, was not directed exclusively at state action, and that Congress's power to enforce it included authority "to enact all necessary and proper laws for the obliteration and prevention of slavery with all its badges and incidents." Bradley denied, however, that discrimination against blacks by proprietors of hotels and restaurants, which had been common in the free states during the antebellum years, was a badge of servitude. "It would be running the slavery argument into the ground," he concluded, "to make it apply to every act of discrimination which a person may see fit to make as to the guests he will entertain, or . . . take into his coach . . . or admit to his . . . theater. . . ."

Bradley's opinion did not go unchallenged. The black press likened it to Taney's infamous *Dred Scott* opinion, and one week after it was announced, Frederick Douglass denounced the decision at a mass protest meeting in Washington, D.C. On the Court itself, Justice John Marshall Harlan, a Kentucky Republican who had once owned slaves, penned an eloquent dissent. Hearkening back to the idealism that had animated the Republican party's civil rights program, he characterized Bradley's analysis as "entirely too narrow and artificial," charging that its "subtle and ingenious verbal criticism" sapped "the substance and spirit of the recent Amendments." "Constitutional provisions, adopted in the interest of liberty, and for the purpose of securing . . . rights inhering in a state of freedom, and belonging to American citizenship," he explained, "have been so construed as to defeat the ends . . . which they attempted to accomplish. . . ."

Although the Court narrowed the scope of national power under the postwar amendments, it by no means abandoned the framers' commitment to equality. In *Strauder v. West Virginia* (1880), it held that a law that restricted jury service to white men violated the Fourteenth Amendment's equal protection clause. In the process, it reaffirmed that the amendment had been designed to protect the former slaves from hostile state action and to guarantee that "all persons, whether colored or white, shall stand equal before the laws of the States." Moreover, the Court suggested that it would not tolerate laws establishing racial classifications. As Justice William Strong explained,

> The words of the [Fourteenth] Amendment . . . are prohibitory, but they contain a necessary implication of a positive immunity, or right, most valuable to the colored race—the right to exemption from un-friendly legislation against them distinctively as colored; exemption from legal discriminations, implying inferiority in civil society . . . and discriminations which are steps towards reducing them to the condi-tion of a subject race.

The justices also proved willing to provide remedies against state officials who were guilty of enforcing nominally impartial laws in a discriminatory fashion. In *Ex parte Virginia,* decided at the same term as *Strauder,* the Court upheld the prosecution of a Virginia judge charged with systematic exclusion of blacks from juries in his court. Justice Strong noted that the Fourteenth Amendment was designed "to take away all possibility of oppression by law because of race or color," but denied that its reach was limited to formal enactments of the legislature. "Whoever, by virtue of a public position under a state government, . . . takes away the equal protection of the laws, violates the constitutional inhibition; and as he acts in the name and for the States, . . . his act is that of the State," he explained. "This must be so or the constitutional provision has no meaning." In 1880, in *Neal v. Delaware,* the justices indicated that blacks might prove discrimination even if they did not introduce testimony showing that officials had consciously intended to keep blacks off juries. In reversing the conviction of a black man who had been indicted by an all-white grand jury and tried by an all-white petit jury, the Court held that the fact that no black had served on a jury in a state that was fifteen percent black constituted adequate proof of discrimination. . . .

In *Ex parte Yarbrough,* decided in 1884, a unanimous Supreme Court endorsed [Chief Justice] Waite's position. Jasper and Dilmus Yarbrough and seven other white Georgians (all members of the Pop and Go Club, a Democratic terrorist organization) had been convicted for violation of the Enforcement and Klan Acts for their part in violence against blacks who had voted in a hotly contested congressional election in 1882. The defendants appealed, contending that under the Court's rulings in *Cruikshank* and *The Civil Rights Cases,* the federal government did not have the authority to punish private citizens for civil rights violations. Justice Miller unequivocally rejected their argument. He pointed out that Article I, section 4 of the Constitution gave Congress power to regulate the election of its members and justified legislation (like the provision of the Klan Act under which Yarbrough was prosecuted) punishing persons who attempted to control congressional elections by fraud and violence. According to Miller, Congress had ample authority to protect the Republic by guaranteeing that "the votes by which its members . . . are elected shall be the *free* votes of the electors, and the officers thus chosen the free and uncorrupted choice of those who have the right to take part in that choice."

The Court's ruling in *Yarbrough* recognized that the government had broad authority to protect blacks against political terrorism. Although it merely upheld the government's authority to punish violence at congressional elections, federal and state elections were generally conducted at the same time. As a practical matter, therefore, the ruling enabled federal officials to police most state elections. In fact, Miller's opinion strongly suggested that the government had authority to use the Enforcement Act against persons who attempted to intimidate black voters in any election, regardless of whether candidates for national representative were on the ballot. He expressly reaffirmed the constitutional guarantee of exemption from racially motivated discrimination against voters. In addition, because he held that Congress possessed authority to protect this right from infringement by private individuals as well as by state officials, the opinion strongly suggested that the national government could prosecute parties who sought in any election to intimidate voters because of their race.

While hardly a champion of blacks, the Court thus supported limited federal protection of civil rights, especially in the area of voting rights. Sections of the Enforcement Act of 1870 and the Klan Act punishing infringement of the right to vote, intimidation of voters, and election fraud remained on the books and, in fact, had been reenacted by Congress in 1874 as part of *The Revised Statutes.* Encouraged by the Court's rulings in *Reese* and *Yarbrough,* the Justice Department vigorously enforced these measures throughout the 1880s and the early 1890s. Indeed, for attorneys general and their subordinates, Reconstruction did not end in 1877; prosecuting voting rights cases and ensuring "a free ballot and a fair count" continued to be a high priority. Federal attorneys and marshals in the South won indictments against thousands of election officials who refused to permit blacks to register or vote, stuffed ballot boxes, and engaged in other types of skullduggery aimed at neutralizing the votes of blacks and their allies. They also prosecuted hundreds of individuals who resorted to violence to keep blacks away from the polls or to punish those who had dared to vote.

Despite this effort, the Justice Department won few convictions. Defendants were generally regarded by their white neighbors as heroes persecuted by meddling outsiders. Communities contributed generously to their defense funds, and when cases went to trial, federal attorneys faced batteries of highly skilled defense lawyers. In order to put together cases that experienced defense counsel could not pick apart, harried federal attorneys needed the services of detectives to help them assemble evidence. They also required the assistance of experienced trial lawyers who could help them develop strategies for prosecution and present cases effectively in court. These hotly contested cases frequently involved large numbers of witnesses and lengthy trials, thus resulting in substantial expenses for summoning witnesses and jurors. Congress, however, facing considerable pressure to reduce federal spending, consistently denied the department adequate resources. While federal attorneys' overall caseloads quadrupled during the last quarter of the nineteenth century, Justice Department appropriations only doubled. Consequently, department officials frequently denied prosecutors' requests to hire detectives and additional attorneys. In fact, they occasionally ordered federal attorneys to dismiss cases because they did not have sufficient funds to cover the costs of prosecution.

Juries proved an even greater obstacle to success. Although federal juries continued to be racially mixed, they also included white Democrats who sympathized with defendants and denied the legitimacy of the prosecutions. Because a guilty verdict required the assent of the entire jury, prosecutors had to convince some jurors who were not only skeptical, but often downright hostile. Moreover, because blacks were often eyewitnesses to or victims of the crimes and because community pressure prevented most whites from coming forward to testify against defendants, federal attorneys had to rely heavily on black testimony. Convincing hostile white jurors to change their minds on the basis of evidence offered by blacks was not easy. As one distressed federal attorney explained, "The law is plain—the facts are plainer, but I can't make a white democratic juror believe colored witnesses nor force him to vote [for conviction]. I can't keep politics out of the human mind and I can't make the jury commissioners select more impartial men."

Although it produced few convictions, the Justice Department's effort was not completely without effect. It served notice that northern Republicans had not abandoned support for civil rights and suggested that any systematic effort to deny blacks the right to vote through literacy tests and poll taxes would meet resistance. To underscore this, Republicans in Congress conducted regular investigations of southern election fraud and violence. Combined with opposition from poor whites, who feared that poll taxes and literacy tests would disfranchise them, the government's campaign to protect the voting rights of blacks helped keep the disfranchisers in check during the 1870s and 1880s. Before 1890, only Georgia and Virginia (which experimented with poll taxes in the 1870s) and South Carolina (which in 1882 established a complicated system of balloting effectively disfranchising illiterate blacks) had enacted legislation designed to disfranchise blacks.

As long as they were not legally barred from voting, southern blacks refused to be pushed out of politics. Equating the franchise with freedom, personal dignity, and equal citizenship, they were well aware that political decisions had a significant bearing on their lives. Consequently, in most states of the former Confederacy, blacks continued to vote at a high rate and occasionally mounted serious challenges to Democratic hegemony. In a number of heavily black counties, redemption did not bring an end to Republican control; candidates elected by former slaves continued to serve as state legislators, local officials, and sometimes even congressmen. In addition to retaining power in black belt enclaves, Republicans mounted periodic challenges that threatened Democratic control at the state level. In Tennessee, where Unionist whites in the mountainous eastern counties joined with blacks in the central and western counties to support Republican candidates, the party remained a threat to Democratic control. Indeed, the Republican gubernatorial candidate won election in 1880, when the Democrats divided, and the party won more than forty percent of the vote in statewide elections during the remainder of the decade. In North Carolina, support from mountain Unionists in the west and blacks in the east enabled Republicans to come within a whisker of regaining control of the state in 1880. During the next two decades, Republicans would remain a force to be reckoned with in North Carolina politics. . . .

Northern blacks' continued success in the battle against discrimination did not mean that racism was dead in the North. Social contact between whites and blacks was rare, aversion among whites to contact with blacks in public places was still widespread, and most whites denied that blacks were their equals. If anything, northern racism became stronger during the 1880s and 1890s, as respected biologists and social scientists placed the imprimatur of science on the myth of black inferiority by asserting that blacks had not reached the same intellectual or moral level as whites. Given the persistence of racism, northern blacks continued to suffer discrimination and, despite the new public accommodations laws, were frequently denied admission to white theaters, hotels, restaurants, and amusements. The public accommodations laws gave blacks remedies against such abuses, and they frequently sued those who discriminated against them; however, because confrontations with hostile proprietors were unpleasant and lawsuits were expensive, many blacks chose to avoid places where they knew they were not welcome. White prejudice also consigned most blacks to menial, low-paying jobs, depriving them of the opportunities offered by an expanding economy. And whether or not they were willing to sue, state law offered no redress against employment discrimination.

Nevertheless, northern blacks' political and legal victories were not meaningless. In practical terms, they gave black children access to white schools, which were better funded and offered greater educational opportunities than were available in the South's separate and unequal schools. Even though discrimination continued, greater fluidity in race relations existed in the North. Consequently, northern blacks, unlike their southern counterparts, were not subject to constant and blatant reminders that they were regarded as an inferior caste, unfit to associate with whites. Furthermore, the victories of the 1870s and 1880s established the principle of colorblind citizenship as part of the North's dominant public philosophy. As the Michigan Supreme Court noted in 1890, "there must be and is an absolute, unconditional equality of white and colored men before the law. . . . Whatever right a white man has in a public place, the black man has also." This marked a significant change from the antebellum era, when most Republicans had assured their constituents that they did not support black suffrage, much less blacks' right to equal access to public accommodations. While the principle of colorblind citizenship often amounted to little more than empty rhetoric, it nevertheless upheld a standard that blacks could press whites to honor in practice as well as in name. And given the political and legal techniques they had learned and the confidence they had gained in over half a century of agitation for reform, blacks would not be bashful about holding whites to their promises.

The Triumph of Racism

While northern blacks' campaign for civil rights accelerated during the years after Reconstruction, southern blacks' gains were swept away by a rising tide of white supremacy. During the late 1870s and 1880s southern blacks had refused to accept the Democratic counterrevolution, using political and legal means to defend their rights. Yet while they had won occasional victories, their position generally had deteriorated. Beginning in the late 1880s and stretching into the first two decades of the twentieth century, southern Democrats launched a ferocious new offensive that reduced blacks to second-class citizenship.

Despite Democrats' efforts to deter them, blacks had continued to vote at a high rate in most states during the 1870s and 1880s. Indeed, they had frequently joined with poor white farmers who had bolted the Democratic party because of dissatisfaction with its economic policies, forming coalitions that forced the dominant Democrats to resort to even greater violence and fraud in an effort to maintain their power. This pattern continued in the 1890s, as many economically distressed white farmers left the Democratic party to join the Populists. The new party pledged itself to use the power of government on behalf of working people, advocating nationalization of the railroads, a vigorous campaign against big business, wholesale reform of the financial system, and establishment of producer-operated cooperatives that would free farmers from dependence on merchants. Like the independent parties of the 1870s and 1880s, the Populists hoped to attract black voters to their cause, uniting poor whites and blacks in a coalition that would drive the Democrats from power. In North Carolina, where Populists fused with the Republican party, the strategy worked, at least temporarily; and in a number of other southern states, only widespread violence and unprecedented fraud by the Democrats defeated it.

Shaken by this challenge, southern Democrats moved to undercut the opposition by disfranchising blacks. Aware that the Fifteenth Amendment prohibited them from openly denying blacks the right to vote, Democrats sought to accomplish their objective indirectly. By requiring voters to pay poll taxes (small annual head taxes usually amounting to less than three dollars per year), they could reduce the black electorate substantially. The great majority of southern blacks were desperately poor agricultural laborers and sharecroppers. Trapped in a vicious credit system that kept many in debt from year to year, precious little cash passed through their hands. Consequently, a tax of only three dollars could put the ballot beyond their reach. The literacy test offered disfranchisers an even more effective tool. Given the legacy of slavery and the meager support for black schools in the aftermath of Reconstruction, illiteracy among blacks was widespread. In 1890, more than half of the adult black males in the South could not read, and many others were barely literate. Fairly administered, literacy tests (which required prospective voters to prove that they could read a provision of the state or federal constitution) would deny the ballot to most black men; applied by partisan white officials who were bitterly opposed to black suffrage, they would cut even further into the black electorate.

For Democratic leaders, literacy tests and poll taxes had an added attraction. Although publicly they emphasized the effect these measures would have on blacks, Democrats were well aware that they would also take their toll on poor whites. The region's depressed agricultural economy affected whites as well as blacks, leaving many white farmers on the brink of ruin and forcing many others into the poverty of tenancy and sharecropping. Poverty also bred illiteracy; in 1900, twelve percent of southern whites could neither read nor write. The new voting requirements, therefore, would exclude many whites from voting, and happily for Democratic leaders, these would be the men who had defected from the party during the 1880s and 1890s.

Although blacks and dissident whites bitterly opposed disfranchisement, conservative Democrats achieved their objective. Beginning with Florida and Tennessee in 1889 and Mississippi in 1890 and concluding with Georgia in 1908, measures designed to prune the electorate were adopted throughout the South. Each of the eleven states of the old Confederacy made payment of a poll tax a requirement for voting, and five heightened the effect of the tax by making it cumulative (i.e., requiring voters to pay poll taxes for previous years as well as for the year of the election). Seven of these states coupled the poll tax with a literacy test, and seven adopted the secret ballot, which served as a de facto literacy test because illiterates were unable to read it. Except for Florida, each of these states supplemented the poll tax with a literacy test or the secret ballot or both. In five states, Democratic leaders established loopholes for whites—a concession necessary to obtain sufficient support for passage of the disfranchisement measures. Several states exempted from the literacy test those who owned a certain amount of property (usually $300) or enacted understanding clauses that enfranchised those who could explain a passage of the constitution when it was read to them by the registrar. Several states supplemented these with grandfather clauses that waived literacy tests for those who were descendents of persons who had been qualified to vote prior to 1867 (the year southern blacks gained the ballot) or who had fought for the Union or Confederacy.

The new requirements had a dramatic effect on the southern electorate; in the years following their enactment, registration among blacks plummeted. By 1910, black registration had decreased to fifteen percent in Virginia and to less than two percent in Alabama and Mississippi. Although loopholes and discriminatory administration of the laws allowed many whites to dodge the effects of the literacy requirements, the new laws took their toll on whites as well. Many were too proud to admit that they could not read and declined to exploit the loopholes, while others were excluded from voting because they were too poor to pay their poll taxes. Therefore while white registration remained at approximately eighty percent in Virginia and Alabama, it decreased to approximately fifty percent in Louisiana and to sixty percent in Mississippi. As J. Morgan Kousser, the leading student of suffrage restriction had noted, the disfranchising measures "insured that the Southern electorate for half a century would be almost all white; yet . . . [they] did not guarantee all whites the vote."

Passage of legislation mandating segregation—the Jim Crow laws—coincided with disfranchisement. Separation of the races in churches, schools, public transportation, hotels, and restaurants had become customary in the decades following the war. During the late 1870s and 1880s, however, some states began to codify custom, mandating segregation in prisons and public schools. Beginning in the late 1880s and continuing through the first two decades of the twentieth century, southern legislatures and city councils went to work with a new fervor, enacting a mountain of laws and ordinances to formalize and to put the force of law behind what had been largely customary arrangements.

The move to give white supremacy the force of law was a natural product of a turbulent era. As white Democrats launched their disfranchisement campaigns, they stoked the fires of racial prejudice white hot in order to focus attention on blacks (rather than poor whites) as the primary targets and to convince those who were concerned about the impact on poor whites that disfranchisement was necessary at all costs. The disfranchisers repeatedly denounced blacks as ignorant, lazy, criminally inclined, and venal, a race demonstrably unqualified to exercise political rights. In an atmosphere poisoned with racial hatred, it is hardly surprising that laws designed to further degrade blacks attracted broad support. Continued black assertiveness and activism in the decade after Reconstruction also contributed to the emergence of segregation. It reminded southern whites that they had not fully established white supremacy, the goal of the redeemers. In fact, many whites feared that a new generation of blacks who had never known slavery was coming to maturity and that they might pose an even stiffer challenge to white supremacy than had their parents. Frustrated by their failure to restore black deference and concerned about the future, the establishment of legally sanctioned segregation offered white southerners a powerful means of asserting their power and dominance. Moreover, given the deep racism that existed throughout the South, adoption of segregation statutes by one or two states led legislators in neighboring states to follow suit, quickly spreading the laws across the region.

Jim Crow came to the South in three waves. Between 1887 and 1891 most states of the former Confederacy adopted laws requiring railroads to provide separate but equal accommodations for the two races. Then, beginning in 1901 with Virginia, most southern states passed laws requiring urban street railroads to separate black and white passengers. Finally, during the 1910s, states and localities created a complex web of regulations designed to extend the logic of separation to all spheres of southern life. A number of states forbade whites and blacks to be taught together, even in private schools, and barred teachers and nurses from serving students or patients of another race. States and cities established separate parks and mandated residential segregation. Some states required manufacturers to designate different entrances for white and black employees, to maintain separate pay windows, toilets, and water buckets, and to separate workers by race on the job. Not content with segregating school children, North Carolina and Florida required that public school textbooks used by children of different races be stored separately. And, though not required by law, many courts kept separate Bibles for swearing black and white witnesses. . . .

Blacks' constitutional claims, . . . were unequivocally rejected by the Supreme Court. During the 1870s and 1880s the Court had been dominated by northern Republicans who, although quite conservative, nonetheless had come of age at the height of the struggle against slavery and who shared their party's commitment to emancipation and equal rights. Their rulings had narrowed the compass of the post-war amendments, restricting the government's authority to punish civil rights violations by private citizens. However, they had empha-sized that the postwar amendments had been adopted to guarantee the former slaves equal rights and that they clearly barred discrimi-natory state action, whether it was carried out through blatantly discriminatory laws or by more subtle means. The six new justices who came to the Supreme Court between 1888 and 1894 were of a different generation. Although most were northern Republicans, they had come of age at a time when northern interest in Recon-struction was dimming and scientists were giving respectability to racism. Consequently, the new justices were less inclined than their predecessors to protect the constitutional rights of blacks.

The first major test of the new justices' position on civil rights came in 1896, when the Court decided *Plessy v. Ferguson*. The case had been initiated by the American Citizens Equal Rights Asso-ciation, a group organized by New Orleans blacks to challenge an 1890 Louisiana law requiring railroads to provide separate but equal accommodations for blacks. The association was represented by Albion Tourgee of New York, who had served on the front line of the Reconstruction-era battle for equality as a Republican leader in North Carolina and who had remained an eloquent advocate of the cause after returning to the North. Hewing to the arguments developed by abolitionist legal theorists and Reconstruction-era Republican congressmen, Tourgee denied that the law's guarantee of equivalent facilities satisfied the requirements of the Fourteenth Amendment's equal protection clause. The entire purpose of the postwar amendments, he emphasized, was to eradicate caste and es-tablish a colorblind Constitution. By separating blacks from whites, he concluded, the Louisiana statute stigmatized and degraded blacks, subjected them to invidious discrimination, perpetuated the spirit of caste, and therefore was patently unconstitutional.

The Court's response suggested that the arguments of Reconstruction-era Republicans rang hollow to the new justices. Justice Henry Brown, a Michigan Republican who in 1890 had replaced Justice Samuel Miller, wrote the Court's opinion, sustain-ing the law's constitutionality. Reading the scientific racism of the 1890s back into the 1860s, Brown asserted that the amendment's framers must have understood that there was a deep natural aversion to racial intermingling. Consequently, he asserted, they had merely intended to guarantee "the absolute equality of the races before the law," not social equality. Brown concluded therefore that the amendment was satisfied by the Louisiana statute's requirement of equal but separate facilities. Blind to the campaign of racial hatred that was then raging in the South, he denied Tourgee's assertion that the statute "stamps the colored race with a badge of inferiority." "If this be so," the justice blithely explained, "it is not by reason of anything found in the act, but solely because the colored race chooses to put that construction upon it." Only John Marshall Harlan, a veteran of Reconstruction-era political battles who had served on the Court for nearly twenty years, dissented, predicting that "the judgment this day rendered will . . . prove to be quite as pernicious as . . . the *Dred Scott case*."

Three years later, when it decided *Cumming v. School Board of Richmond County, Ga.,* the Supreme Court suggested that it would not be overly scrupulous in guaranteeing that segregated facilities were actually equal. The case was brought by Augusta, Georgia blacks to challenge the school board's decision to close the county's only black high school. Since the board continued to support several white high schools, the plaintiffs charged that it had deprived black children of opportunities afforded whites, thereby denying them equal protection. A unanimous Court turned aside their argument, however, signaling that under the guise of separate but equal blacks might be consigned to grossly unequal schools, services, and accommodations.

The Court also sustained disfranchisement. While the new voting requirements disfranchised many poor whites, they were directed principally at blacks. Not only did many states include understanding clauses, property tests, and grandfather clauses offering whites ways around the literacy tests, but the new laws had a much more drastic effect on blacks than on whites. Moreover, the rhetoric accompanying disfranchisement suggested that southerners were determined to eliminate blacks from politics. Despite the fact that the disfranchisement laws were racially neutral on their face, therefore, a good case could be made that they violated the Fifteenth Amendment.

In 1898, when it decided *Williams v. Mississippi,* the Court rejected such an argument. Justice Joseph McKenna, a California Republican who had recently joined the Court, admitted in his opinion that the Mississippi Supreme Court had openly suggested that the state's poll tax and literacy test were designed to disfranchise blacks. . . . Nevertheless, McKenna concluded that "nothing tangible can be deduced from this," adding that the state's voting requirements did not deny anyone the right to vote on the basis of race. In sum, states might devise clever strategies to defeat the spirit of the Fifteenth Amendment so long as they did not expressly violate its provisions.

By the end of the century, then, the postwar amendments' revolutionary promise of a colorblind Constitution that empowered the national government to guarantee its citizens civil equality lay unfulfilled. Given the ferocity of southern resistance, most white Americans' unwillingness to centralize power in the national government, the waning of concern for black rights in the North, and the resurgence of racism nationwide, the nation reneged on promises made in the heat of the Civil War and Reconstruction. During the 1870s and 1880s the Supreme Court had significantly restricted the scope of national power to protect individual rights, effectively curtailing (although not destroying) the revolutionary potential of postwar amendments and civil rights laws. With the addition of new members to the Supreme Court in the 1890s, the Court capitulated to the racist fury that was sweeping the South. Placing form above substance, ignoring the purpose of the postwar amendments, and demonstrating a perverse ignorance of southern legislators' intent, the Court accepted segregation and disfranchisement.

Consequently, blacks entered the new century stripped of the promise of the Reconstruction revolution. Northern blacks were in a better position than black southerners, but with no thanks to federal Constitutional guarantees. Through political and legal action they had been able to win passage of legislation guaranteeing them equal civil rights, and state courts, relying on state constitutional provisions and statutes, had handed down decisions protecting these rights. Despite the law, however, racism remained powerful among northerners, as evidenced by the behavior of northerners who served on the Supreme Court, and frequently undercut the rights to which blacks were entitled. It was in the South, however, where ninety percent of the nation's blacks lived in 1900 that the capitulation to racism was most evident. There blacks were subjected to a humiliating system of segregation in all aspects of their lives, a system that, despite the legal fiction of separate but equal, consigned them to schools and other facilities that were separate and visibly unequal. They were also systematically denied the ballot, the principal symbol of citizenship in the Republic. Marked by the law as members of an inferior caste and denied political power, they were left by the law to the tender mercies of their white neighbors.

Charles M. Payne

SETTING THE STAGE

For the first third of the twentieth century, Jim Crow was universally established in the South. While blacks and whites were segregated in education and public accommodations, blacks universally endured inferior accommodations, had no voting rights, and were subject to human rights violations. In order to maintain this oppressive social order, whites used various forms of violence (legal and extralegal) to intimidate black people. Charles Payne studies the use of violence in Mississippi during the years before the modern civil rights movement. Payne describes mob violence, which included lynching, as well as other methods of violence used to curb black lawlessness against whites, that in effect became tools of political repression.

Charles Payne is a professor of history at Duke University and is the author of *I've Got the Light of Freedom: The Organizing Tradition and the Mississippi Freedom Struggle.*

Everything that took place in Mississippi during the 1960s took place against that state's long tradition of systematic racial terrorism. Without some minimal protection for the lives of potential activists, no real opposition to the system of white supremacy was possible. Lynching is only one form of racial terror and statistics on it virtually always underestimate the reality, but between the end of Reconstruction and the modern civil rights era, Mississippi lynched 539 Blacks, more than any other state. Between 1930 and 1950—during the two decades immediately preceding the modern phase of the civil rights movement—the state had at least 33 lynchings.

The first victim was Dave Harris, shot to death in 1930 by a crowd of 250 white men who believed Harris had killed a young white man near Gunnison, Mississippi. The second and third victims were Pig Lockett and Holly Hite. Arrested for robbery, they were taken from the law enforcement officers by a mob, which hung them. In 1931, Steve Wiley was accused of attempting to assault the wife of a grocery store owner while he was drunk. She shot him three times. A mob hung what was left of him from a railroad trestle. A week later, in Vicksburg, Eli Johnson, also accused of an attempted assault on a white woman, was lynched. In November of that year, the body of Coleman Franks was found hanging from a tree limb near Columbus. He had been charged with shooting and wounding a local white farmer. There were no lynchings in 1932, but two in 1933. In July an unnamed Negro man in Caledonia, Mississippi, was hung, accused of insulting a white woman. In Minter City that September, Richard Roscoe got into a fight with a white man. A mob shot him to death, tied his body to the rear of the sheriff's automobile, and paraded it through town before dumping it in front of his home.

Nineteen-thirty-four saw three killings. In Bolivar County, a mob overpowered sheriff's deputies and seized Isaac Thomas and Joe Love, who had been arrested for an alleged attack on a white woman. The men were hung from a railroad trestle. Less than two months later, in Pelahatchie, Mississippi, four white men beat seventy-year-old Henry Bedford to death. A tenant farmer, he was accused of having spoken disrespectfully to one of the whites in the course of a dispute about land rental. The sheriff arrested four whites—for which he suffered some criticism—but no indictments were ever handed down. About a month later, Robert Jones and Smith Houey were hung from a tree near Michigan City. They were accused of killing at least one white man.

There were seven killings in 1935, three in the month of March alone. On March twelfth, Ab Young was hung from a tree in a school yard near Slayden. Young was wanted in connection with the shooting death of a white highway worker. When he was captured, the mob had an argument about whether to burn him or turn him over to the sheriff in Holly Springs. The brother of the murdered man had made a plea that Young not be mutilated. While the argument was still going on, a group of about fifty went off to hang him. He was allowed to sing a hymn, which he was able to do in a clear, unfaltering voice, apparently unnerving some of his captors. After he was dead, several in the crowd used his swinging body for target practice. When the lynchers got back to town the burn-him or give-him-to-the-sheriff argument was still going on. Ten days later in Lawrence County, R. J. Tyronne was shot to death, apparently by neighbors who thought he had become too prosperous. On the thirtieth of the month, the body of Rev. T. A. Allen, weighted down with chain, was found in the Coldwater River. Allen had been involved in an attempt to organize sharecroppers. In June, R. D. McGee in Wiggins was both hung and shot for his alleged attack on an eleven-year-old white girl. In July, Bert Moore and Dooley Morton, both young farmers, were hung near Columbus, also for an alleged attack on a white woman. Bodie Bates was hung from a bridge in August for the same reason. In September, a mob in Oxford, site of the University of Mississippi, hung Ellwood Higginbotham, who was being tried for the murder of a white planter.

In 1936, J. B. Grant, seventeen years old, was shot over a hundred times by a mob, tied to an automobile, and dragged through the streets of Laurel before being hung from a railroad trestle. What he had done to deserve this is not known. It was a record fifteen months before the next killing, but that one proved particularly brutal: Roosevelt Townes and "Bootjack" McDaniel, both in their mid-twenties, were accused of murdering a white man and were taken from the sheriff by a mob. Three or four hundred people, including women and children, took them to a clearing in the woods near Duckhill, where they were chained to trees. According to one report, the mob turned on McDaniel first. A blowtorch was applied to his chest until he confessed, after which he was shot. The blowtorch was applied to Townes for as much as an hour; it was used to burn off his fingers and ears individually. While he was still alive, brush and wood were piled at his feet and fired with gasoline, finally burning him to death.

During the first half of 1938, there were no lynchings anywhere in the South, perhaps in part because, in the wake of the Duckhill slayings, federal anti-lynching legislation was gaining new support. In the second half of the year, there were seven lynchings, four in Mississippi, in which the NAACP estimated a total of six hundred people took part. Only a few were involved in the murder of Wash Adams, who was beaten to death in Columbus for failing to pay the ten-dollar balance on his wife's funeral bill. In the Delta town of Rolling Fork, a blacksmith named Tom Green refused to do some work ordered by the plantation manager. Green was fired and then got into an argument with R. Purdy Flanagan, the plantation owner, about who owned which tools. Shooting started; Green was wounded but Flanagan was killed. Green holed up in his cabin where he was killed after a fifteen-minute gun battle with a mob of three hundred. His body was dragged by car to the place where he had killed Flanagan, doused with gasoline and burned, then dragged into town and burned again. That was near the beginning of July. Near the end of the month a mob in Canton shot and killed Claude Banks as he was driving home. In November, a mob of perhaps two hundred killed Wilder McGowan in Wiggins. McGowan was accused of assaulting a white woman.

Where we have more than fragmentary details about these cases, it is often because of the work of NAACP investigators, usually native white southerners. Their work repeatedly demonstrated that the underlying stories were much at variance with reported versions. Stories about sheriffs being "overpowered" by mobs often turned out to be cases of collusion between sheriffs and the mobs—although they also found cases where law-enforcement people did everything they could to protect their prisoners, sometimes successfully. Of course, investigators frequently found that the actual reasons victims were selected had no relationship to their alleged transgression. The crowd at Duckhill may have seized Roosevelt Townes partly because he was a bootlegger in a part of the state where that occupation was thought a white man's prerogative.

Wilder McGowan was probably killed because he had trouble grasping the whole idea of white man's prerogative. On November 20, a Mrs. Murray reported that at about eight P.M. she had been attacked and robbed by a light-skinned colored man with straight hair. The seventy-four-year-old Mrs. Murray was a member of one of the area's prominent white families. A posse estimated at two hundred men descended upon the local Negro quarters and ordered that no one leave. One woman, thinking the order applied only to men, tried to leave for her job; she was hit on the head with a pistol butt and told to "git back." Bloodhounds led the posse through a rooming house. Learning that one resident, Wilder McGowan, age twenty-four, was not there, the mob became interested in him. When he returned home, he was taken into the nearby woods and hung.

In many respects, McGowan was an unlikely choice. Several witnesses could have accounted for his whereabouts during the time the crime was committed. He was dark-skinned, so he didn't fit Mrs. Murray's description. He was never taken before Mrs. Murray for identification. The NAACP investigator concluded that McGowan was selected because he had had several altercations with whites:

> On one occasion when he refused to run as other Negroes did when ordered to do so by some armed whites in an automobile, he was attacked but beat his assailants and took a revolver from one of them. Recently, he was suspected of having slashed with a knife one of a group of whites who visited a Negro dance hall "looking for some good-looking nigger women." It is known that he was one of two or three young Negro men who resented the slur on their women and had a fist fight with the whites. He called for the lights to be put out and in the darkness the whites were badly beaten and one cut on the arm.

"After they had Linched him," McGowan's uncle wrote the NAACP a year later, "they claim that they caught the right negroes But still Wilder is dead." In a larger sense, Wilder was the right Negro.

The McGowan case was closer to the rule than to the exception. Southwide, allegations of rape were made in about one-sixth of all lynchings (but probably in one hundred percent of all southern speeches about lynching). Immediately after it was founded, the Association of Southern Women for the Prevention of Lynching (ASWPL) made an attempt to find out how many of the charges of rape had any validity:

> These investigations showed that white men, determined to get rid of a certain Negro, would accuse him of an attempted sex crime. They know that officers would approve without question their action for this offense. . . . While in some instances the weight of the evidence supported the charge of attempted rape, investigations of many lynchings indicated so strongly that white women . . . were merely a front for lynchers that no report of a lynching for the protection of a white woman could be accepted as true until it was verified.

Of course, mobs had their own understanding of what constituted "assault"; looking a white woman in the eye could be enough.

Near the end of the thirties, Canton, Mississippi, had two killings, both of which, according to an NAACP investigator, reflected, in different ways, a trend toward "quieter" lynchings. In July of 1938, a white man named A. B. McAdam visited the city to see his daughter who was hospitalized there. After he left the hospital, he was, he claimed, attacked and robbed by a Black man. Law-enforcement officers and citizens decided to blockade the part of town where the incident was supposed to have taken place. At the same time, Claude Banks, twenty-two-year-old son of a prosperous Negro funeral home owner, was driving home from a party. As he drove by the blockade, members of the mob opened fire with pistols and shotguns, apparently making no effort to stop the car. Witnesses said that both deputies and police officers were among those doing the shooting. Banks was killed. His companion, Willie Jones, was arrested and roughed up before being released with the warning that if he ever said anything he would catch "sudden pneumonia"—that is, be killed. Canton's mayor did what he could to keep the story quiet, refusing to cooperate with a photographer who wanted to get a picture of the body—a departure from the older tradition in which murderers, smiling and grinning, posed with the bodies of their victims or pieces thereof, for photos that were sometimes turned into postcards. Claude Banks's father did what he could to keep the issue alive. He went to the mayor and requested the city render some form of compensation for his son's death and then asked a local judge if there were any legal avenues of redress. Both told him that nothing could be done. . . .

By the end of the thirties, NAACP officials and members of the ASWPL thought howling mobs were becoming passe. Small groups of men were doing quietly what large crowds used to do publicly. Kangaroo courts and charges of "killed while resisting arrest" were giving racial murder a quasi-legal air. Even when large groups were involved, there were more attempts to suppress news of murders—this in a state where lynchings had previously been announced in the newspapers a couple of days in advance in order to give the country people time to get to town.

World War II brought new possibilities of racial tension. On the one hand, whites worried that those Blacks who served in the armed forces would come back with "biggity" ideas. On the other hand, some whites felt that not enough Black men were going to war. Blacks were more likely to be excluded from service for reasons of health or illiteracy, leaving some whites feeling that there were too many Black men around. Nonetheless, the state's lynching rate did not change much during the war years; there were three in 1943, one more in 1944.

The 1943 killings were only a week apart, separated by only a few miles. The first involved two fourteen-year-old boys, Charlie Lang and Ernest Green, arrested for attempting to rape a thirteen-year-old white girl near the small town—population fourteen hundred—of Quitman. The sheriff claimed the boys had confessed. On October 12, a small group of men supposedly overpowered the constable at the jail and took the boys. They were found hanging from a beam of the bridge where the incident had taken place. The bridge was a traditional site for lynching in Clarke County. In 1918, four Negroes, two of them pregnant women, had been hung there for alleged complicity in the death of a local dentist.

Subsequent investigations of the 1943 killing by the NAACP again raised doubts about just what had happened. The girl and the two boys were friends, and they frequently played together, often around the bridge. On that day, according to the report of the NAACP's Madison Jones,

> they were running and jumping when the girl ran out from under the bridge and the boys behind her. A passing motorist saw them and the result you know. The boys were mutilated in the following fashion. Their reproductive organs were cut off. Pieces of flesh had been jerked away from their bodies with pliers and one boy had a screw driver rammed down his throat so that it protruded from his neck.

The Quitman killings may have inspired the killers of Howard Wash, killed just five days later about thirty miles away. Wash had been tried and found guilty of murdering his employer, a local dairy farmer. He had pleaded self-defense, and the fact that the jury that convicted him refused to recommend the death penalty may indicate that some of its members found some validity in his claim. He was sentenced to life imprisonment, but a crowd broke into the jail and seized and hung him.

In 1944, the Reverend Isaac Simmons was farming 295 acres of land in Amite County. For a couple of years, a group of white men had been trying to get him to sell the land, but he had no interest in that. Simmons, sixty-six years of age, went to a lawyer to make certain that there would be no trouble about transferring the property to his children. Word of his visit to the lawyer got out. On the morning of March 26, six armed white men picked up Simmons and one of his sons and drove them to a thicketed area where Simmons was told to get out of the car. He tried to run, but two shotgun blasts caught him in the back. The killers then reloaded the shotgun, walked over to where he had fallen, and shot him a third time. His son, who had been forced to watch, was beaten and given ten days to get off the land. When the son returned with friends to reclaim his father's body, he found that all of his father's teeth had been knocked out with a club—presumably after he was already dead—and his arm broken and his tongue cut out.

Such mutilations—parading dead bodies around the town, shooting or burning bodies already dead, severing body parts and using them for souvenirs, using corkscrews to pull spirals of flesh from living victims or roasting people over slow fires—were as much a part of the ritual of lynching as the actual act of killing. They sent a more powerful message than straightforward killing would have sent, graphically reinforcing the idea that Negroes were so far outside the human family that the most inhuman actions could be visited upon them.

There were two more killings after the war. In 1946, Leon McTate of West, Mississippi, was whipped to death by six white men who accused him of stealing a saddle. In July of 1949, Malcolm Wright was riding in his wagon with his wife and four children near Houston, Mississippi. Three white men in an automobile, angered because they could not pass the wagon on the narrow road, beat Wright to death while his family watched, the last Mississippi killing listed by the NAACP before the fifties.

The Wright killing, perhaps more eloquently than the more brutal slayings or the spectacle lynchings, underscores how tenuous Black life was. The point was that there did not have to be a point; Black life could be snuffed out on whim, you could be killed because some ignorant white man didn't like the color of your shirt or the way you drove a wagon. Mississippi Blacks had to understand that viscerally. Those who wanted to work for change had to understand that they were challenging a system that could and would take their lives casually.

The Structural Background of Change

As terrible as the lynchings of the thirties and forties were, the system of racial violence was by then in decline, in part because the cotton-based political and economic system from which it had grown was declining. The increasing difficulty of maintaining a way of life in Mississippi based on cotton was a particularly important change for the Mississippi Delta.

Roughly the northwestern quarter of the state, bounded on the west by the Mississippi River, the Delta is flat and treeless, with soil so rich that it frequently produced a tenth of the nation's cotton crop, cotton of very high quality. In 1935, David Cohn, a Delta native and a firm believer in white supremacy, wrote "Cotton is more than a crop in the Delta, it is a form of mysticism. It is a religion and a way of life"—a way of life, as he noted elsewhere, dependent above all else upon Black labor. Most Delta counties were three-quarters Black, and the Blacks were overwhelmingly agricultural laborers, tenant farmers, and domestics. They were a poor and suppressed population even as compared to Blacks in the rest of Mississippi. As Blacks from other states feared going to Mississippi, Blacks from the hill counties or piney woods of Mississippi were frequently reluctant to venture into the Delta. SNCC's Dorie Ladner, who had grown up in Hattiesburg, recalls being terrified on her first trip into the Delta and being amazed to learn that in 1962 there were still places where there were curfews for Negroes. It seemed to her that whatever was left over from slavery had been left in the Delta.

One of the most detailed portraits we have of traditional Delta life is that by the anthropologist Hortense Powdermaker. Her *After Freedom* is a study of the Delta town of Indianola in Sunflower County during the early 1930s. She describes a world structured around cotton production. Delta cotton production was organized around vast plantations rather than the smaller farms that dominated other parts of the state. The great majority of Delta Blacks were either sharecroppers or renters on a plantation. Individual landlords could be better or worse, but the system itself was profoundly corrupt, a form of life Blacks repeatedly said was only marginally better than slavery.

Sharecroppers were vulnerable to all manner of exploitation. Powdermaker estimates that twenty-five or thirty percent of them may have gotten an honest settlement at the end of the year. Since sharecroppers and tenants were largely illiterate, without recourse to the law, and often unable even to move to a different plantation without the permission of their landlord, less scrupulous landowners were free to do as they chose. Indeed, it was for just this reason that Black tenants were preferred to white ones. Blacks could be more easily squeezed; poor whites were thought to be too "independent." Even without the rapacity of landlords, cropping on shares barely allowed much more than a subsistence existence except in boom years. In 1932, Powdermaker's first year in the Delta, she estimates that seventeen or eighteen percent of those cropping on shares in Sunflower County made some profit, ranging from $30 to $150 for the year. The rest broke even or ended the year in debt. If the one study she cites is representative, half the Black families in the Delta could not afford a minimally decent diet. Most could not even hope that their children, through education, could make a better life. The school calendar was built around the cotton season, which meant that most Black youngsters were in school only when they weren't needed in the fields. (Aaron Henry, who as an adult would be among the most important Black leaders in Mississippi, as a child asked his mother why he could only go to school for five months while the white kids went seven. She answered that it was because he was smarter than white kids; they needed extra time.)

Powdermaker did her work in the 1930s, the last decade in which she could have seen the cotton economy in relatively pure form. Change had been in motion at least since tractors first appeared in the Delta during the First World War. In the 1930s, flame cultivators were introduced that for thirty-five cents an acre cleared land that cost a dollar to clear by hand, even when hoe hands were only making a dollar a day. The 1940s saw the development of the first commercially viable cotton harvester, a machine capable of doing the work of forty or more pickers.

While cotton production was being mechanized, competition from synthetics and cheap foreign cotton made cotton a less valuable crop. During the Depression, the bottom fell out of the cotton market. Across the South, the average price of a pound of cotton, which had been thirty-five cents in 1919, dropped to six cents in 1931. In Mississippi it fell to nine cents. Delta farmers began switching to other crops—corn, oats, soybeans—all requiring much less labor than cotton. By the 1960s, modernized plantations found they needed barely a fifth of their former work force.

Suddenly most Blacks had no economic function. Schemes to reduce the size of the Black population became a popular subject of discussion. The Great Migration during World War I had generated near-panic among wealthier whites. Labor agents from the North were shot at, beaten, harassed with every legal device planters could think of. Blacks caught trying to leave might be jailed or even strung up as a lesson to others. By the 1950s, gubernatorial candidates were competing to see who could promise to drive the greatest number of Negroes from the state in the shortest period of time.

The separation of Negroes from the soil unraveled the balance of political and economic forces that had defined their place since shortly after the Civil War. It meant, for example, increased out-migration of Blacks from the South to the North and West, a process accelerated by the northern demand for labor during World War II. During the 1940s, 1.6 million Blacks left the South, to be followed by almost 1.5 million during the 1950s. The North's new Black voters created a counterforce to the Dixiecrats who had previously enjoyed a virtual stranglehold on national policy concerning race. The new Black vote mattered enough that by 1940 the national Democratic platform spoke to the question of equal protection under the law for the first time. Referring to that period, historian David Lewis says, "Although isolation of any single election factor risks presenting a false picture, the reality that Afro-American votes were now determinative in 16 non-South states with 278 electoral votes escaped no serious political strategist." In contrast, the white South controlled only 127 electoral votes.

Since the end of Reconstruction, the federal government had essentially taken a hands-off stance to the South's way of doing business. It amounted to tacit national support for southern racism. The withering of that support constituted a fundamental shift in the balance of forces. It meant, for example, that the South could be threatened with federal anti-lynching legislation. No such legislation ever passed, but the threat of it was salutary. Southwide, 1923 saw the sharpest one-year decrease in the number of lynchings in thirty-five years—from sixty-one the previous year to twenty-eight in 1923—a decrease attributed by the NAACP partly to the northward migration and partly to the first sustained agitation for a federal anti-lynching bill. By 1938, Senator Wagner of New York thought a clear pattern had been established: "Experiences in 1922, 1934 and 1935 demonstrated that the number of lynchings declined with significant regularity while anti-lynching legislation was pending in Congress, only to rise again when hope for passage of such legislation died." The pattern repeated itself in 1938, which saw a complete cessation of lynching across the South for the first six months of the year, while another bill was being discussed, only to have lynchings start up again almost as soon as Congress adjourned.

Under the new political order, it became possible to have the FBI investigate racial murders. By the end of 1942, they had investigated at least five killings. Even though they took the position that there were grounds for federal involvement only in cases where state officials were involved in lynchings, their investigations did lead, directly or indirectly, to some people being indicted, including some in both the Howard Wash and the Isaac Simmons lynchings cited above. In Mississippi, of course, it was impossible to find a jury that would convict, but even the idea that lynchers could be indicted was a new thought for Mississippi, a clear reminder that the outside world was beginning to impinge in uncomfortable ways.

An equally important factor in the gradual decline of racial terror may have been the collapse of the cotton economy, which led to less need to control Blacks, either through the near-peonage of sharecropping or through violence. Prior to the turn of the century racial lynchings across the South averaged around one hundred a year. Between 1900 and 1920, they fluctuated between fifty and seventy. By 1935, after the arrival of nickel-a-pound cotton, the number dropped to eighteen, and for the next twenty years it would not rise above eight in any one year. There continued to be non-economic reasons for controlling Blacks, obviously, but economic changes removed one of the traditional pillars of the system.

In the early 1930s, according to Arthur Raper's classic study of lynching, Mississippi officials prevented fourteen lynchings, more than they allowed to take place. Hortense Powdermaker, conducting her study of Sunflower County at the same time, concluded that the fear of outside opinion was a potent factor in reducing community support for the mob. By the thirties, newspapers in larger Southern cities typically criticized lynchings, at least in principle. By the forties, their criticisms were clearly linked to fear of outside scrutiny. In 1943, for example, the Jackson *Clarion-Ledger* warned that the federal government was trying to find a way to bring lynching under federal jurisdiction, "a fact which all citizens, all law officers, and all court officials, should keep in mind constantly." The only absolutely certain way to block the menace of federal encroachment, they stressed, "is to prevent lynchings in the future, through education, through suasion, and by giving every prisoner or suspect full and adequate protection until the guilty are punished through due process of law."

While political agitation was becoming more effective, the collapse of the cotton-based economy simultaneously removed the most fundamental reason for controlling Blacks. Lynching patterns had always been related in complicated ways to economic factors. In the Delta, the most common months for lynching were June and July, the months of the cotton season when cotton needs the least labor. Between the turn of the century and the Depression, there was a consistent relationship across the South between the price of cotton and the number of lynchings. In relatively prosperous times, lynchings were fewer. When whites were feeling more economic pressure, they were more likely to turn to rope and faggot. In the midst of the Depression, with cotton at a nickel a pound, the correlation was broken. Instead of going up, as one would have predicted from past patterns, the number of lynchings went down. Economic insecurity during the Depression affected different classes of whites in different ways. Poor whites traditionally made up the majority of the mobs. Jessie Daniel Ames of the Association of Southern Women for the Prevention of Lynching pointed out that those poor whites reached by New Deal programs actually may have had more cash money in their pockets than they were accustomed to and thus had less need of "finding a Negro to lynch to prove their supremacy." For wealthier whites in the South, lynching was beginning to look counterproductive. In 1939, Ames noted, "we have managed to reduce lynchings . . . not because we've grown more law-abiding or respectable but because lynchings became such bad advertising. The South is going after big industry at the moment and a lawless, lynch-mob population isn't going to attract very much outside capital." . . .

The Black Response

Changes in the structural underpinnings of racism wouldn't have mattered if Black Mississippians weren't willing to challenge the system. There were always people who resisted, as witnessed by the slayings of Wilder McGowan and the Reverend T. A. Allen, killed in 1935 for organizing sharecroppers. In the 1940s, the pace of activism picked up, often in direct response to changes originating outside the state.

The generation of Black Mississippians coming to adulthood in the late 1940s had a stronger sense of entitlement than their parents. By 1947, the Delta's David Cohn could lament:

> The younger generation of Negroes is sharply at odds with their elders. If the latter suggest moderation in racial points of view, if they say that the world cannot be changed in a day, younger Negroes are likely to dismiss them contemptuously as "handkerchief heads" or "Uncle Toms"—epithets taken from the Northern Negro press, whose often reckless and irresponsible outpourings they avidly read.

It wouldn't take much for a man of Cohn's disposition to see a militant behind every other plow, but more judicious observers saw similar changes. Samuel Adams, studying one hundred sharecropper families in the Delta in the mid-1940s, found "evidence of a growing race consciousness" in their changing musical tastes. Increasingly, the songs that were popular were those that ridiculed whites, made subtle protests against segregation, or tried to stimulate racial pride.

Hortense Powdermaker detected more aggressive attitudes emerging among Blacks in the early 1930s. While she found every possible shading of opinion among Blacks of every age and every status grouping, there were discernible patterns, with the most consistent patterns centering on age. The oldest generation, those over sixty at the time of the study, had been born either in slavery or just after the Civil War. They were the generation most prone to put their trust in "good" white people and most prone to believe that Blacks were indeed inferior to whites. Still, they resented the suffering the system imposed on them. Among this generation, both belief and behavior tended to acknowledge white superiority.

Their children, though, born just before the turn of the century, more typically continued to behave as if they accepted the superiority of whites but seldom really believed it. They grew up having less intimate contact with whites than had their parents, and many of them, with at least the rudiments of literacy and exposure to newspapers, movies, and the radio, were more aware of the world beyond the plantation. They held that Blacks were just as good as whites but recognized as a plain fact of life that such a belief could not be acted on publicly. In the presence of whites, they presented the countenance whites typically wanted to see—respectful, content, subservient. Some derived a fleeting sense of superiority from their ability to deceive whites.

The children of that generation, people born in the early years of the century, exhibited a great deal more resentment at their station in life. They considered themselves entitled to equal treatment and were much less comfortable than their parents had been with the elaborate codes of ritual deference, a dilemma they resolved by trying to avoid contact with whites as much as possible. Similarly, the better-educated Blacks of whatever generation tended to be more visibly angry about the injustices and indignities of the system, and they, too, reacted by minimizing their contact with whites. For those who had too much pride to greet a white man with the traditional "Howdy, boss," or some equally humiliating variant, avoiding contact altogether was the next best thing.

Powdermaker is careful to say that the more bitter, resentful attitudes characterized only a "dissenting minority," but "it is their attitude that is spreading and the more passive one that is on the wane as . . . ideas of what is due the individual citizen penetrate ever more deeply into the Negro group." While these attitudes in the 1930s seldom expressed themselves politically, that potential was clearly present. She reports that one young man, whom she presents as typical of the better-educated Negroes, "recognizes his inability to vote as the crucial point. For him the vote has become the symbol of the kernel of the inter-racial situation. He maintains that . . . only a need for the votes of the Negroes will bring justice to them in work, in conditions of living, in the courts."

By the 1940s, that attitude among Mississippi Blacks had begun to grow into various forms of political mobilization, much of it based in Jackson, the state's largest urban center. In the middle of the decade, T. B. Wilson, secretary of the Jackson NAACP ("Niggers, Apes, Alligators, Coons and Possums," according to the old racist joke), organized a chapter of the National Progressive Voters League.

The *Jackson Advocate,* like many Black papers of the day, supported the drive vigorously. Response was slow at first but quickened with the 1944 Supreme Court decision outlawing the white primary. Before that decision, Wilson said, people were "indifferent, disinterested, but when we worked up this case of registering and voting them because the Supreme Court decision gave us to understand that we could vote, then they began to go register."

The importance of the white-primary decision is still not widely appreciated. In much of the South, allowing only whites to vote in primary elections had been the most effective means of wholesale disenfranchisement. Once that became illegal, there was an almost immediate surge in Black registration, which historian David Garrow sees as the true beginning of Black political emergence in the South. In 1940, only three percent of Southern Blacks were registered, a figure that had not changed much since the turn of the century. By 1947, twelve percent were registered; by 1952, twenty percent. . . .

[Black] veterans became a factor in what was probably the most significant mobilization of Mississippi Blacks in the forties, the hearings on Senator Theodore Bilbo. For all of his long career, Bilbo had been a symbol of the most virulent sort of racism, best summarized by his famous admonition that the best way to keep a Negro from the polls on election day was to pay him a visit at home the evening before, a message he spread with increased vigor after the all-white primary was outlawed. Indeed, some observers thought many white Mississippians would have accepted the decision had not Bilbo and others whipped up a campaign against it.

After Bilbo's reelection in 1946, the national NAACP, in conjunction with organized labor and other groups Bilbo had offended, led a drive to convince the Senate to refuse to seat him, on the grounds that Bilbo had been a leader in the disenfranchisement of Blacks. At the hearing held in Jackson, Black veterans testified for three days. Moreover, Negroes packed the courtroom, perhaps the most significant act of public defiance from Negroes the state had seen in decades. County registrar after county registrar faced the national press and detailed with great honesty exactly how hard they worked to keep the voting rolls white, by advising Negroes not to try to register, by threatening those who didn't recognize good advice when they heard it, by employing a double standard on the literacy requirement. Their candor was a gauge of how little some Mississippians of that period worried about the opinions of the outside world.

Bilbo died before the Senate reached a final decision on his seating, but he had served a purpose, providing Blacks with a symbol so universally hated that Mississippi Blacks with some help from out of state were able to mobilize publicly against it. In the context of this mobilization, Black voter registration rose steadily. There were an estimated two thousand registered Negroes in the state in 1940, twenty-five hundred in 1946, but five thousand in 1947, a one-hundred-percent increase in a year. (Even so, that amounted to about one percent of the eligible Negroes in the state, the lowest figure in the South. In 1946 in rural Leflore County, where Greenwood is located, twenty-six of the county's thirty-nine thousand Negroes were on the rolls, none of whom voted.) "Negro leaders in the state point out that perhaps the most crucial factor in this remarkable increase was the stimulation and courage" provided by the Bilbo hearing. The surge in Black registration started immediately after the war and continued for several years. There were seventeen thousand on the rolls by 1952, of whom perhaps fifty-six hundred were voting. The number of registrants peaked around 1954 or 1955, somewhere between twenty and twenty-five thousand, the highest figure in the twentieth century.

Characteristically, Mississippi made less progress between the late forties and the early fifties than did nearby states. In that period, Mississippi saw a fourfold increase in Black registration. Both Alabama and Louisiana, the two states which, after Mississippi, were considered most determined to keep Blacks from the polls, changed more rapidly during the same years. In Louisiana, Black registration went from ten thousand to one hundred thousand. Even in Alabama, it went from six thousand to fifty thousand, an eightfold increase.

The southern states as a whole, of course, had developed a long list of tactics to minimize Black voting. Among them were requiring one or more white character witnesses; requiring only Black applicants to show property tax receipts; strict enforcement of literacy tests against Negro applicants; rejecting Black applicants because of technical mistakes in filling out registration forms or requiring Black applicants to fill out their own forms while those of whites were filled out by registration officials; a variety of evasive tactics, such as claiming that registration cards had run out, that all members of the registration board had to be present, or that it was closing time; putting difficult questions about the Constitution to Negro applicants; holding registration in private homes, which Blacks were reluctant to enter. Where other sections of the South relied primarily on a few such tactics, Mississippi, according to Margaret Price, appeared to use them all. As late as 1954, in the thirteen Mississippi counties that had majority Negro populations a *total* of fourteen votes were cast by Blacks in that year's elections. . . .

The figure of twenty or twenty-five thousand registrants in Mississippi by the mid-fifties is hardly impressive in a state with an adult Negro population of nearly half a million. Still, it represents a tenfold increase in fifteen years, a rapid enough change to suggest some underlying qualitative shift in the political activity of Blacks. The same is suggested by the growing state NAACP membership. In 1949, the records of the national office listed twenty-three branches with a total of one thousand members. Southern branches were frequently short-lived. By 1951, there were only seventeen branches in the state, but they still claimed about one thousand members. In 1952, membership crept up to thirteen hundred; by the end of 1954, it reached twenty-seven hundred, still a small number but double the 1952 figure.

The rising numbers of Black voters and NAACP members were not the only reasons in the early 1950s for thinking that the South, even Mississippi, had begun to turn away from the past. In Mississippi, median Negro family income was up, with almost all the increase associated with urban families. Racist violence across the South was less common than it had been. In Mississippi between 1946 and 1949, one observer found no evidence of significant Klan activity. In 1952, for the first time in seventy years, Tuskegee Institute could not find an example of a lynching in the South. The more underground forms of racial killings continued, of course, and race-related bombings continued to occur, but observers thought even the latter might have their silver lining. A bombing may be the act of a lone individual or two and is a form of violence preferred by people who are afraid of being caught.

In urban areas and the upper South, barriers to Negro registration were lowered, and Blacks even ran for office. In all areas of the South, even Mississippi, interracial groups such as the Southern

Regional Conference had begun to work publicly for change. "Mississippi Negroes," said a Jackson newspaper in the mid-fifties, "have a gleam in their eyes and a feeling that they have a foot in the door." Another observer, sympathetic and well informed, said "It is to be hoped that the 1950s may be a decade of citizenship fully realized."

Some very experienced Black activists were similarly optimistic. The NAACP's Ruby Hurley, in a memo written as late as 1955, noted an increase in the number of threats against NAACP officers in the state but also observed that people did not seem unduly worried by them. "Although our people are terribly annoyed, they are not frightened as they might have been a few years ago." She was meeting some determined Negroes, people who were telling her, "We just want our rights; we want to vote like the white folks do. . . . And they can pressure all they want, it won't make no difference. We ain't always eaten so high on the hog, we can eat poor again."

In his year-end report for 1954, E. J. Stringer, who had suffered various forms of harassment for serving as president of the NAACP State Conference of Branches, was full of optimism. In 1955, he thought, it should be possible to have at least one branch in each of the state's eighty-two counties; successful school integration was forthcoming. T. R. M. Howard, president of the Regional Council of Negro Leadership (RCNL), had also been harassed—at the age of 47, his draft board reclassified him 1-A—but still thought the future looked promising. In 1954, he noted that while three-fourths of Mississippi whites would take up arms to defend segregation, another year or so might change a great many attitudes.

Partly because of economic change inside the state, partly because of Mississippi's increasing involvement with the social currents of the world outside the state, racial terror was no longer as common or as effective as it had been. If some observers were optimistic about the state's future, we may be sure that many others had to be uncertain. There was no way to tell how meaningful the apparent changes were until someone tested them.

II

The Development

of a Movement

Civil rights activism continued to increase in the years following World War I.
The National Association for the Advancement of Colored People (NAACP),
founded in 1909, protested various forms of racial subjugation—from disenfranchisement and segregation to job discrimination. Here NAACP members
picket a 1934 crime conference in Washington, D.C. to protest lynching.
(Corbis)

and first heard these cases under the rubric of *Brown*. Public school segregation, according to the NAACP's legal brief, was a violation of the Fourteenth Amendment's equal protection clause. An integral element of the effort to make blacks part of the nation during the Reconstruction period (1863–77), this 1867 amendment clearly defined U.S. citizenship to encompass all blacks. Furthermore, it stated that all citizens were equal under the law. Consequently, the NAACP lawyers argued, the blatantly unequal racially segregated schools were unconstitutional and had to be integrated. In each case, local lawyers in conjunction with NAACP lawyers sought the immediate end of Jim Crow schools as intrinsically separate and unequal. The lawyers also argued that state-sanctioned segregation stamped blacks with a stigma of inferiority that undermined their self-esteem. In effect, the aim in *Brown*—the total and unconditional abolition of Jim Crow schools—represented a critical move in the black freedom struggle.

Historical Backdrop: The Constitution, the Law, and Fighting Jim Crow

The continuing African American freedom struggle has produced simultaneous, often overlapping, battles on many fronts: political, economic, social, cultural. The nineteenth-century war against slavery featured moral as well as political and economic campaigns in the North. This effort required that slaves and free blacks in the South struggle as best they could until conditions were ripe for seizing freedom for the enslaved, as they were in the Civil War. Abolitionism—various northern-based movements to emancipate the slaves—was a divisive national issue that alienated most whites, especially the proslavery forces in the North and South. Like the war against Jim Crow, abolitionism was a war waged by a dissenting black minority and its stalwart white supporters: a multifaceted and far-reaching struggle. . . .

The Evolution of the NAACP Legal Campaign Against Jim Crow

"The problem of the twentieth century," African American scholar and leader W. E. B. Du Bois perceptively noted in 1903, "is the problem of the color line." This often quoted prophecy speaks directly to the uncharted road leading to *Brown:* how best to alleviate the "color line," a primary manifestation of Jim Crow. At this time, Du Bois increasingly favored public agitation, particularly political organization and political action. Booker T. Washington, the most famous and influential black leader from 1895 to 1915, publicly advanced an accommodationist strategy emphasizing black self-help and the cultivation of goodwill between the races, not agitation. These two positions reflected a continuing debate on how best to advance the interests of African Americans.

In spite of Washington's accommodationist public persona, behind the scenes he was actively engaged in lawsuits challenging Jim Crow. Du Bois, however, took the more publicly activist route and along with prominent blacks such as Ida B. Wells and William Monroe Trotter and whites such as Mary White Ovington and Oswald Garrison Villard launched the interracial National Association for the Advancement of Colored People (NAACP) in 1909. Founded in part as a response to a series of antiblack race riots, most notably the 1908 Springfield, Illinois racial conflagration, the NAACP soon emerged as the leading black civil rights organization.

The NAACP pursued several lines of attack in its assault on the "color line." Lobbying for favorable legislative, judicial, and executive action; waging a publicity war through the media, most effectively in the *Crisis* magazine, initially edited by Du Bois; and working with grassroots chapters on specific issues of local concern such as discriminatory ordinances, the organization endeavored to advance a black civil rights agenda. Intensely fought battles against antiblack discrimination in jobs, housing, voting, public accommodations, and education demanded functional knowledge, savvy, and flexibility. Given its limited resources and the awesome power of the racist status quo, the NAACP favored significant yet workable battlegrounds where its members could realistically achieve the upper hand. Victories with far-reaching impact were thus highly desirable.

From the beginning, litigation proved to be a particularly important and effective tool in the organization's armament. The legal struggle against segregated schools in mid-nineteenth-century Boston and Jim Crow railway cars at the turn of the century clearly presaged the NAACP legal campaigns. In the Boston school integration (1849), *Dred Scott* (1857), and *Plessy* (1896) cases, the decisions went against the individual black claimants and the collective aspirations of blacks. Nevertheless, hope remained that the rule of law would eventually be squared with constitutional claims for full black equality, especially following the enactment of the Fourteenth Amendment.

The legal endorsement of equality in *Brown* was a capstone to an extraordinary series of battles against de jure (legal) and de facto (actual) Jim Crow. The Fourteenth Amendment's guarantee of equal protection under the law epitomized the legal tradition undergirding *Brown*. Early American legal tradition (1787–1830) was built on English common law and emphasized freedom, equality, and justice for all citizens as framed in the Constitution (1787) and Bill of Rights (1791). With its powerful Enlightenment grounding, this compelling vision of constitutional law stressed reason, order, and progress as inseparable from freedom, equality, and justice. The United States ideologically embraced a republican form of government that deepened the young nation's commitment to these tenets.

This libertarian, or pro-freedom, reading of the Constitution and the law is fundamentally antithetical to the slavery and racism the nation's founders embraced. In fact, the founding patriarchs countenanced freedom for whites fully predicated upon black slavery and black debasement. This haunting paradox has decisively shaped the American nation since its founding. However, the libertarian view of the Declaration of Independence (1776) and the Constitution, along with the radical egalitarianism of the former, provided indispensable ideological bases for the black freedom struggle from the beginning until now. . . .

A deep-seated belief in the prospects for advancing black civil rights through the legal system earmarked the highly influential career of Charles Hamilton Houston, who was most responsible for charting the various legal paths that led to *Brown*. In 1983, Judge A. Leon Higginbotham Jr. wrote that "Houston was the chief engineer and the first major architect of the twentieth-century civil rights legal scene." He "almost single-handedly . . . organized and led the legal battalion in the critical early battles seeking equality for black Americans."

Harvard-trained and the first black elected to *Harvard Law Review*, Houston left a private practice he shared with his father in Washington, D.C., to become dean of Howard University's law school (1924–35). . . . Besides Thurgood Marshall, who would be instrumental in *Brown* and later would be a Supreme Court justice,

Houston taught a number of prominent attorneys who would distinguish themselves in civil rights litigation, including Edward P. Lovett, James G. Tyson, Oliver W. Hill, Coyness L. Ennix, and Leslie S. Perry. Second, he pioneered in two fields of legal study and practice: civil rights law and public interest law. Third, he engaged in a whirlwind of civil liberties, civil rights, and antidiscrimination activities, beyond his university duties, including the defense in the highly publicized Scottsboro case in which nine young Alabama blacks were accused of raping two white women on a freight train. By 1935, Houston had emerged as the most influential black lawyer in the United States.

In light of that status, it is not surprising that when the NAACP sought a new special counsel in 1934, Houston was chosen. Having taught law and litigated a variety of cases, he was now charged with the responsibility of directing the litigation activities of the most important black civil rights organization in the country. Houston stressed that the law was a potentially useful means to promote social change, especially in the context of a complicated social struggle. Why the judicial system? As historian Genna Rae McNeil has noted: "With little power to compel congressional or presidential concessions and with virulent racism ever a possible consequence of direct action, blacks were in a better position to seek redress through the courts." . . .

Believing that carefully executed litigation could contribute to local grassroots activism and the development of a mass movement, the NAACP and its legal staff supported local legal struggles. NAACP lawyers worked hand in glove with local lawyers, whether the issue was black political exclusion, disparities between white and black teachers' salaries, a black falsely accused or convicted of a crime, or some other miscarriage of racial justice. The NAACP also mounted a vigorous legal and educational campaign against the most virulent forms of legal racism, such as the highly visible terrorism of state-sanctioned white rule through mob action and lynch law. In far too many instances in the first half of the twentieth century, a black accused of a crime—especially a black man accused of raping a white woman—was murdered publicly by angry white lynch mobs with no concern for niceties like court trials or convictions. Although the NAACP had waged an unrelenting and highly public battle against white lynch law since 1919, the group—like others struggling against

this heinous injustice—was unable to persuade the federal government to pass an antilynching law. Southern white opposition, notably
in the Congress, effectively blocked all such efforts.

Battered but undaunted, the NAACP went forward. The seemingly impregnable state-sanctioned world of Jim Crow fueled extensive debate within the organization around what tactics to use to
dismantle institutionalized racism. Two related debates in the 1930s
illuminate the nature and impact of this spirited discourse: (1) the
kind of legal strategy to pursue and (2) more broadly considered,
legalism versus alternative strategies.

The first debate was over whether the NAACP lawyers should
attack the entire edifice of Jim Crow forthrightly by seeking a ruling
nullifying *Plessy*—a direct attack strategy—or, whether they should
work incrementally, building a series of legal victories that paved the
way for the eventual dismantling of *Plessy*—a developmental strategy.
A principal goal of the developmental strategy was to force the South
to equalize its separate black and white worlds through litigation by
making Jim Crow fiscally and politically unworkable. Given the rela-
tive poverty of the South and the declining respectability of Jim
Crow, equalization would undermine American apartheid.

Nathan Margold, Houston's predecessor as head of the
NAACP legal team, had pushed for the direct attack strategy. Like
Houston, Margold was a protégé of Felix Frankfurter and was committed to both legal realism and judicial activism. In 1931, a year
after his hiring, Margold issued a bold report strategically arguing
for a direct attack on segregation, leaving open the issue of equalization. A frontal assault would cut immediately to the heart of the
issue—cogent legal demonstration of the fundamental wrong of
state-sanctioned racial segregation—and would require an immediate end to Jim Crow. Margold preferred that the issue of equalization be treated as a related but subordinate concern.

Margold maintained that a direct attack was preferable as it
required fewer suits and the NAACP's legal staff could devote its
attention to precedent-setting cases. Similarly, this approach avoided
litigating overlapping suits at the state and local levels and thus the
often confusing and conflicting welter of federal, state, and local
statutes. Also, as the Margold report explained, a direct attack was
a better use of the NAACP's limited fiscal resources and its small
legal staff.

Houston and Marshall after him firmly believed that the Margold report put forth a position which the NAACP and the larger black freedom struggle should support in theory; however, in reality, they realized that the times were inauspicious for such an aggressive strategy. In the Depression years, economic hardships intensified among blacks and spread among whites. Economic turmoil further exacerbated racial tensions and did not provide the most supportive setting to battle Jim Crow. In addition, the NAACP lacked sufficient mass black support and progressive white support on the one hand and the necessary strategic support within the legal establishment on the other. In the 1930s in particular, many blacks still had to be convinced that a legal assault against Jim Crow was viable. Otherwise, local blacks facing the extraordinary pressures brought to bear against those who filed anti–Jim Crow suits might not have the uncommon courage and the black community support necessary to proceed. Another important impediment which had to be overcome was the widespread lack of trained black lawyers. Therefore, Houston decided to employ a more moderate strategy of equalization as a way to build support for a direct attack later. Cultivating a network of popular and professional support became a vital tactical goal.

Houston chose to focus the legal assault on education because of its centrality to advancement and fulfillment within American culture. As such, the blatant denial of equal educational opportunities to black youth touched a powerful nerve in the American psyche. The terrible realities of segregated education in the South offered compelling evidence of gross racial disparities in facilities, budgets, and salaries. Also, Houston contended, "discrimination in education is symbolic of all the more drastic discriminations," such as lynch law. Furthermore, Jim Crow education represented the deeply ingrained stigma of innate black racial inferiority.

Houston's strategy featured three related aspects. Desegregation of public graduate and professional schools was one. Here the battle was fought at a less contentious level than that of elementary and secondary schools. Equalization of white and black teachers' salaries was the next aspect. The NAACP legal team achieved a number of important victories in salary cases. As a result, many southern school boards masked salary differentials through the use of so-called merit criteria, and the cases became much harder to argue. It was not until the late 1940s that the next level of the legal plan—equalization of elementary and secondary school facilities—became feasible. Until then, overcoming the local and tactical obstacles hindering these cases proved too difficult.

Another challenge was finding and sustaining the morale of litigants whose character and resources would have to withstand intense public scrutiny and white reprisals—typically economic, sometimes physical and violent. The prolongation of many cases caused litigants to lose enthusiasm and even drop out. Racist southern school districts used various legal strategies to tie up the proceedings and to exhaust black litigants financially and emotionally. Often these districts admitted to the disparities in their educational offerings but exaggerated or lied about efforts under way to ameliorate them. The defense used this tactic in the South Carolina district court case of *Briggs v. Elliott.*

Other obstacles faced the legal team. First, the fact that the states and local school districts themselves were primarily responsible for public school education policy and funding inhibited litigation at the federal level. Second, with the awesome weight of tradition and social custom, *Plessy* was the precedent upon which pro–Jim Crow rulings rested. Third, it followed that courts did not consider state-sanctioned Jim Crow to violate the Fourteenth Amendment rights of blacks to equal protection under the law and therefore left Jim Crow intact. Fourth, the defendants and courts alike variously ignored, trivialized, masked, neutralized, explained away, and accepted the pervasive reality of separate and unequal. All of these tactics naturalized Jim Crow as fundamental to a "higher law" of white supremacy, or integral to the organic order of society. According to Mary Frances Berry, the controlling factor in legal decisions was the ubiquity of constitutional racism. Ultimately, as Derrick Bell maintains, the law functioned to sustain white supremacy.

The NAACP's Legal Strategy Challenged

It is not surprising, then, that searching questions were raised about the NAACP's growing commitment to legalism as a primary strategy: the group's second pivotal 1930s controversy. Many committed to the black freedom struggle called for greater emphasis on economic issues because of the Depression's ravaging effects. As one would expect, economic critique was widespread: it could easily be found on the street, in colleges and universities, and among radicals and progressives. Bluesman Carl Martin observed:

> Everybody's crying: "Let's have a New Deal,"
> 'Cause I've got to make a living,
> If I have to rob and steal.

At the same time, economist Abram Harris and political scientist and future United Nations stalwart Ralph Bunche, both young professors at Howard University, called for interracial labor unity and an understanding of the centrality of economics, or material forces, to the historic oppression of blacks. They maintained that the oppression of blacks was not merely a problem of race but was a question of class as well. Broadly speaking, the struggle had to be one of ameliorating capitalism's most flagrant abuses. Far more oppositional, albeit less influential, voices like black Alabama Communist Party activist Hosea Hudson found capitalism itself to be the problem, socialist revolution the solution.

The venerable W. E. B. Du Bois was the most provocative and powerful voice questioning the NAACP's focus in the 1930s. His perceptive critique cut two ways. First, harking back to the ideas of Booker T. Washington at the turn of the century, Du Bois now wanted the fiercely interracialist and integrationist NAACP to promote black economic development—and in turn black elevation—through aggressive support of a separate black economic world. Du Bois's Marxist-socialist-inspired critique of capitalism, calling for greater workers' control over the economy, spoke more and more of the necessity for black networks like consumer cooperatives. This message did not sit well with the intensely pro-capitalist NAACP.

Du Bois and others emphasized that legalism had to be prefaced by the redistribution of wealth and across-the-board leveling of power and influence. Reliance on legalism as a remedy for the problems confronting black Americans signaled a reformist agenda at best, they felt, certainly not a revolutionary one. After leaving the association in 1934, once the ideological rift became irreparable, Du Bois continued to offer an increasingly militant socialist and internationalist approach. The "road to *Brown*," however, was clearly being plotted through capitalism, not socialism.

Du Bois's call for black economic nationalism vividly exposed the tensions between voluntary and imposed segregation, between separatism and integrationism, between black nationalism and American nationalism. Seeking to get beyond these tensions, he stressed that blacks had to strengthen the institutional infrastructure and social fabric of their own communities. The critical issue was to forge more effective forms of collective organization and action aimed at intraracial uplift. In this vision, integration assumed a decidedly secondary, even ancillary, position. He emphasized the importance of black institutions and black culture in structuring and propelling the black freedom struggle and in nurturing the black psyche. The thrust of NAACP politics, from this point of view, increasingly now collided with rather than meshed with black needs and aspirations.

The historical and rhetorical development of *Brown* reflected a profound discomfort with racial separatism. Essential to the social-scientific discourse behind *Brown* was the argument that racial segregation, even voluntary segregation, was responsible for the psychological damage and sociocultural pathology among blacks. Du Bois clearly perceived that this negative characterization of a distinctive black life and culture as well as of blacks as victims was one-sided and misleading. This potentially baneful argument, increasingly vital to the NAACP's liberal indictment of Jim Crow, failed to make the crucial distinction between what Du Bois saw as the benefits of voluntary segregation—autonomy and psychic health—and the harm of state-imposed segregation—dependency and dehumanization. The point was not that white racism had deformed black life and culture, but rather that it had deformed the American experience. . . .

The Growing Anti-Racist Offensive: *An American Dilemma* Confronts World War II

Another vital development fueling the NAACP's crusade was the declining intellectual and cultural respectability of racism. In *Brown* and the various cases the NAACP lawyers argued leading up to it, the growing scientific and humanistic consensus in favor of egalitarianism was crucial. Nowhere was this point more effectively put forward to national and worldwide audiences than in Gunnar Myrdal's magisterial study of race relations in the United States, *An American Dilemma* (1944). The Swedish economist directed a large staff in an exhaustive study, four years in the making, of the evidence and significance of the discrepancy between the American creed and the American reality for African Americans. The awesome final product consisted of more than 1,000 pages of text, ten appendices, and more than 250 pages of notes.

For 1950s America and beyond, the *Brown* decision and *An American Dilemma* constitute twin pillars in the evolving liberal racial orthodoxy: America had no choice but to live up to the American creed in its treatment of its black citizens. Evidence of the impact of *An American Dilemma* can be seen in its extensive use in the theory and practice of civil rights law—where its findings became crucial—and its influence on the Supreme Court that decided *Brown*. It became the authoritative work on black-white race relations until the mid-1960s when its assimilationist and integrationist approach came under attack (notably within the black insurgency) as being too liberal, too reformist, and complicitous in the negative construction of black life and culture. From World War II up to the radical Black Power movement beginning in 1966, *An American Dilemma* defined the liberal orthodoxy on American race relations. The *Brown* decision experienced a similar path. . . .

As in *Brown*, the argument and the remedy in *An American Dilemma*—like most American efforts to deal with racial inequality—did not go far enough. What became increasingly clear in the period from *An American Dilemma* to *Brown* was a growing yet insufficient national will to tackle this thorny problem. In spite of brief moments to the contrary, such as the noteworthy government efforts spawned by black insurgency between 1954 and 1974, the national will has proven insufficient to the challenge.

Even the explosive wartime economy that brought the nation out of the Depression and the subsequent thirty years of sustained economic growth were insufficient to create racial equality. Neither was postwar U.S. global supremacy. Nonetheless, in this broad context of sustained economic growth and "Pax Americana," or worldwide U.S. dominance, the black freedom struggle surged. *Brown* represented a turning point in its building momentum.

The pulsating wartime economy transformed the American landscape. Streams of rural blacks leaving the South during the Depression reached flood proportions during the war as job opportunities

when he was refused admission to the University of Maryland's law school. The state's alternative of providing scholarships for blacks to attend out-of-state schools was viewed as a violation of Murray's Fourteenth Amendment right to equal treatment under the law. Because the constitutional injury to Murray was "present and personal," the remedy had to be immediate. Murray either had to be admitted at once to Maryland's School of Law or a separate and equal school of law for Maryland blacks had to be created forthwith. Since a comparable black law school could not be created overnight, he had to be admitted to Maryland's School of Law.

Nevertheless, with the possibility that a separate black law school might satisfy the letter of the ruling, *Plessy* clearly remained intact. In the *Gaines* and *Sipuel* cases, similar circumstances resulted in similar rulings, this time in the Supreme Court. The decisions in these cases turn on the issue of the inequality between the reputable all-white state-supported law schools in Missouri and Oklahoma and the makeshift all-black arrangements those states scrambled to provide to avoid admitting blacks to their all-white law schools. Notwithstanding the impact of the sociological arguments on the behind-the-scenes discussions of these cases, the Court was deeply divided on the issue of overruling *Plessy* and thus did not go that far. . . .

In *Henderson v. United States* (1949), a case coupled with *Sweatt* and *McLaurin,* the federal government issued a friend-of-the-court brief vigorously condemning segregated railroad dining cars, which the Court subsequently declared illegal. Earlier, in *Shelley v. Kraemer* (1947) and *Sipes v. McGhee* (1947), the Supreme Court outlawed restrictive covenants (contracts forbidding the sale of property to blacks and other "stigmatized" groups and individuals) as invidious and unconstitutional forms of racial discrimination. Charles Houston himself, in concert with his NAACP colleagues, argued this series of cases. In its friend-of-the-court brief to support the government's opposition to restrictive covenants, the Department of Justice revealed the growing importance of cold war concerns. That brief made it clear that Jim Crow was a very serious problem for the United States in its propaganda war with the Soviets for the hearts and minds of the Third World, especially in Africa. Indeed, this was an issue that the NAACP legal team and its cohorts increasingly exploited to good effect.

In *Henderson,* Attorney General Howard McGrath maintained before the Supreme Court that "segregation signifies and is intended to signify that a member of the colored race is not equal to the white race." Jim Crow, McGrath further explained, represented "an anachronism which a half-century of history and experience has shown to be a departure from the basic constitutional principle that all Americans, regardless of their race or color or religion or national origin, stand equal and alike in the sight of the law." This ringing endorsement of constitutional egalitarianism by the nation's number one lawyer meshed well with the Justice Department's earlier argument for desegregation on cold war grounds. This kind of ammunition, including President Harry Truman's official initiation of desegregation of the armed forces, verified strong opposition within the government to state-sanctioned racial segregation. The stage was now set for a full-fledged direct attack against *Plessy*-sanctioned segregation: the "road to *Brown*" was taking shape.

Politics, Social Change, and Decision-Making within the Supreme Court: The Crafting of *Brown*

Brown v. Board of Education of Topeka, Kansas, as well as *Briggs v. Elliott, Davis v. County School Board of Prince Edward County, Belton v. Gebhart,* and *Bolling v. Sharpe*—the cases eventually argued collectively as *Brown v. Board of Education*—all wound their separate ways toward the Supreme Court in the early 1950s. In each case, and in spite of anticipated lower court setbacks, the NAACP legal staff remained hopeful about a positive Supreme Court ruling in favor of equal educational opportunity. Third World nationalist struggles, most importantly growing assertiveness within America's own communities of color, pervaded the international community, which was reeling from the Holocaust, the dropping of the atomic bomb on Hiroshima and Nagasaki, and an escalating cold war. Worldwide as well as at home, white supremacy was under furious assault. Even though the "Red scare" repressed left-progressive forces in this country, seriously undermining the most radical elements within the black struggle, that insurgency soon reinvigorated itself via the civil rights movement. *Brown* contributed significantly to the ethos and spirit of this revitalized social movement, which was fast becoming a mass movement. . . .

[B]oth sides in *Brown* mounted strong cases. From the lower courts, *Briggs v. Elliott* is included because the case featured two legal titans: the celebrated establishment lawyer John W. Davis for the defense and Thurgood Marshall for the plaintiffs. In oral arguments, they both provided high drama as well as astute argumentation. In their legal briefs, they compellingly presented their cases. *Briggs v. Elliott* encapsulated the twin battles in the NAACP's all-out war on segregated schools. First was the clear-cut evidence of the denial of equal educational opportunity owing to gross physical and funding disparities between white and black schools. Second was the inter-related argument of psychosocial harm inflicted on black school-children as a result of Jim Crow schools. Although only the lower court dissent of Judge J. Waties Waring responded favorably to the second argument, it clearly made an impact on both sides.

Indeed, the sociological argument figured in all of the component cases in *Brown* except *Bolling v. Sharpe*. The NAACP lawyers relied heavily on the social-scientific work of many influential scholars such as Otto Klineberg and Gordon Allport. The most important of these experts, however, were social psychologists Kenneth and Mamie Clark. The Clarks had devised a doll test as a way to gauge evidence of personality dysfunction among black children under Jim Crow. When shown two dolls—one white and one black—the children were asked which one they preferred. The fact that a preponderance of the black children expressed a preference for the white doll was most revealing for the Clarks. From this finding, they extrapolated that the damage done to the self-esteem of these children reinforced notions of black inferiority and white superiority. Racial segregation did indeed damage the black psyche. The issue was not, as the majority opinion in *Plessy* had contended, that the antiblack stigma was all in the minds of blacks. Rather, the stigma was all too real, for whites as well as blacks. . . .

The arguments in *Brown* proceeded in three stages. First, the initial presentation of the case did not give the justices all the time and evidence they needed to decide definitively. To gain more time to sift through the evidence and try to sway one another on various points, the justices called for a second stage to the proceedings: reargument on the intentions of the Fourteenth Amendment's framers.

Had the framers created that amendment as opposing or supporting segregated public school education? The third and final stage,
after the decision to strike down *Plessy* on the merits of the case was
reached—often called *Brown I*—the court called for arguments
about the remedy, or how to enforce the ruling. That decision regarding implementation is often referred to as *Brown II*.

During the first stage of deliberations, a consensus emerged
that overall the claimants' case was powerful enough to be sustained
and in turn to be used as a platform to overrule *Plessy*. Speaking to
the sociological argument, Justice Tom Clark privately observed that
"we need no modern psychologist to tell us that 'enforced separation
of the two races stamp[s] the colored race with a badge of inferiority,' contrary to [the argument in] *Plessy v. Ferguson*." Agreement on
racial equality and the related imperative of equality of educational
opportunity emerged early on. Two other issues loomed as more
contentious. In spite of much debate, the evidence of the intentions
of the Fourteenth Amendment's framers was not very convincing. A
modest preponderance of the evidence suggested that they saw the
amendment as favoring segregated public school education. Ultimately, however, the justices found the evidence inconclusive and
wholly insufficient to sustain a judgment one way or the other.

There was also much interesting behind-the-scenes debate
about whether the case could be decided principally on its legal merits
or whether political and social considerations were primary. Once the
focus shifted away from the traditional issues of original intent and reliance on precedent to considerations of the impact or consequences
of an admitted error—*Plessy*—the die was cast. As Mark Tushnet
demonstrates in the reasoning of Justice Robert Jackson, "an appropriate premise for overruling *Plessy*" did not necessitate compelling
explanations of either "the failure of the representative branches
[Congress and the president] or the intentions of the framers." Instead, the appropriate legal premise was a profound mid-twentieth-
century global paradigm shift: an emerging and increasingly powerful
consensus regarding racial equality. Within a legal framework based
on this premise rather than the fallacy of white racial superiority, the
view of racial equality as a fundamental principle of law as well as of
society and culture meant that state-sanctioned racial segregation in
education, and beyond, was a dead constitutional letter.

A consensus within the Court about overruling *Plessy* was easier to reach than an agreement regarding remedy. Indeed, much of the debate among the justices about overturning *Plessy* pivoted around how, in effect, to implement such a potentially cataclysmic decision. This deeply felt sensitivity about how the nation, especially the white South, would react clearly circumscribed the whole of the Court's lengthy deliberations, not just the third stage where remedy was the explicit subject. The justices, like many Americans, feared what Justice Clark prophetically referred to as "subversion or even defiance of our mandates in many communities." In an early closed conference of the justices on the case, Alabama-born Justice Hugo Black had pointed to the issue agitating all of the justices: the extraordinary depth of racial caste in the South, the "deep seated antagonism to commingling" across racial boundaries. He argued that many southern school districts would shut down "rather than mix races at grade and high school levels." Ultimately, however, the issue of the differences between desegregating at the level of colleges and universities as opposed to the primary and secondary levels, where social intercourse between the races was seen as far more explosive, did not prove determinative.

What did prove compelling was agreement that the remedy had to be gradual. Without this commitment to incrementalism, the commitment to overturning *Plessy* weakened. The contending briefs on this issue fully aired both sides: immediatism and gradualism. Fears of an extremely volatile southern white response to an immediate implementation decree rendered gradualism the only viable option. At the point of remedy, therefore, legal concerns were plainly secondary. The NAACP brief argued strongly for immediate relief given that egregious violations of constitutional rights had been established. But the Court wanted to weigh the effects of immediate or gradual implementation. This delicate situation led to the ambiguous and in many ways ill-fated compromise of the eventual relief decree: implementation "with all deliberate speed."

The Court's fundamental lack of nerve and will mirrored that of the executive and congressional leadership as well as of the vast majority of white Americans. As Tushnet has shown, "It was not so much that the Justices understood that it would be difficult for courts to accomplish what they wanted through judicial decrees: the more acute problem was that they never truly decided what they wanted the courts to accomplish."

While they hoped and prayed for the best, the NAACP lawyers and perceptive observers everywhere were fully aware that the relief decree lacked muscle. A less radical and perhaps more effective decree might have been the middle ground option—immediate desegregation tempered by modifications sensitive to local conditions. On the cusp of the twenty-first century, the continuing national scandal of separate and unequal schools for children of color is a tragedy of epic proportions. The same is true of the persistence of racial apartheid in many areas of American life, including housing and employment. Tushnet has provocatively offered in retrospect that "had the Court followed through on the promises of *Brown,* political resistance to desegregation might have been smaller, the courts might not have had to develop intrusive remedies, and the reaction against 'judicial activism' . . . might not have occurred." Perhaps the "shock therapy" of immediatism would have served the short-term future better. It is hard to imagine it serving worse than "all deliberate speed."

The *Brown* Decision: Immediate Responses and Immediate Consequences

As soon as Chief Justice Warren announced the decision on May 17, 1954, the reaction was swift and predictable. Most commentators did not emphasize the exceedingly moderate and measured language of the decision. The legal rhetoric neither soared nor inspired. The text stressed that segregation is wrong and had damaged all Americans, especially blacks. It also emphasized that in midcentury America, Jim Crow was morally and intellectually indefensible. There was no ringing rejection of segregation as a profound legal error in *Plessy.* There was no pointed legal argument against race as an arbitrary and thus indefensible category or for a color-blind society. The egalitarianism of the decision's text was dutiful and restrained.

Far more important than the modest substance of the text of the decision has been its awesome symbolic resonance—what Americans have read into the decision, how they have interpreted it. Blacks and their allies in the black liberation struggle were pleased and hopeful, but often cautious. Pro-segregationists and their allies were deeply alarmed. Both camps fretted about the immediate and long-term consequences of this momentous decision. In particular, racial liberals and supporters of the black freedom struggle felt vindicated. Richard Kluger writes that the decision "represented nothing short of a reconsecration of American ideals. . . . The Court had restored to the American people a measure of humanity that had been drained away in their climb to worldwide ascent." Not surprisingly, therefore, within an hour of the decision's announcement, "the Voice of America would begin beaming word to the world in thirty-four languages: In the United States, schoolchildren could no longer be segregated by race."

Nationwide editorial comment reflected a predictable range of opinion. Notwithstanding an undercurrent of caution, black newspapers throughout the country lauded the decision as heralding a new age in race relations. The white press more clearly reflected local and regional perspectives. Northern and western newspapers saw the ruling as positive and hopeful. Pro-segregationist southern papers uniformly condemned the decision, while the liberal southern white press summoned up a guarded hope for the best.

Black response ran the gamut from elation to occasional opposition. Cleophus Brown, a labor and civil rights leader in Richmond, California, remembered that moment as "the point at which 'black folks in Richmond saw the light' and really began to believe they could break through." Black cultural racialists like anthropologist and writer Zora Neale Hurston rejected the logic of *Brown* as self-defeating at best, antiblack at worst. Reflecting a tactical position uncommon among blacks, she chose to emphasize the strengths of all-black institutions rather than the inequities under which they labored. From Hurston's perspective, the decision plainly reiterated notions of black inferiority, with its insinuation that black schoolchildren could learn best under the tutelage of white teachers, sitting next to white students. For Hurston, this was a brutal slap in the face of black teachers and administrators as well as black schoolchildren. She charged: "How much satisfaction can I get from a court order for somebody to associate with me who does not wish to be near me?" In fact, a critical failure of the egalitarianism of the liberal and social-scientific consensus undergirding *Brown* was its devaluation of black culture and black institutions and, ultimately, of blacks themselves.

While W. E. B. Du Bois lauded *Brown,* he shared Hurston's concern about its limitations and possible consequences. He was especially troubled by the decision's blindness both to the potential for the mistreatment of black children in integrated schools and to the strengths of a distinctive black culture. Still, on balance, he viewed *Brown I* and *II* as important but imperfect steps along freedom's bumpy journey. . . .

White resistance to black equality and empowerment has historically been fierce, and the reaction to *Brown* was no different. In August 1955, three months after *Brown II* had been announced, Emmet Till, a fourteen-year-old black teenager visiting relatives in Mississippi, was lynched for allegedly whistling at a white woman. In December of that year blacks in Montgomery, Alabama, launched the successful year-long Montgomery bus boycott. In September 1957 President Dwight D. Eisenhower was forced to send federal troops to Little Rock, Arkansas, to protect black schoolchildren integrating previously all-white Central High. The conclusion of Cyrus Cassell's poem "Soul Make a Path Through Shouting" poignantly captures the riveting drama and complex historical context of that most revealing moment:

> I have never seen the likes of you,
> Pioneer in dark glasses;
> You won't show the mob your eyes,
> But I know your gaze,
> Steady-on-the-North-Star, burning—
>
> With their jerry-rigged faith,
> Their spear of the American flag,
> How could they dare to believe
> You're someone scared?;
> *Nigger, burr-headed girl,*
> *Where are you going?*
>
> *I'm just going to school.*

Brown gave us that heroic moment and infinite others. Most important, the struggle to realize the promise of *Brown* endures.

Adam Fairclough

THE LABOR MOVEMENT, THE LEFT, AND THE TRANSFORMATION OF THE NAACP

Adam Fairclough's essay offers a compelling analysis of the convergence of events that gave rise to civil rights organizations in Louisiana, with special attention to the nation's oldest civil rights organization, the NAACP. Struggles to secure civil rights had begun before the Montgomery bus boycott and the *Brown v. Board* decision of 1954. Many historians have attempted to refocus the impetus to the modern civil rights movement on the events that occurred in the 1940s, particularly court cases initiated by the NAACP and the daring March on Washington Movement led by A. Philip Randolph. The generation of workers before the era of the modern civil rights movement was confronted by many exigencies, including the Great Depression and various bouts with political repression. The movement was also buttressed by the labor struggles in Louisiana. The class and color chasms in the New Orleans black community, as Fairclough explains, have often been oversimplified into neat "either/or" interpretations. The truth, he notes, can be more complex. The Creole elite, for example, was often comprised of some of the most militant agents in the NAACP, not the accommodationist proponents of the status quo. To the elements of class, skin color, and labor activism, the radicalism of the Communist Party also added unique ingredients to the struggle for civil rights.

Adam Fairclough is a professor of history at University of Leeds and has examined the civil rights movement from a national perspective with his work on the Southern Christian Leadership Conference, *To Redeem the Soul of America* (1987) and with *Martin Luther King Jr.*

The onset of the Great Depression exacted a heavy toll on the NAACP. Branches that had barely kept alive during the 1920s fell silent. The Alexandria branch regrouped in 1930 but soon became inactive. The chronically unstable Shreveport branch reorganized in

"The Labor Movement, the Left, and the Transformation of the NAACP" from *Race and Democracy: The Civil Rights Struggle in Louisiana, 1915–1972* by Adam Fairclough. Used by permission of The University of Georgia Press.

the same year but collapsed again in 1932, when pressure from whites forced it to cancel a talk by Oscar DePriest, the black congressman from Chicago and at the time the only African-American in Congress. "They felt that DePriest is not a representative type of Negro," the branch president reported, "that his talks are injurious to the Negro in the South, that encouraging the Negro along political lines was not what they felt should be done at this time." In many cases the national office simply lost contact with branches; by 1933 even the New Orleans branch had become so quiet that New York assumed that it had gone under.

The fortunes of the association slowly picked up as economic conditions improved. The New Orleans branch showed signs of activity in 1934 and, under the leadership of James E. Gayle, expanded its membership to 750. New branches appeared in Jennings (1935), Plaquemine (1935), and Lake Charles (1936). Reorganizations revived dormant branches in Shreveport (1936) and Lake Providence (1938). By 1940 the Baton Rouge branch had 800 members. Many branches owed their survival and vitality to the dedication of individuals. In Baton Rouge, for example, insurance man Benjamin J. Stanley, who served as a branch officer from 1930 to 1955, supplied the essential stability, and the Reverend John Henry Scott served as president of the Lake Providence branch for thirty years.

The role of Charles H. Myers in leading the Monroe branch was especially noteworthy. By the 1960s this branch had declined into virtual oblivion, and civil rights workers regarded Monroe as one of the most repressive towns in Louisiana. Yet between 1928 and 1948 Monroe boasted the strongest, the most stable, and arguably the most militant NAACP branch in the state, thanks in large part to Myer's leadership. A native of Texas, Myers moved to Monroe during the 1922 railroad strike and, like many other blacks, became a beneficiary of the companies' efforts to defeat the unions. Recruited as a mechanic by the Missouri Pacific, he quickly gained promotion and gladly joined the company union, since the AFL unions and the independent railroad brotherhoods systematically excluded blacks. Myers also became a successful businessman (at one time he operated two movie theaters in Shreveport) as well as an accomplished magician. As president of the NAACP, he protested the disfranchisement of blacks, took up cases of police brutality, and peppered local editors with complaints about discrimination. When the growing power of the railroad unions caused black workers to be demoted and displaced, Myers wrote to Charles H. Houston, the NAACP's chief legal strategist, who pressed the issue until the Supreme Court declared the unions' discriminatory practices illegal. In 1940 Myers threatened to boycott and picket a Monroe movie theater that had replaced its Negro manager with a white man. He won his point.

Building popular support, however, often proved difficult, especially in the rural areas. As J. H. Scott reported from East Carroll Parish, "one of the biggest problems our branch has had is to have people believe that the association can be helpful in the South. . . . Also in the farming community where old boss has had the say about everything it is hard to get the tenant to stand for the right." Complaints about opposition from teachers and ministers cropped up regularly in branch letters to the National Office; Scott was a rare example of a black preacher providing strong leadership. According to E. L. Fair, secretary of the Lake Providence branch, some preachers urged blacks not to join the NAACP on the grounds that "if the white folks knew that they were organizing anything to go against them they would run them out of the Country." An agent for the *Pittsburgh Courier,* Fair could find only two ministers willing to distribute this militant black newspaper. "Where we gets most of our trubble from is the 2 × 4 pastors." Charlie Myers informed Walter White that he had almost thrown one minister down some stairs "as he attempted one of his Uncle Tomish talks."

In the mid-1930s the NAACP was surviving, in the sense that it could claim a handful of active branches in Louisiana, but it still had no statewide structure to foster its growth and coordinate its activities. With the exception of Monroe, and possibly Baton Rouge, it had failed to attract mass support. This state of affairs reflected the weakness of the organization nationally; as late as 1940 the NAACP had only fifty thousand members.

Black political scientist Ralph J. Bunche deplored the NAACP's failure to recruit a mass base. In a lengthy monograph he wrote for the Carnegie-Myrdal study, "The Negro in the United States," he complained that "the control of the branches rests largely in the hands of an exclusive, often class and color snobbish, self-appointed Negro upper class group, and they are run, more frequently than not, as closed corporations." Bunche further contended that the association's unimaginative pursuit of court cases rendered its program irrelevant to the vast majority of blacks, whose primary concerns—poverty and unemployment—it largely neglected. The NAACP's national leadership, he went on, "has shown a pitiful lack of knowledge of mass technique and of how to pitch an appeal so as to reach the ears of the masses." Bunche's criticisms were tendentious and overstated: as the example of Charles Myers showed, individual branch leaders could sometimes be militant and populist. However, as applied to many of the big-city branches, Bunche's description did not stray far from the truth.

In 1939, for example, the executive committee of the New Orleans branch read like a who's who of the black bourgeoisie. It included nine top executives of the leading black insurance companies, two members of the most prestigious undertaking business, and the city's most eminent black surgeon, Dr. Rivers Fredericks. Actually, this group was not so much middle class as upper class: they were men of considerable means. When he died in 1954 Fredericks left assets worth $1.5 million. . . .

These men had served the NAACP well, nurturing the branch through its difficult infancy. As businessmen and professionals serving a black clientele, they enjoyed the economic independence that enabled them to provide protest leadership as well as vital financial support and organizational competence. Fredericks himself preferred to stay in the background, yet his wealth and social status gave him considerable influence. Some of his protégés, moreover, became community leaders elsewhere: through Fredericks, for example, Dr. A. C. Terrance established a practice in Opelousas. Like other black doctors in rural Louisiana, Terrance kept in touch with the NAACP despite the absence of a local branch.

A social gulf, however, separated the leaders of the New Orleans branch from the black lower classes, inhibiting the NAACP's ability to attract popular support. In their struggle to achieve wealth and status, moreover, black professionals tended towards elitism and clannishness; they prized their credentials, wore their learning proudly, and sometime regarded others with patronizing condescension. Aspects of lower-class black culture that white folklorists celebrated, educated blacks looked upon with embarrassed disapproval. The arguments that swirled around the annual Mardi Gras parade of the Zulu Social Aid and Pleasure Club typified this conflict between lower-class hedonism and middle-class respectability. As the Zulus and their "second-liners" reveled in a display of drunken buffoonery, the people whom they regarded as "stuck-up niggers" condemned the spectacle as grotesque and distasteful. As A. P. Tureaud recalled from the perspective of old age, "Once we climbed the so-called ladder of middle-class America we . . . felt that that was not a good image of middle-class life—to be parading and having the men and women in the streets carrying on these body gyrations; 'shaking,' as they'd say on the street." The persistence of "hoodoo" evoked similar disdain, especially among the physicians and pharmacists who felt they had had to contend against the "credulity and faith of the ignorant."

Thus the New Orleans branch was almost a caricature of the "closed corporation" described by Bunche in 1940. Yet by the time Bunche's views found their way into *An American Dilemma*, published in 1944, his analysis was already out of date. The NAACP's national membership had increased almost tenfold and was approaching the half-million mark. New branches were sprouting like mushrooms, and in most big cities, working-class blacks gained representation on branch committees, sometimes winning outright control. In New Orleans, a two-year struggle resulted in a group of Young Turks, nearly all of them middle class or working class, taking over the leadership.

The spectacular growth of the NAACP during the 1940s is usually attributed to the Second World War, which had a dramatic effect on the outlook and behavior of African-Americans. Yet the cycle of growth started *before* the war. In New Orleans, the Young Turks made their first bid for leadership in 1939, and they took control of the branch before Pearl Harbor. By 1941 the NAACP was showing signs of fresh vigor throughout Louisiana. By then, moreover, the NAACP's national legal staff, led by Thurgood Marshall, had secured important court victories that enabled branches in the South to go onto the offensive. The NAACP was already being transformed.

The leadership shift that took place in New Orleans was closely linked to the explosion of labor militancy associated with the rise of the CIO. The growth of industrial unionism in the late 1930s transformed the political climate and to some extent radicalized the black working class, hitherto discouraged by apathy and fear. The NAACP was a direct beneficiary of this political awakening.

With the arrival of organizers from the Committee for Industrial Organizations in 1936, New Orleans, once a union stronghold but by 1939 a bastion of the "open shop," echoed to the din of industrial strife. On the waterfront the International Longshoremen's and Warehousemen's Union, fresh from its triumphs on the West Coast, slugged it out with the International Longshoremen's Association. The conflict came to a head in the summer of 1938 with a simultaneous strike of dockworkers and truck drivers. After a federally supervised election attended by fraud, bribery, and intimidation, the notoriously corrupt ILA emerged victorious. . . .

The CIO unions soon boasted half a million black members nationwide, and they placed themselves "in the vanguard of efforts to transform race relations." The National Maritime Union promoted blacks to leadership positions and insisted that its contracts with the shipping companies include antidiscrimination clauses. The majority-black National Union of Marine Cooks and Stewards was an exemplar of racial equality. As Jane Record noted, the union's Negro members, mostly from the South, "found in the NUMCS hiring hall the most satisfying hiring experience of their lives." On the New Orleans waterfront the small ILWU local was, to quote Dave Lee Wells, "an example of union democracy, racial solidarity and militance unmatched . . . in the Jim Crow era." Local 206 of the Transport Workers Union "played a significant role in anti-racist activities of all sorts," according to the most thorough history of the TWU. Comprising about six hundred New Orleans truck drivers, most of them blacks, it conducted a successful strike against a contractor who, at the insistence of the Louisiana and Arkansas Railway Company, refused to employ black drivers. The Communist Party exerted a strong influence within each of these unions and played a major role in shaping their egalitarian policies.

The Communist Party also entered rural parishes, trying to organize blacks and whites into a farmers' union. The drive began in 1936 when Clyde Johnson, Communist organizer of the Alabama-based Sharecroppers Union, moved his headquarters to New Orleans. This was the union's first attempt to operate openly—the Party itself still led a twilight existence in Louisiana, police harassment forcing it to operate under cover of a bookstore. Johnson began building what became the Louisiana Farmers Union, soon handing over its leadership to fellow party member Gordon McIntire, a young, tall, gaunt, white Texan. McIntire was assisted by Peggy Dallet, whose brother, Joe, died in Spain as a member of the International Brigade.

The union first established itself as a going concern in St. Landry Parish, where it fought the eviction of twenty farming families, most of them blacks, by the Resettlement Administration. However, although the LFU recruited both blacks and whites, its leaders decided to draw back from directly challenging segregation after an incident in Opelousas. At a mass meeting in the courthouse square a white man yelled, "Nigger union!" The gathering stayed calm, but McIntire recognized the potential for violence if black union members appeared to "crowd out" whites in public. Thereafter the union stuck to a policy of separate locals and separate meetings. . . .

The rise of the People's Defense League (PDL) provided another illustration of how the labor militancy and leftist activism of the 1930s spilled over into the civil rights drive of the 1940s. The PDL was synonymous with Ernest J. Wright. Born in Kenner, just outside New Orleans, Wright attended Xavier University in the 1930s, where he came under the tutelage of Katherine Radke, a German-born nun and head of Xavier's school of social work. With Radke's encouragement, Wright studied social work at the University of Michigan, working on placement in Detroit. Returning to New Orleans, he joined the staff of the *Louisiana Weekly* to promote a "community responsibility program." Using his weekly column as a platform, Wright soon became a well-known lecturer and activist. "Every week in churches, community centers, and labor halls throughout the city," wrote one student of Wright's career, "hundreds turned out as he spoke on the need to obtain the ballot, [and] reviewed the latest local and national developments." He also became a leading light in the SNYC [Southern Negro Youth Congress].

A strike of black insurance agents marked the beginning of Wright's career as a labor organizer and served as the launching pad for the People's Defense League. The dispute started in September 1940 when the four biggest black-owned insurance companies (the Unity, the Louisiana, the Douglas, and the Good Citizens) attempted to quash efforts by their collection agents to form a CIO union. In 1934 the companies had signed a secret anti-union compact, which they now put into effect. At the Unity, the two instigators of the union were fired in the presence of the assembled agents. . . .

In August 1941 Wright founded the People's Defense League, which soon became, in the FBI's estimation, "the most powerful negro organization in New Orleans," thanks to Wright's "personal magnetism and unlimited energy." Wright held regular meetings in Shakespeare Park and wrote a weekly column in the *Louisiana Weekly*. He crisscrossed New Orleans and Louisiana addressing churches, unions, NAACP branches, PTAs, graduation classes—every conceivable audience. He hammered away at the same themes: police brutality, discrimination, organized labor, the vote. In March 1943 he teamed up with the Reverend Abraham Lincoln Davis, pastor of New Zion Baptist Church, to form the Louisiana Association for the Progress of Negro Citizens, which focused exclusively on obtaining the ballot.

The prominence of ministers like Davis in the right-to-vote movement furnished another yardstick of blacks' heightened aspirations and rising self-confidence. During the 1930s black intellectuals had lambasted ministers for their timidity and conservatism. Davis, however, who had moved to New Orleans in 1936 as a young man of twenty-two, embraced social and political causes; through his leadership of the Interdenominational Ministerial Alliance he did more than any other minister to identify the black church with the fight for the ballot. Other ministers joined the fray, among them L. L. Haynes, pastor of Mount Zion Baptist Church, and Gardner C. Taylor, who left New Orleans in 1942 to become pastor of Mount Zion First African Baptist Church in Baton Rouge, one of the largest in the state. Other like-minded ministers included Jetson Davis, A. L. Davis's brother, a pastor in Plaquemine; and Maynard T. Jackson, president of the Baptist Ministerial Union in Lake Charles. As Davis told a meeting in Shakespeare Park in October 1941, "The church cannot, must not and will not distance itself from the everyday problems which face the Negro people."

The revival of white liberalism in New Orleans reflected the rise of the labor movement, the growth of race consciousness among blacks, and the climate of political openness encouraged by Roosevelt and the New Deal. In 1938 the National Urban League organized a branch in New Orleans; numerically, conservative, segregation-minded whites dominated its board, but a handful of Jewish liberals and a prolabor Josephite Catholic priest wielded disproportionate influence. The year 1939 saw the formation of the Catholic Committee of the South; staunchly prolabor and strongly antidiscrimination, the CCS established a stronger presence in New Orleans than in any other city. In 1940 the Southern Conference for

Human Welfare organized a Louisiana committee with an office in New Orleans.

Against the political ferment that provided a backdrop to the late 1930s, the New Orleans branch of the NAACP looked increasingly timid and isolated. Under the presidency of James Gayle, a publisher of church music, the branch staged occasional protest meetings but did little else. His successor, Dr. Aaron W. Brazier, a physician, spurned an opportunity to identify the branch with the defense of Hugh Pierre, a headline-making case that resulted in the first instance in which the U.S. Supreme Court reversed a Louisiana verdict because of the exclusion of blacks from the jury. Brazier attributed the branch's poor showing to the apathy of the masses and the inertia of the membership, but A. P. Tureaud thought that Gayle and Brazier showed "little or no aggressiveness at all. They were just keeping the organization alive." In 1938 James B. Lafourche, a writer at the *Louisiana Weekly,* challenged Brazier and, when defeated, asked the national office to revoke the branch's charter. New York refused—Lafourche was a slippery character who inspired distrust—but it expressed concern over the branch's weak leadership and lack of popular support, especially when the Communist Party was assiduously courting the Negro.

For Brazier's critics, the humiliating outcome of a suit against the Municipal Auditorium proved to be the final straw. The auditorium is an imposing structure that lies on the site of Congo Square, the open space on the edge of the French Quarter that was famous in antebellum days for the dancing of African slaves. Built in the 1930s in the plain, modernist architectural style typical of WPA-financed public buildings, it was run by a commission appointed by the City of New Orleans. In 1937, when a black minister, denied permission to hire the building, decided to take the commission to court, the NAACP agreed to back his action. But the case went awry from the start. Instead of hiring a competent attorney, the branch retained a white man who worked as a postal clerk and lawyered in his spare time. This amateur lawyer then submitted a brief that alleged that the minister had been discriminated against as a taxpayer rather than as a Negro. The failure to allege racial discrimination allowed the federal court to dismiss the case for want of jurisdiction. "You know, he only had to say he was a nigger," the judge told A. P. Tureaud. "I would have had to hear the case."

The loss of the suit discredited the Brazier administration and spurred a group of younger blacks into fielding their own slate of candidates. The insurgent faction called itself "The Group." It included truck drivers, insurance agents, letter carriers, postal clerks, and a doorman at Godchaux's department store. None of these men were remotely upper class, and none of them, with the exception of lawyer A. P. Tureaud and a couple of schoolteachers, could be classified as professionals. The core of The Group consisted of a trio of post office workers: John E. Rousseau Jr., Donald Jones, and Arthur J. Chapital. Jones and Rousseau were clerks, Chapital a letter carrier. With insurance agent Daniel E. Byrd, Jones became The Group's principal ringleader. . . .

Numbering at the outset about two dozen people, The Group sought to recruit enough new members to vote the existing executive committee out of office. Donald Jones told Thurgood Marshall of the planned "coup" and solicited his advice. Marshall encouraged him, but warned The Group to play by the rules. By November 1939 The Group had signed up 319 new members, and it put forward a "balanced ticket" that included Creoles and non-Creoles, people who lived downtown and uptown. As the election approached, a rival ticket led by J. Edwin Wilkins came forward, referring to itself as the "Progressive" ticket. A pharmacist at Flint-Goodridge hospital, Wilkins was also president of the Autocrat Club, a well-known Creole institution. Rivers Fredericks had induced him to stand, promising office space in the Louisiana Life building and money for a full-time secretary. Both factions wrote to New York predicting electoral skullduggery; Walter White admonished them to behave properly.

The election took place in an atmosphere of high excitement. The ticket fielded by The Group held a preelection pep parade through the Seventh Ward, culminating in a rally at Jeunes Amis Hall with music and refreshments. When the votes were counted the following evening, the, "Progressive ticket" defeated The Group by 324 to 294. Brazier himself, who received but seven votes, praised the "hectic and enthusiastic" campaign. "The sight was unbelievable," he wrote Walter White. "More than one thousand people came out, including spectators to watch the contest and spur their friends on."

This healthy exercise in democracy swelled the branch's membership and brought about a near clean sweep of the offices: only three members of the old guard won places on the seventeen-member executive committee. But the clash of "tickets" produced a badly divided branch. The Group complained that Fredericks had hastily cobbled together a slate of wealthy "big shots" for the sole purpose of excluding them. Wilkins had won, moreover, with the help of a bloc vote from the corrupt longshoremen's union, the ILA, which had purchased memberships for all its men. "Practically the entire interested NAACP membership remains under the leadership of the losers, The Group," Donald Jones complained. "In other words, you have there a Democratic cabinet and a Republican congress."

Actually, Jones overstated the matter: although the new board was dominated by businessmen and professionals, it also included Clarence Laws, the young executive secretary of the Urban League and himself a member of The Group. Wilkins also reached out to The Group by inviting A. P. Tureaud to serve as the branch's legal adviser; the old leadership had strenuously opposed using Negro lawyers. Responding to charges that he had presented his slate of candidates as the "downtown," or Creole, ticket, Wilkins insisted that he wanted to bridge the old division between downtown and uptown. "The objective of the NAACP is to get the 180,000 Negroes of New Orleans together," he explained. "The southern white man tries to divide them—to make the educated Negro feel he is superior to the uneducated Negro, the urban to the rural, the light to the dark. . . . But Negroes must come together under all conditions."

A renewal of the Municipal Auditorium controversy gave Wilkins a chance to practice what he preached. In the spring of 1940 Marian Anderson was booked to give a concert in New Orleans. Then at the height of her fame as a singer, Anderson had just won "a smashing victory over segregation" in the nation's capital that thrilled blacks everywhere. When the Daughters of the American Revolution denied her permission to sing in Constitution Hall, Secretary of the Interior Harold Ickes, a longtime supporter of the NAACP, invited her to give her recital on the steps of the Lincoln Memorial. Widely condemned for its bigotry, the DAR later lifted its color bar on Constitution Hall.

Marian Anderson, however, was neither a racial crusader nor a political activist: her art and her career came first. Thus she accepted the invitation to sing in New Orleans despite the fact that the organizers of the concert planned a whites-only event. After vociferous black protests, the auditorium allocated seats for blacks in the balconies. The NAACP protested that "horizontal" segregation of this kind insulted blacks: only "vertical" segregation, whereby blacks and whites sat on opposite sides of the hall but on the same level, would be acceptable. When the auditorium commission rejected this demand, refusing to allow blacks to sit on the ground floor, the NAACP voted to boycott the concert. The branch's action split the black community. The fraternities and sororities wanted the concert to go ahead, seeing it as an opportunity for an internationally renowned black singer to perform in New Orleans. The *Louisiana Weekly* lashed Wilkins in print, accusing him of "fighting to keep Negroes from hearing a great Negro artist." The NAACP failed to persuade Anderson to cancel her appearance and failed to dissuade blacks from attending. The branch found itself out on a limb.

Frederic Morrow, the NAACP's coordinator of branches, saw the split in the black community as evidence of the old "class-caste fight between the native Negroes and the Creoles," who had never managed to cooperate. "The biggies are fighting," he believed, "because cancellation will deny them an opportunity to put on the dog and entertain." Actually, Morrow cited the Creole/American division to explain something considerably more complex. After all, the branch's leaders, largely Creole and upper class, were themselves "biggies," yet they instigated the boycott. The Group, largely Creole too, but mainly working class and middle class, supported the boycott. In fact, the protest generated support that cut across both class and cultural lines. The dispute over the Anderson concert seems to have been a division between the race-conscious NAACP and the black upper class, not between Creoles and non-Creoles.

Outsiders frequently made the same error when viewing New Orleans black society, explaining everything in terms of the alleged conflict between Creoles and Americans and equating that division with a light-skinned/dark-skinned dichotomy and a split between the upper class and the lower class. Thus simplification was piled upon simplification until caricature obscured reality. By the 1930s there was little correspondence, in fact, between the black class structure and the division between Creole and non-Creole. And while many Creoles still placed a high social value on light complexion, culture rather than color had become the main reference point of Creole identity. A Creole such as A. P. Tureaud remained proud of what his ancestors, the free people of color, had achieved in antebellum days, but he did not believe that Creoles could remain apart from other blacks. Nor did he draw attention to his light complexion.

The celebration of the free people of color by black writers such as Marcus Christian, Clarence A. Laws, and Octave Lilly Jr. expressed a similar outlook. Employed by the Federal Writers Project to produce a study of "The Negro in Louisiana," these scholars described with pride the literary, military, and economic achievements of the *gens de couleur libre,* but they stressed that after Emancipation the free colored class had united with the freed slaves, realizing that they shared a common interest in obtaining equal rights. As Joan Redding has pointed out, to these writers "the convergence of the freed and free black cultures . . . provided a model for solutions to the political and social issues of their own day." Thus they viewed cultural differences as a source of strength rather than a source of division: "Rather than finding professionalism and elite culture at odds with the interests of the black masses, they found both folk and elite culture integral to the improvement of the race." In this way they could prize their Creole heritage and their own educational attainments while pressing the cause of all blacks through the NAACP. Clarence Laws and Octave Lilley both joined The Group.

The controversy surrounding the Marian Anderson concert marked a watershed in the evolution of the NAACP in New Orleans: the boycott movement represented the branch's first serious protest against inequalities within segregated public accommodations. Although the NAACP lost that fight, the affair illustrated a marked tendency for blacks to unite across class and cultural lines, exemplified by large public meetings and cooperation between organizations. The NAACP won the backing of the Interdenominational Ministerial Alliance and the Southern Negro Youth Congress; one mass meeting drew three thousand people. Shortly afterward an array of organizations, and black leaders of virtually every political persuasion, jointly lobbied the city's public housing authority, HANO, to employ black managers in its new Negro projects. Under the auspices of this coalition, the Committee of 100, blacks attended protest meetings and boycotted the Magnolia project's "open house" day. Faced with such opposition, HANO agreed to take on black personnel.

The Group, however, remained dissatisfied with the NAACP's leadership and frustrated by their own exclusion from power. They also complained that the existing black newspapers in New Orleans, the *Louisiana Weekly* and the *Sepia Socialite,* were insufficiently militant. Worse, in the recent gubernatorial election, they had allowed themselves to be manipulated by the Long organization. The Group therefore decided to launch its own weekly newspaper, each man chipping in $100 of his own money. The first issue of the *New Orleans Sentinel* appeared in June 1940. It was edited by the two postal clerks, Donald Jones and John E. Rousseau (three years earlier Rousseau had founded NAPE's local newsletter, *The Postscript*). A. P. Tureaud contributed copy, including occasional editorials, and Ernest Wright wrote a regular column. The paper supplemented its local material with articles from the *New York Times* and press releases from the NAACP and the Southern Negro Youth Congress. The *Sentinel* was left-of-center and prolabor. "We dared to publicize the coming of Negro candidates on the Socialist ticket with Norman Thomas," Tureaud recalled. In contrast to the *Louisiana Weekly,* the *Sentinel* supported the agents in the insurance strike of late 1940.

That strike exemplified the way in which the old division between Creole and non-Creole had to a large extent been superseded by the economic conflict between class and class. It also showed how such conflicts could spill over into the NAACP: the leaders of the strike were all members of The Group; the branch's executive committee included five representatives of the struck companies. Daniel Byrd specifically charged J. E. Wilkins of favoring the owners because he owed his election to Rivers Fredericks, president of Louisiana Industrial Life. The "insurance vote" had indeed assisted the Wilkins ticket; the Louisiana, for example, counted forty-seven NAACP members among its employees. The strike damaged the standing of the branch leadership, and at the 1940 annual general meeting, held during the tail end of the dispute, Rev. C. C. Taylor defeated Wilkins. But The Group still failed to elect its own ticket, and two of the insurance owners, Rivers Fredericks and Henry E. Braden, remained on the board.

Nevertheless, The Group stayed together, with the *Sentinel* their campaigning organ. Impatient with the branch leadership and keen to find an issue that would boost the paper's circulation, The Group laid plans for a suit in federal court to challenge the differential in the pay of black and white schoolteachers. Black teachers in

New Orleans were keen to file an equalization suit, and in March 1939 three high school principals advanced the money to bring Thurgood Marshall to New Orleans to discuss strategy. Despite their defeat in the 1939 and 1940 branch elections, The Group kept in touch with Marshall, proceeding with their plans independently of the local NAACP. . . .

A few months later, The Group finally captured control of the New Orleans branch of the NAACP. Daniel Byrd, Donald Jones, Raymond Tillman, Ernest Wright, Arthur J. Chapital, John E. Rousseau, and A.P. Tureaud all joined the executive committee. So did Rev. A. L. Davis. The social and class character of the branch's leadership had altered decisively. If not exactly a revolution, it did signal the most important change in the branch's history: members of The Group dominated the New Orleans NAACP for the next twenty years, some of them remaining active into the 1960s and even the 1970s. Three of them, A. P. Tureaud, Daniel E. Byrd, and Arthur J. Chapital, merit particular attention, for they provided stable and strong leadership for both New Orleans and Louisiana.

Of the three, A. P. Tureaud deserves to be considered first, for his name became virtually synonymous with that of the NAACP in Louisiana. Like other black lawyers in the South at that time, Alexander Pierre Tureaud used his initials rather than his given names so that whites would not address him on a first-name basis. Known to all as "Tureaud," he first joined the NAACP in 1922 after hearing James Weldon Johnson, the organization's first executive secretary, give a speech at Howard University, and he remained active in the association until his death in 1972. For most of that half-century, Tureaud's name appeared on every school and university integration suit filed by the NAACP in Louisiana, as well as on suits integrating buses, parks, and public buildings. Tureaud represented the first Louisiana students to be arrested in the sit-in movement of 1960, and his case resulted in the first Supreme Court decision quashing the convictions of sit-in demonstrators. The fact that Tureaud was the most experienced and competent black lawyer in Louisiana—indeed, in 1947 he was the *only* black lawyer in the state—made him uniquely important. He always worked closely with the experts of the NAACP Legal Defense Fund, particularly Thurgood Marshall, the fund's top lawyer and chief strategist between 1940 and 1961;

in key integration cases the briefs filed by Tureaud were drafted, partially or in their entirety, by the fund's New York staff. Yet Tureaud himself participated in the formulation of legal strategy and tactics, and his local knowledge enhanced the value of his contribution. . . .

. . . Tureaud's commitment to legalism did not simply reflect professional self-interest or political conservatism: it must also be understood in terms of his background, generation, personality, and religious faith. Tureaud had a sense of history, an appreciation not only of his particular Creole heritage but also of what black Louisianians had achieved as a whole. His knowledge of the past gave him a faith in the future; temporary setbacks did not faze or discourage him. Moreover, Tureaud grew up during the so-called nadir of the Negro's post-Emancipation odyssey. Born three years after *Plessy v. Ferguson* and one year after Louisiana disfranchised virtually all black voters, he passed his youth and early adulthood during a time when lynching was commonplace. As with many of his generation who made the decision to stay in the South, Tureaud had no choice but to practice patience and forbearance, enduring setbacks and humiliations in the faith that God and the Constitution would enable blacks to ultimately triumph. Tureaud did not wear his religion on his sleeve, and he was privately critical of the racism that sullied the Catholic Church. Yet like other Creoles of color who stayed within the church, his faith reinforced his commitment to a certain methodical, patient, and moderate approach to social and political change.

Patience and moderation, however, were also part of Tureaud's personal makeup. As long as he could do so without compromising his principles, he preferred to do things amicably; he would bend over backward to appear reasonable and moderate. White politicians sometimes shamelessly exploited this characteristic. DeLesseps S. "Chep" Morrison, mayor of New Orleans, often prevailed upon him not to press NAACP suits during his all-too-frequent election campaigns. But Tureaud's palpable fairness, and his unfailing courtesy, won him universal respect. He was a man of complete integrity, relentless dedication, and uncommon decency. . . .

Arthur J. Chapital was New Orleans born and bred, and his importance as an NAACP activist stemmed largely from his long service to the New Orleans branch. Born in 1901, Chapital attended the public schools and Straight University. Raised a Catholic, he rebelled against the church's segregation policy and joined Beecher Memorial

Congregational Church, which had both black and white members. A postal worker for thirty-eight years, he helped to organize NAPE and served as the union's branch president. He joined the NAACP in 1939 and, elected to the executive board in 1941, was a mainstay of the New Orleans branch until his death in 1969. He served as branch president between 1951 and 1962 and briefly held the post of full-time executive secretary in the late 1960s.

Chapital was stubborn, argumentative, and cantankerous, but also utterly dedicated and completely honest. That earned him the kind of respect accorded to Byrd and Tureaud. Moreover, Chapital had deep and wide roots in the New Orleans black community. His breadth of contacts and network of personal relationships made him a key individual—*the* key individual—when it came to rallying and uniting blacks around a particular issue. "The association's strength was in individuals as opposed to being in an organization," recalled Harvey Britton, who became the NAACP's Louisiana field secretary in 1966. "You had individuals who could issue a call, like Arthur J. Chapital. When Chapital wanted to pull people together, he was part of the fabric of the community, he could pull those people together."

Britton was right to stress the importance of key individuals in the NAACP, yet the association also derived its strength from black organizations and institutions. These provided the social context within which individuals could accumulate influence. Arthur Chapital, for example, was not only a respected and well-known individual, he was also a leader of the postal workers union and the Supreme Commander of the Scottish Rite Masons in Louisiana. Similarly, A. P. Tureaud could drum up support for the NAACP among black Catholics by virtue of his high rank within the Knights of Peter Claver.

The ability of the NAACP to build popular support depended on these institutional building blocks. The two black Masonic orders were an obvious example; by the 1940s they boasted a combined membership of twenty thousand in three hundred lodges. Their histories went back a long way, and they both functioned as quasi-political organizations.

The history of the Prince Hall Masons in Louisiana dated from 1842, when free Negroes formed the first of several lodges in New Orleans. Repressed and forced underground in the late 1850s, the lodges reemerged during the federal occupation and, under the leadership of Oscar J. Dunn, combined to form the Eureka Grand Lodge. Dunn himself went on to become lieutenant governor of the state, and the Eureka lodge of the Prince Hall order, to quote Joseph Logsdon and Caryn Bell, "provided an important nucleus for political activism" during the Reconstruction years. The link between the Prince Hall Masons and the Republican party survived the demise of Reconstruction. James Lewis Sr., who headed the lodge after Dunn's death, held public office long after 1877 and remained active in the party until his death in 1914. The son of a white planter and a mulatto slave, Lewis had raised the first black regiment for the U.S. Army during the Civil War. In the 1890s he supported the challenge to segregation mounted by the *Comité des Citoyens*. His son James Lewis Jr. continued the family tradition of Republican politics, attending every national convention between 1928 and 1940.

Another Lewis dynasty revived the fortunes of the Prince Hall Masons in the early twentieth century and dominated the order for a remarkable span of seventy years. John G. Lewis Sr. took over the state organization in 1903; his son Scott became grand master in 1931, and another son, John G. Lewis Jr., headed the order between 1941 and 1979. The elder Lewis was born either in England or Canada—accounts differ—in 1851 and came to New Orleans in 1865. After serving as an inspector of Customs for the Port of New Orleans at the tender age of eighteen, he moved to Natchitoches and opened a school (according to Masonic lore, "the first public school north of Rapides Parish"). By the turn of the century he had become a substantial businessman and landowner; in 1910 he started *The Plumb Line,* a Masonic paper produced by his own printing company, the Dawn of Light.

Under the leadership of John G. Lewis Jr., the Prince Hall Masons became closely associated with the NAACP. The Masons provided members and meeting places; they organized voter registration schools; they furnished generous financial support. Lewis himself played an important part in the formation and growth of the Louisiana State Conference of NAACP Branches. Daniel Byrd was a keen Mason, and another Mason, Dr. E. A. Johnson, succeeded Tureaud as president of the LSC.

The Masonic network was national in scope. Like [Daniel E.] Byrd, his staff worker in Louisiana, Thurgood Marshall was a devoted Mason. He counted John Lewis Jr. among his closest friends, and he provided free legal representation when the Prince Hall order took its rivals to court. Substantial donations to the Inc. Fund [NAACP Legal Defense and Education Fund]—sometimes exceeding twenty thousand dollars a year—cemented the Prince Hall-NAACP alliance at the national level. . . .

The Louisiana Colored Teachers Association also gave the NAACP vital backing. Under the presidency of George Longe (Arthur Chapital's predecessor as Grand Commander of the Scottish Rite Masons) the LCTA made its first solid commitment to the NAACP by agreeing to help defray the cost of the Orleans Parish salary equalization suit. The alliance became firmer under Longe's successor, J. K. Haynes. A native of Lincoln Parish, Haynes assumed the presidency in 1942, and his election softened the old rivalry between New Orleans and the northern part of the state, smoothing the way for a formal agreement in 1943 between the LCTA and the NAACP Legal Defense and Education Fund. Under its terms, the LCTA undertook to finance all the Inc. Fund's education suits, with A. P. Tureaud handling the litigation under the supervision of Thurgood Marshall. The arrangement represented a kind of "package deal" whereby the LCTA secured the Inc. Fund's assistance by placing Tureaud on a permanent retainer. The pact also enabled black teachers to support the NAACP without putting their jobs on the line—an especially important consideration in north Louisiana, where the repressive atmosphere made teachers doubly reluctant to take out memberships. In Bossier Parish, for example, where the NAACP had no branch, teachers financed a successful voter registration suit litigated by the NAACP.

Although historians of the civil rights movement have often exaggerated the importance of the black church, some Baptist and Methodist ministers did support the NAACP. Ministers headed perhaps a third of the association's branches, including, at one time or another, those in Shreveport, Alexandria, Monroe, and New Orleans. But the significance of ministerial support did not lie merely in their individual participation, or even in their general prestige within the black community; in many instances, ministers brought about the bloc enrollment of their congregations. In New Orleans, for example, Rev. L. L. Haynes persuaded 820 members of his 900-strong congregation to join the NAACP. Unfortunately, black ministers often proved to be poor organizers. They were accustomed to acting unilaterally, especially the Baptists, and their authoritarian style was ill-suited to the NAACP's democratic and bureaucratic structure. Branches headed by ministers tended to be weak ones. However, there was one outstanding exception: Rev. J. H. Scott led the Lake Providence branch, one of the strongest in rural Louisiana, for thirty years.

The paucity of NAACP branches in southwestern Louisiana can be explained, in part, by its large population of black Catholics. The Catholic churches, in every case pastored by white ministers, provided the association with no direct assistance. The Knights of Peter Claver, which had more members in Louisiana than in any other state, supported the NAACP financially, but it did not have the same close association with the NAACP that, for example the Prince Hall Masons did.

Throughout Louisiana, but especially in the Catholic half of the state, black professionals still provided the strongest leadership. Doctors, dentists, and pharmacists composed an influential elite; although few in number (black doctors and dentists actually *declined* in number during the 1930s and 1940s) they were educated, organized, and economically independent. A black physician, Dr. E. A. Johnson, founded the NAACP branch in Natchitoches; a group of medics organized the New Iberia branch. These professionals, moreover, often had interlocking business interests with insurance companies and funeral homes, the largest black-owned enterprises in the state. The insurance companies, with 2,500 employees and branches throughout Louisiana, provided a network of communication and another source of NAACP leadership. Even in communities without NAACP branches, doctors and insurance agents provided a point of contact with the state and national organization. In Opelousas, for example, A. P. Tureaud worked with Dr. D. D. Donatto, president of the Negro Chamber of Commerce. Another local doctor, A. C. Terrance, served on the NAACP's National Medical Committee.

Black newspapers prepared the soil for the NAACP's growth. Virtually all literate blacks read at least one paper a week, and many read more than one. Apart from the *Shreveport Sun* and the New Orleans-based *Louisiana Weekly,* which had both achieved commercial stability, other local papers were launched from time to time and had a short-lived impact: the *Alexandria Observer,* the *Monroe*

Broadcast, the *New Orleans Sentinel,* and the *Sepia Socialite,* also published in New Orleans. Blacks in southwestern Louisiana sometimes read the *Houston Informer;* copies of the *Kansas City Call* and the *Oklahoma City Black Dispatch* found their way to northern Louisiana. Far more influential than any of these local papers, however, were the nationally distributed *Chicago Defender* and *Pittsburgh Courier.* The latter included a Louisiana supplement, a single sheet that covered the paper front and back, four pages of state news. A New Orleans schoolteacher, O. C. W. Taylor, provided the local copy and arranged for the *Courier's* sale in Louisiana. John E. Rousseau Jr. later became its Louisiana correspondent. By the 1930s, both papers reached every corner of the state; their distribution networks formed important lines of communication. They also provided the NAACP with priceless free publicity, and their news coverage and militant editorials helped to mold the political and racial consciousness of two generations. "It was the *Defender* that kindled in me a fire for civil rights," recalled Rev. J. H. Scott.

After 1940 the NAACP experienced exponential growth. By 1944 its membership had increased from 50,000 to 429,000, and the number of branches had tripled. Most of that expansion took place in the South, and Louisiana shared in it. By 1944 the branches in Baton Rouge, Shreveport, Monroe, and Lake Charles each claimed at least a thousand members. The New Orleans branch, which in 1938 had barely three hundred members, now boasted six thousand.

Criticized by the left and loathed by the right, slow-moving and bureaucratic, often riddled with factionalism and petty rivalries, the NAACP emerged during the early 1940s as the spearhead of the civil rights struggle in Louisiana. By 1943 A. P. Tureaud had filed salary equalization suits in the parishes of Orleans, Jefferson, and Iberville. In 1944 the NAACP intensified its campaign for the ballot, and in the months leading up to the autumn elections blacks registered in larger numbers than any time since 1896. The following year Edward Hall sued the registrar of voters of St. John the Baptist Parish in what Tureaud expected to be a decisive test case. By 1945 the NAACP had been transformed. Previously ineffectual and largely inactive outside New Orleans, it was now a statewide organization with a fast-growing membership and increasing legal clout.

Of all the factors contributing to that transformation, one deserves a chapter to itself: World War II. The war revived the economy and boosted union membership. It placed some blacks in skilled jobs from which they had formerly been excluded. It put black men in uniform and sent them overseas. It eroded the isolation and parochialism of rural communities, facilitating travel and involving blacks in home-front activities. Above all, the war interrupted the status quo and gave blacks an all-pervading sense that white supremacy, increasingly discredited as an ideology, could be successfully challenged.

Tactics and Strategies

The civil rights movement was a complex and multifaceted struggle that was not led by any single person or organization. One of the keys to success was the grassroots effort of field workers who trained, assisted, and learned from local people. In this photo, Bob Moses, a leader of the Student Nonviolent Coordinating Committee, is addressing a training group in preparation for Freedom Summer 1964. Thousands of black and white young people fanned across Mississippi registering blacks to vote. Many were beaten, jailed, and some were even murdered. (Black Star)

Harvard Sitkoff

WE SHALL OVERCOME

The Birmingham campaign of 1963 is the central focus of this essay which
discusses the strategies of the Southern Christian Leadership Conference,
the Congress of Racial Equality, and the Student Nonviolent Coordinating Committee as well as the NAACP and the National Urban League.
Harvard Sitkoff's essay is an overview of the major national organizations
and their tactics in conquering "the most segregated city this side of
Johannesburg, South Africa." Sitkoff gives particular attention to the strategies of the movement, including the militant direct action challenges to
racist laws. Through their commitment to nonviolence, the activists were
effective in generating some white sympathy and federal action. As Sitkoff
reveals, civil rights organizations were not always united in righteous harmony, but clashed in ideological conflict at times. In addition, they found
themselves competing for resources and prestige as the Birmingham campaign got underway.

Harvard Sitkoff is a professor of history at the University of New Hampshire. He is the author of several articles as well as the book *Fifty Years
Later: The New Deal Evaluated.*

Martin Luther King's determination to provoke a confrontation
in Birmingham in 1963 resulted in a massive wave of nonviolent
action—"the Negro Revolution." Birmingham decisively changed
both the nature of the struggle for racial justice and white attitudes
toward civil rights. After more than twenty thousand blacks were
jailed in hundreds of demonstrations, King's action eventuated the
passage of the most comprehensive anti-discrimination legislation in
American history.

The decision to launch a campaign to end segregation in Birmingham had been reached in a three-day strategy session conducted by the SCLC [Southern Christian Leadership Conference] at
its retreat near Savannah at the end of 1962. The motives were both
personal and political, practical as well as philosophical. Albany
weighed heavily on King and his aides. Malcolm X had said "the civil

rights struggle in America reached its lowest point" in Albany, and many in the movement agreed. Albany brought into the open doubts about King's leadership and disillusionment with the established techniques of protest. The head of the SCLC wanted desperately to prove that nonviolence could still work, that "you can struggle without hating, you can fight without violence." King also believed it imperative to demonstrate his own courage and effectiveness, to dispel rumors that he was a reluctant and losing crusader. His reputation and SCLC's importance necessitated a daring, dramatic effort, especially since 1963 would be the year of the one hundredth anniversary of the Emancipation Proclamation.

King realized the need for some decisive achievement to rekindle the morale and momentum of the freedom struggle. Social movements require victories for sustenance, and civil-rights gains had not kept pace with the rising expectations of blacks. Despair mounted in 1962, and King feared that if the movement faltered, blacks would turn to leaders like Malcolm X, who mocked nonviolence and had nothing but scorn for "integration"—a word, Malcolm said, "invented by a northern liberal." Gaining converts, and far more sympathizers, Malcolm dismissed the aspirations of civil-rights leaders as fantasy and condemned their conciliatory style as debasing. "Our *enemy* is the *white man*," he insisted as he preached black nationalism, stressing that blacks must take control of their own livelihoods and culture "*by any means necessary.*" Proudly, Malcolm accepted the label of extremist. "The black race here in North America is in extremely bad condition. You show me a black man who isn't an extremist and I'll show you one who needs psychiatric attention!"

Worried that blacks would flock to extremists like Malcolm X if he did not succeed, King decided that the time had come to force Kennedy's hand. The President's policy of trying to show concern for blacks while at the same time avoiding action to inflame the white South, said King, had brought the movement nothing but delay and tokenism. By 1963, thirty-four African nations had freed themselves from colonial bondage, but more than two thousand school districts remained segregated in the South. Only 8 percent of the black children in the South attended class with whites. At this rate of progress, civil-rights leaders moaned, it would be the year 2054 before school desegregation became a reality, and it would be the year 2094 before blacks secured equality in job training and employment. Kennedy would have to be pushed, and pushed hard. "We've got to have a crisis to bargain with," King's right-hand man Wyatt Tee Walker explained at the SCLC retreat. "To take a moderate approach hoping to get white help doesn't help. They nail you to the cross, and it saps the enthusiasm of the followers. You've got to have a crisis."

Birmingham appeared to answer King's diverse needs. The Reverend Fred Lee Shuttlesworth, the fearless head of the Alabama Christian Movement for Human Rights, an SCLC affiliate, had just invited King to conduct nonviolent demonstrations in Birmingham, the most segregated big city in America. No other undertaking would be more audacious. Absolute segregation was the rule—in schools, restaurants, rest rooms, drinking fountains, and department-store fitting rooms. Municipal officials closed down the city parks and playgrounds rather than desegregate them. Birmingham abandoned its professional baseball team rather than allow it to play desegregated clubs in the International League. It even banned a textbook because it had black and white rabbits in it. Although over 40 percent of the population was African-American, fewer than ten thousand of the 80,000 registered voters were black. White racism permeated the city; and it was reinforced daily, wrote a reporter in *The New York Times,* "by the whip, the razor, the gun, the bomb, the torch, the club, the knife, the mob, the police and many branches of the state's apparatus." To crack this solid racist wall would be a mighty achievement.

Birmingham was more than unyielding on segregation. It had the reputation of a dangerous city. Blacks dubbed it "Bombingham" for the eighteen racial bombings and more than fifty cross-burning incidents that occurred between 1957 and 1963. Leading the vanguard of the brutal, last-ditch defenders of segregation was Eugene T. "Bull" Connor, who vowed: "We're not going to have white folks and nigras segregatin' together in this man's town." The jowly, thickset police commissioner prided himself on being as vigilant as he was cruel in "keeping the niggers in their place." The SCLC could count on Conner to respond viciously to any effort to alter the city's racial order; they believed this could create the crisis that would force the President to act. "We *presumed* that Bull would do something to help us," recalled Wyatt Walker. Connor's unwitting assistance to them would thus enable SCLC to "turn Bull into a steer." King decided to aid Shuttlesworth, but to avoid having their nonviolent campaign used as a political football, they postponed the demonstrations until after the April 2 mayoralty runoff election. In the meantime, King and his associates prepared a top-secret plan which they called "Project C"—for *Confrontation.*

King and his task force arrived in Birmingham the day after the election. They promptly issued a manifesto calling for an immediate end to racist employment practices and Jim Crow public accommodations, and for the rapid formation of a biracial committee to plan for further desegregation. "We're tired of waiting," Shuttlesworth told a packed church meeting that evening. "We've been waiting for 340 years for our rights. We want action. We want it now." As the congregation responded with spirited renditions of "Woke Up This Mornin' with My Mind Stayed on Freedom" and "Ain't Gonna Let Nobody Turn Me 'Round," King rose to vow that he would lead an economic boycott and demonstrations against the downtown merchants until "Pharaoh lets God's people go."

The first stage of Project C began the next morning. Small groups of protesters staged sit-ins at the segregated downtown lunch counters. The anticipated arrests followed. King continued this tactic for several days, patiently piquing the concern of the Kennedy Administration and the interest of the national news media while arousing the black community.

On April 6 the second stage of Project C began with a march of fifty African-Americans, led by Shuttlesworth, on City Hall. Connor arrested them all. The next day, Palm Sunday, Connor similarly intercepted and jailed a column of blacks marching on City Hall headed by Martin Luther King's brother, the Reverend A. D. King. Day after day the public marches and arrests continued, in the full glare of newspaper photographers and television cameras. King had counted on these incidents and the economic boycott accompanying them to activate larger numbers of Birmingham blacks, to focus national attention on the issue of civil rights, and to discomfort the city's economic elite. He had calculated right. On April 10, city officials secured an injunction barring racial demonstrations. They thought it would stop the SCLC campaign in its tracks, dampening the fervor of the black community. But King announced that he saw it as his duty to violate this immoral injunction and that he would do so on Good Friday, April 12. Accompanied by Abernathy and Al Hibbler, the popular blind blues singer, King led some fifty hymn-singing volunteers on yet another trek toward City Hall. Chanting "Freedom has come to Birmingham!" nearly a thousand blacks lined their route. An infuriated Connor, escorted by a squad of snarling, snapping police dogs, ordered their arrest.

While in jail, King composed an essay justifying the strategy of the black freedom struggle. Ostensibly written to the eight Birmingham clergymen who had condemned the SCLC campaign as "unwise and untimely," King addressed his reply to the many whites and blacks who apparently shared his goals but questioned his tactics, especially those who urged the movement to be patient, moderate, and law-abiding. Begun in the margins of newspapers and continued on bits of scrap paper smuggled to him by a prison trusty, King worked for four days on his nineteen-page "Letter from the Birmingham Jail." Soon after, several national periodicals published it in its entirety and reprints were distributed across the nation. Widely quoted, the epistle proved to be a potent weapon in the propaganda battle to legitimate the direct-action movement. By depicting the protesters, rather than the forces of "law and order," as the defenders of the Judeo-Christian heritage and the Constitution, King quieted some influential critics of civil disobedience.

King's letter began with a refutation of the charge of "outside agitator," arguing that as a Christian and an American he had the duty to combat injustice wherever it existed. Then King explained how the white leadership of Birmingham left blacks no alternative but to demonstrate at this time. He detailed the broken promises and refusal to negotiate by the white elite, juxtaposing them against his portrayal of the dismal, brutal plight of black Birmingham. Something had to be done to break the crust of apathy and indifference that enabled white America to ignore such injustice; something had to be done to create a crisis so the city could no longer evade a solution. To those who asked blacks "to wait," King retorted that "wait" generally meant "never." He had never "yet engaged in a direct action movement that was 'well timed,'" King observed, "according to the timetable of those who have not suffered unduly from the disease of segregation." . . .

King next turned to a philosophical vindication of civil disobedience. Because segregation laws injured the soul and degraded the human personality, he defined them as unjust, and then contended that one has a moral responsibility to disobey unjust laws.

He reminded his fellow ministers that the laws of Hitler had been "legal," and further emphasized the undemocratic nature of the segregation ordinances by indicating that blacks had been excluded from the political process which enacted these state and local laws. To those still unwilling to accept the justness of nonviolent civil disobedience, King underlined the alternative: "Millions of Negroes, out of frustration and despair, will seek solace and security in black nationalist ideologies, a development that will lead inevitably to a frightening racial nightmare." Disappointed with the moderates who cared more about law and order than about justice, King hoped they would someday recognize the nation's true heroes. . . .

D Day, May 2, an astonished national audience generated by the sit-ins, protest marches, police brutality, and the slaying of William Moore, watched over a thousand black children, some only six years old, march out of the Sixteenth Street Baptist Church to demonstrate and be arrested. Before the cameras, the young blacks sang freedom songs, chanted freedom slogans to the hundreds of cheering adult spectators, and knelt to pray as the police corralled them. They offered no resistance to Connor's stupefied forces, clapping, dancing, laughing, and skipping to the patrol wagons waiting to take them to jail. "Black and glad," determined yet not somber, the children stunned the nation.

Criticism of King for his "children's crusade" came from every quarter. Moderates anguished about the safety of the children. Conservatives denounced the tactic as cynical and exploitative. Radicals demeaned it as unmanly. "Real men," objected Malcolm X, "don't put their children on the firing line." King retorted, that, by demonstrating, the children gained a "sense of their own stake in freedom and justice," as well as a heightened pride in their race and belief in their capacity to influence their future.

In fact, King had accepted Bevel's plan to use Birmingham's black children as demonstrators because most adults had been reluctant to march and the campaign would have soon fizzled out. Bevel had also asserted that the news photographs of young girls and boys being hauled off to jail would dramatically stir the nation's conscience. The needs of victory were all that mattered; and the rules of the game had changed. Another thousand black children of Birmingham packed the Sixteenth Street Baptist Church that evening to shout their approval of King and his promise: "Today was D Day. Tomorrow will be Double-D Day."

The *New York Times Account* of the May 3 demonstrations began: "There was an ugly overtone to the events today that was not present yesterday." No one would accuse the report of overstatement. An enraged "Bull" Connor, watching a thousand more students gather in the church to receive their demonstration assignments, abandoned all restraint. He ordered his forces to bar the exits from the church, trapping inside about half the young protesters, and then had his men charge into those who escaped and had gathered in Kelly Ingram Park. The police, swinging nightsticks indiscriminately, beat demonstrators and onlookers. Attack dogs set loose sank their fangs into three fleeing children. Horrified at this mistreatment of their young, adults in the park hurled bricks and bottles at the policemen. "Let 'em have it," Connor commanded the firemen with the high-pressure hoses. With a sound like gunfire, streams of blistering water roared from the nozzles, blasting blacks against buildings and sweeping kids down slippery streets. The hundreds of pounds of pressure ripped the bark off trees; it also tore the clothes off young people's backs, cut through their skins, and jerked their limbs weightlessly. Those jailed that Friday brought the number of children arrested in two days to nearly thirteen hundred.

King had his confrontation, and more. On Saturday, an additional two hundred students were arrested, and several thousand adult blacks skirmished with the police, pelting them with rocks. Again, graphic illustrations of clubbings, police dogs, and fire hoses appeared on the front pages of newspapers and on television sets throughout the country. The appalling pictures of snarling dogs lunging viciously at youthful marchers, of bands of policemen ganging up to beat children and women, of high-pressure hoses knocking the very young and the very old off their feet, brought a surge of anger and determination across black America and aroused the conscience, or guilt, of millions of previously indifferent whites. King suddenly had massive support. Kennedy now had to act.

The pictures of violence in Birmingham made him "sick," the President admitted to a delegation from the Americans for Democratic Action that Saturday. Yet he doubted aloud that he had a constitutional mandate to act. He termed impossible the liberals' suggestion that he intervene immediately and forcefully in Birmingham, but acknowledged: "I am not asking for patience. I can well understand why the Negroes of Birmingham are tired of being asked to be patient." Privately, the President knew that the time had come to act. He had to resolve the conflict with the least possible political damage to himself. He shared the sense of national outrage at Southern white atrocities yet shrank from the prospect of using federal force to impose a new racial order. Kennedy simply wanted the quickest possible restoration of civil peace. Secretly he ordered Justice Department mediators to Birmingham to persuade the contending groups to negotiate a settlement. Concurrently, key Administration officials began an intensive campaign to pressure Birmingham's most influential businessmen, especially those connected with U.S. Steel, to accept a compromise agreement.

Until this moment in the crisis, the Senior Citizens' Committee, covertly organized by the Birmingham Chamber of Commerce to deal with desegregation problems, would not even talk with King and his associates. They were the so-called white moderates of the South—the gentlemen who said "nigra" rather than "nigger"—supposedly too busy making money to hate, yet for a month they had avoided even a hint of willingness to end the disorder and violence. Now, suddenly, they were ready to talk. They had felt the heat from Washington. They feared the city was on the verge of a major bloodletting. And they had reckoned the toll of the black boycott: sales in April had dropped more than a third in the downtown stores. So Birmingham's economic elite started to negotiate in earnest on May 4, even agreeing to hold all-night sessions. They talked and listened but would not accede. The SCLC would not back down. Deadlock. King ordered the demonstrations to continue. . . .

A shocked nation demanded federal action to end the conflict. Kennedy's mediators pressed King to yield on his demands for immediate desegregation and an end to discrimination in employment. They warned him of the folly of prolonging the crisis in the expectation of intervention by federal troops. Separately, the Justice Department officials urged the city's business establishment to make real concessions, not merely promises of future action. They threatened the white elite with the probable consequences of federal action and the economic effects of a bloodbath in Birmingham. Neither negotiating team would budge. The talks resumed, and so did the confrontation.

Tuesday, May 7, the conflict peaked. A larger number of students than ever before, and far less submissive, appeared on the streets. Rather than march from the church and court arrest, some two thousand young blacks suddenly converged on the downtown area at noon. Most staged sit-ins. Others picketed the major stores. Some held pray-ins on the sidewalks. Several thousand adult spectators then spontaneously joined a raucous black parade through the business section. Over and over they shouted "Freedom! Freedom! Freedom!" "We're marching for freedom!" Others chanted "The police can't stop us now. Even 'Bull' Connor can't stop us now."

Connor certainly tried. Adding an armored police tank to his arsenal, he ordered his men to drive the protesters back into the black ghetto. Brutally, they did so, penning nearly four thousand in Ingram Park. Connor commanded that the high-pressure hoses be turned on the trapped blacks. The water shot from the nozzles whacked the bark off trees. It tore bricks loose from the walls. The crowd screamed. Rocks flew. SCLC aides circulating in the crowd pleaded for nonviolence. Few could even hear them over the crashing of the huge hoses; and not many who could hear wanted to listen. Soon after Shuttlesworth entered the park to try to calm his followers, a blast of water slammed the minister against the side of a building. On hearing that an injured Shuttlesworth had just been placed in an ambulance, Connor laughed. "I waited a week to see Shuttlesworth get hit with a hose. I'm sorry I missed it. I wish they'd carried him away in a hearse." Not until the crowd had been thoroughly pacified and dispersed did the dogs cease biting, the clubs stop crashing bones, and the hoses end knocking blacks down and washing them along the sidewalks. A reporter who watched in despair mumbled "God bless America."

That afternoon, as the downtown demonstrations erupted, a secret emergency meeting of the Senior Citizens' Committee resolved to end the disorder that had caused Birmingham to become an international byword for unrestrained police brutality. With the din of freedom chants in their ears, the business leaders directed their negotiators to come to terms with the SCLC. A three-hour bargaining session brought the two sides close to agreement. Differences remained, but the premonition of unchecked violence affected both negotiating teams. Following three more days of talk, they reached agreement.

The SCLC had won its demands for the "desegregation of lunch counters, rest rooms, fitting rooms and drinking fountains"; for the "upgrading and hiring of Negroes on a nondiscriminatory basis throughout the industrial community of Birmingham"; and for the formation of a biracial committee. It accepted, however, a timetable of planned stages, relenting on its insistence that these changes take effect immediately. The SCLC, moreover, acceded to the release of arrested demonstrators on bond, giving up its demand for the outright dismissal of all charges against them. Although this was a compromise that pleased neither black nor white hardliners, King claimed with pride "the most magnificent victory for justice we've ever seen in the Deep South."

Before returning to Atlanta, King pleaded for reconciliation and brotherhood in Birmingham, but too many in that steel town, black and white, wanted neither. That Saturday, Connor and other leading local and state officials broadcast their denunciations of the biracial accord. They assaulted the Senior Citizens' Committee and the Kennedy brothers as well as King and the SCLC. At nightfall, over a thousand robed Ku Klux Klansmen met to hear further diatribes against the agreement. Shortly after the rally ended, two dynamite bombs rocked the home of A. D. King, strewing glass and timber in every direction. Sullen neighbors milled about, vowing vengeance. The Police and Fire Department officials inspecting the rubble were jostled and threatened. As the crowd grew, so did calls for retribution.

Minutes later, another bomb exploded, blasting a gaping hole in the Gaston Motel, the SCLC's headquarters in Birmingham. Thirsting for vengeance, the black underclass of Alabama's steel town streamed out of the bars and pool halls in the ghetto. They pelted the arriving police and firemen with stones and bottles. They stabbed one officer and assaulted several others. When some of King's aides urged them to stop throwing rocks and go home, the mob responded, "Tell it to 'Bull' Connor. This is what nonviolence gets you." . . .

King hurried back from Atlanta the next day to calm black Birmingham and to see that the accord held. He and other SCLC officials made the rounds of black bars and pool halls, schools, and churches, preaching the necessity of avoiding any provocation that might jeopardize the agreement. King pleaded that blacks stay on the nonviolent road to freedom. "Don't stop," he urged. "Don't get weary. There is a great camp meeting coming." How long? He was asked; not long, he promised. "We *shall* overcome." The familiar refrain reassured and comforted. The furor subsided. City officials and business leaders began to implement the desegregation pact on schedule. Order returned to Birmingham. . . .

Birmingham fully awakened blacks to a sense of their new power; it ignited a mighty confidence in the potency of mass social dislocation to overcome white intransigence. If such a bastion of segregation could be defeated then any other city or area could be brought to heel by an aroused black community. Birmingham also spurred self-pride, a spirit of black unity, a willingness to join the struggle. James Farmer termed this optimistic assertiveness "a spiritual emancipation" and journalists trumpeted the emergence of a "New Negro," dwelling endlessly on their loss of fear, their readiness to go to jail, and their urgent quest for Freedom Now! "The most important thing that happened," Wyatt Tee Walker later acknowledged, "was that people decided that they are not going to be afraid of white folks anymore. Dr. King's most lasting contribution is that he emancipated black people's psyche. We threw off the slave mentality. Going to jail had been the whip which kept black folks in line. Now going to jail was transformed into a badge of honor."

In part, the bravery of Birmingham's black children inspired this commitment. The image of the young, first seen on television and then seared in memory, volunteering to face down Connor's bullies and dogs and hoses, goaded thousands more to demonstrate. The same images also shamed blacks into the struggle. If children could court jail so that all blacks could be free, how could their elders do less. Simultaneously, the pictures of violence against women and kids engendered new depths of anger and widespread bitterness. The catalysts of hatred and retaliation in part dissolved black apathy and helped spark a brushfire of "little Birminghams" across the country in mid-1963.

More significant than the numbers, the nature of the struggle changed after Birmingham. Nearly a decade after *Brown*, African-American parents no longer would wait patiently for their children to attend desegregated schools. The militant "never" of hard-core segregationists would be matched by their own militancy. En masse, they forsook gradualism for immediacy. Tokenism and, for some, even nonviolence, no longer sufficed. *Freedom Now* meant, at a minimum, sweeping basic changes without either delay or dilution. "The package deal is the new demand," wrote Bayard Rustin. Instead of accepting further protracted, piecemeal alterations in the racial system, blacks clamored now for "fundamental, social, political and economic change." The price of racial peace, they insisted, must be decent jobs and housing for blacks as well as the franchise, an end to police brutality as well as immediate desegregation of all schools and public accommodations. To underscore their determination, moreover, blacks demonstrated for these concerns in an exceedingly relentless manner.

Birmingham also induced the previously torpid, very poorest blacks to participate in the racial struggle. Their entry into the movement both reflected and accelerated the radicalization of strategies and goals. The unemployed and working poor had little interest in the symbolic and status gains that the college students, professionals, and religious Southern middle-class blacks, who had constituted the bulk of the movement prior to Birmingham, had centered their energies on. They had even less sympathy for, or knowledge of, the spirit of *Satyagraha*. King's talk of love left them cold. His request that they nobly accept suffering and jailing made them snicker. As the black struggle became more massive and encompassing, impatience multiplied, disobedience became barely civil, and nonviolence, at best, a mere stratagem.

In addition, both deliberately and inadvertently, all the major civil-rights organizations further radicalized the movement. All responded to the changes wrought by Birmingham with an increasing militancy. "There go my people," King often quoted Gandhi at this time. "I must catch them, for I am their leader." And as King hurried to capitalize on the new spirit and participants in the struggle, so did James Forman of SNCC [Student Non-violent Coordinating Committee], James Farmer of CORE [Congress of Racial Equality], Roy Wilkins of the NAACP, and even Whitney Young, the executive director of the National Urban League since 1961. Far more outspoken than his predecessors, Young in 1963 constantly harped on the themes that civil rights are not negotiable, that the time for compromise or delay had passed, and that the nation owed blacks a "domestic Marshall Plan." "The only fair and realistic way of closing the gap and correcting historic abuses," Young insisted, "calls for a transitional period of intensified special effort of corrective measures in education, in training and employment, in housing and in health and welfare." Although never a direct-action organization, the Urban League in 1963 publicly defended that strategy and urged blacks to demonstrate and protest.

So did the NAACP. Wilkins, who had chided black demonstrators in Jackson in 1961, returned to that city two years later to be arrested for picketing a Woolworth store that refused to desegregate. At the NAACP annual convention in July, Wilkins demanded that the association "accelerate, accelerate, accelerate" the civil-rights attack. For the first time, the national office provided support for its local branches engaging in direct action, especially in the Carolinas, Mississippi, and Philadelphia, where Cecil Moore, the branch president, led blockades of the job sites of lily-white construction unions and boasted: "My basic strength is those 300,000 lower-class guys who are ready to mob, rob, steal and kill."

CORE, however, took the lead in the North in 1963. It organized rent strikes and school boycotts, demonstrated against job bias and for compensatory employment, and focused public attention on police brutality in the ghetto. And a CORE involved more urban blacks in the struggle, its stridency escalated. Militancy begat militancy, spurring ever more radical demands and tactics. At the same time, responding to pressure from local blacks, CORE put forth a greater effort in the South, mounting voter-registration campaigns and demonstrations against segregation. To the extent that it could, CORE tried to harness the uncompromising impatience of its many new adherents; but, in the main, events were in the saddle: the followers were leading, the leaders following. . . .

Variances between the groups, in style and substance, once easily glossed over, now began to appear insurmountable. CORE, SNCC, SCLC, and the NAACP each hungered for the lion's share of the resources they believed would enable them to set the terms of future agreements and legislation. Each tried to outdo the others, to be more successful in its campaigns, to be more devoted to the struggle. The NAACP and CORE demonstrated that in their competing efforts in a score of cities in the North and in the Carolinas; the same was true of the rivalry of SNCC and SCLC in Danville, Virginia, and in Gadsden and Selma, Alabama; and the contest for primacy in the civil-rights struggle in Mississippi among the NAACP, SNCC, and CORE generated still further momentum and militancy within the movement.

Impatience and demands escalated, moreover, because the civil-rights leadership recognized that the new mood in black America would not be long sustained. They feared that delay could dissipate the intense involvement generated by Birmingham. Worrying that anything smacking of "business as usual" might precipitate individual blacks' hasty withdrawal into the private struggle for a better life, the leaders pressed for "all, now!" The civil-rights organizations concertedly demanded as much as they could as quickly as possible. . . .

From southwest Georgia across the Black Belt to the Louisiana delta, white supremacists mobilized for a last-ditch stand. They viewed themselves as the defenders of an isolated outpost—abandoned by the rest of white America, outnumbered by blacks, and under attack by an alliance of the federal government and civil-rights agitators. Embattled and endangered, they grew desperate, anxious to go down fighting and wound the hated black movement in whatever ways they could. First they tried all manner of harassment and intimidation, especially economic coercion. When that failed to stop the civil-rights troops, they called on sheriffs and deputies, who arrested thousands of demonstrators in the Deep South during the summer and fall of 1963. In each citadel of white racism, police brutally clubbed protesters, teargassed them, scarred their bodies with electric cattle prods, and turned biting dogs and high-powered hoses on the volunteers in the movement. Still, the demonstrations continued.

Fearful, frustrated, furious whites turned to terrorism and murder. Fiery crosses placed on the lawns of civil-rights spokesmen and carloads of whites night-riding ominously through the black part of town served a preludes to the burning and bombing of homes and businesses owned by integrationists, or the destruction of schools due to be desegregated. In Mississippi, the closed society, where cars owned by whites bore license-plate legends such as MOST LIED ABOUT STATE IN THE UNION, FEDERALLY OCCUPIED MISSISSIPPI, KENNEDY'S HUNGARY, whites put to the torch several NAACP leaders' homes and stores in Gulfport, demolished the cars of civil-rights workers in Biloxi, wounded five SNCC staffers by shotgun blasts in Canton, and shot and killed a young movement organizer in Tchula. In Greenwood, 1963 brought the destruction of the SNCC office, the gasoline bombing of at least a half dozen black businesses and homes, the shooting of as many voter-registration workers, and the machine-gunning of SNCC's Jimmy Travis. Not to be outdone, whites in Jackson burned a restaurant that agreed to hire blacks, ravaged the homes and churches of integrationists, and fired rifles at cars driven by civil-rights workers. Returning from a mass meeting to his home in the capital shortly after midnight on June 11, Medgar Evers, the NAACP field secretary in Mississippi, was murdered by a sniper lying in ambush. Evers had just vowed to fight to end "all forms of segregation in Jackson."

Three months later, after two dozen black youths in defiance of Governor George Wallace had desegregated several previously all-white schools in Birmingham, a bomb constructed from fifteen sticks of dynamite shattered the Sunday-morning peace of the Sixteenth Street Baptist Church, the staging center of the spring protests. Dozens of children attending a Bible class were injured by the explosion. Four black girls, two of them fourteen, one eleven, and one ten, who had been changing into choir robes in the basement, lay dead and buried under the debris. Later in the day, a sixteen-year-old black youth was shot in the back and killed by a policeman with a shotgun, and a black thirteen-year-old riding his bicycle was shot to death by some white boys.

The next day a visibly agitated white attorney, Chuck Morgan, addressed the all-white Young Men's Business Club. Responding to the question on their minds, *who* bombed the church, an angry Morgan exclaimed:

> The "who" is every little individual who talks about the "niggers" and spreads the seeds of his hate to his neighbor and his son. . . . The "who" is every governor who ever shouted for lawlessness and became a law violator. . . . Who is really guilty? Each of us. Each citizen who has not consciously attempted to bring about peaceful compliance . . . each citizen who has ever said, "They ought to kill that nigger." Every person in this community who has in any way contributed to the popularity of hatred is at least as guilty, or more so, as the demented fool who threw that bomb.

After Morgan finished, a member moved that the Business Club admit an African-American to membership. The motion died for lack of a second.

Revulsed by the South's racist violence, embarrassed by the proponents of white supremacy, white Northern opinion swung behind the call for a civil-rights law. Attracted by the religious and patriotic idealism of the movement, dozens of student associations, labor unions, and religious organizations provided financial and political backing. Hundreds of liberal groups went on record in resolutions of support for the movement. Polls and surveys in the summer of 1963 disclosed overwhelming majorities in favor of laws to guarantee blacks voting rights, job opportunities, good housing, and desegregated schools and public accommodations. For a season, at least, Birmingham had altered the minds and hearts of millions of white Americans. . . .

"The sound of the explosion in Birmingham," wrote King, "reached all the way to Washington." The profound consequences of the SCLC campaign forced the President's hand, altering his perception of what needed to be done and what could be done. In response to Birmingham and the rush of spring and summer events that followed, Kennedy traveled in fits and starts toward a commitment to civil rights, and an identification with the movement, that he had previously resisted. Although he never fully reached that destination, he moved nearer to it than any previous American President. . . .

With the ebbing of Cold War tensions now allowing the President to focus on domestic issues, Kennedy demonstrated his resolve shortly after the Birmingham accord had been reached. On May 21, a federal district judge ordered the University of Alabama to admit two black students to its summer session. . . . Several hours after the first black students at the University of Alabama had registered, just a couple of hours before the assassination of Medgar Evers, Kennedy spoke to the nation on the race issue in a televised address that most of his advisors had counseled him against. He had decided to assert his leadership on what he called "a moral issue . . . as old as the Scriptures and . . . as clear as the American Constitution." It ought to be possible, Kennedy intoned,

> for American students of any color to attend any public institution without having to be backed up by troops. It ought to be possible for American consumers of any color to receive equal service in places of public accommodation, such as hotels and restaurants and theaters and retail stores, without being forced to resort to demonstrations in the street, and it ought to be possible for American citizens of any color to register and to vote in a free election without interference or fear of reprisal.

The President reviewed with intense emotion the plight of the American Negro, and asked:

> If an American, because his skin is dark, cannot eat lunch in a restaurant open to the public; if he cannot send his children to the best public school available; if he cannot vote for the public officials who represent him; if, in short, he cannot enjoy the full and free life which all of us want, them who among us would be content to have the color of his skin changed and stand in his place?
>
> Who among us would then be content with the counsels of patience and delay? One hundred years of delay have passed since President Lincoln freed the slaves, yet their heirs, their grandsons, are not fully free. They are not yet freed from the bonds of injustice; they are not yet freed from social and economic oppression. And this nation, for all its hopes and all its boasts, will not be fully free until all its citizens are free.

Then Kennedy warned that "events in Birmingham and elsewhere have so increased the cries for equality that no city or state or legislative body can prudently choose to ignore them. The fires of frustration and discord are burning in every city," and the moral crisis "cannot be met by repressive police action" or "quieted by token moves or talk. It is a time to act in the Congress, in your state and local legislative body, and, above all, in all our daily lives."

A week later, saying that the time had come for a national commitment "to the proposition that race has no place in American life or law," Kennedy asked Congress to pass a civil-rights law that included provisions for desegregating public accommodations; granting authority to the Attorney General to initiate school-desegregation suits; establishing a Community Relations Service to prevent racial conflicts; improving the economic status of blacks; and empowering the government to withhold funds from federally supported programs and facilities in which discrimination occurred. Mississippi's Senator James Eastland termed the bill a "complete blueprint for a totalitarian state," but congressional liberals moved quickly to strengthen it further, adding provisions for a permanent Fair Employment Practices Commission and for federal registrars to enroll black voters.

On August 28, over two hundred thousand Americans, black and white, and from almost every state in the union, converged on the Capitol, chanting: "Pass that bill! Pass that bill! Pass that bill!"

Joyously, harmoniously, they marched to signify their belief in equal rights. Gathered in unity before the Lincoln Memorial, the vast, exalted throng cheered the nation's religious and civil-rights leaders' concerted declarations of support for black freedom. They accepted with delight the approval offered by the scores of government officials and dignitaries crowded on the platform behind the speaker's stand. Afterward, the President stated publicly that he had been "impressed with the deep fervor and the quiet dignity" of the marchers, and he lauded the demonstration as one of which "this nation can properly be proud." It appeared to be the apogee of the civil-rights movement. But it had not been so conceived, the unanimity was deceptive, and many of those who participated in and praised the march had opposed it when first announced by seventy-four-year-old A. Philip Randolph, the civil-rights movement's elder statesman.

The legendary head of the Brotherhood of Sleeping Car Porters, Randolph had long nurtured a hope for a march on Washington. He had previously broached the idea in 1941 to force President Roosevelt to open defense jobs to blacks, and in 1948 to pressure President Truman to desegregate the armed services. In December 1962, he and Bayard Rustin began to plan a march for economic justice, centered on demands for a hike in the minimum wage and passage of fair-employment legislation. With little enthusiasm, CORE, SCLC, and SNCC approved Randolph's call for a mass pilgrimage to Washington to dramatize the black-unemployment crisis. The NAACP and NUL [National Urban League] bowed out. The idea drifted until Birmingham. Then it picked up steam as Rustin oriented it toward civil rights, rather than economic legislation, and Randolph agreed to a renamed March on Washington for Jobs and Freedom.

The President met with the civil-rights leadership on June 22 to dissuade them from encouraging blacks to march on Washington. "We want success in Congress, not just a big show at the Capitol," he stressed. "Some of these people are looking for an excuse to be against us; and I don't want to give any of them a chance to say 'Yes, I'm for the bill, but I am damned if I will vote for it at the point of a gun.'" There had been talk of encampments on the White House lawn and mass sit-ins in the legislative galleries. Kennedy warned that their only effect would be "to create an atmosphere of intimidation—and this may give some members of Congress an out." The NAACP and NUL concurred, fearing that a mass demonstration might erupt into violence, discredit the movement, and harm congressional prospects for a civil-rights bill.

Randolph, King, and Farmer stood fast. "The Negroes are already in the streets," Randolph informed the President. "It is very likely impossible to get them off. If they are bound to be in the streets in any case, is it not better that they be led by organizations dedicated to civil rights and disciplined by struggle rather than to leave them to other leaders who care neither about civil rights nor about non-violence?" Sustaining the argument, King stated that it was not a choice of a demonstration or legislation. The march "could serve as a means through which people with legitimate discontents could channel their grievances under disciplined non-violent leadership. It could also serve as a means of dramatizing the issue and mobilizing support in parts of the country which don't know the problems at first hand." "We understand your political problem in getting the legislation through," Farmer added, "and we want to help in that as best we can." Then the head of CORE reinforced the contentions of King and Randolph. "We could be in a difficult if not untenable position if we called the street demonstrations off and then were defeated in the legislative battle. The result would be that frustration would grow into violence and would demand new leadership." The President seemed almost persuaded, but he held off approving the march until he felt secure in its content and logistics.

The march organizers turned their energies to alleviating the qualms of the President and the moderates in the civil-rights camp who still did not back the proposed demonstration in Washington. They blurred Randolph's original focus on economic demands, and shelved plans for a sit-in at the Capitol in favor of staging a mass rally to support Kennedy's legislation. . . .

The turnout exceeded all expectations. Nearly a quarter of a million attended the March on Washington to petition for black rights, including at least seventy-five thousand whites. They took heart in their numbers. The day became a celebration. The assemblage clasped hands as Joan Baez intoned "We shall overcome," sang along with Peter, Paul, and Mary when they asked "How many times must a man look up before he can see the sky?" and hushed to hear Bob Dylan sing a ballad about the death of Medgar Evers. They clapped and cried their accompaniment to Odetta's "If they ask you who you are, tell them you're a child of God" and Mahalia

Jackson's rendition of "I been 'buked and I been scorned." Good-naturedly, they endured the heat and humidity and the seemingly endless introduction of notables and repetition of clichés by speaker after speaker. As the afternoon wore on, some grew listless, and chose to nap, to play with the many children brought by parents, and to wade in the Reflecting Pool between the Washington Monument and the Lincoln Memorial. It did not matter. They had made their point by their presence and demeanor. Then Randolph introduced Martin Luther King, Jr., who had been, as Wilkins put it, "assigned the rousements." . . .

King's rich baritone melodiously praised the "veterans of creative suffering" and urged them to continue the struggle. "*Now* is the time to make real the promises of Democracy. *Now* is the time to rise from the dark and desolate valley of segregation to the sunlit path of racial justice. *Now* is the time to open the doors of opportunity to all of God's children. *Now* is the time to lift our nation from the quicksands of racial injustice to the solid rock of brotherhood." He reminded the nation that there "will be neither rest nor tranquility in America until the Negro is granted his citizenship rights," and in rising tones answered those who asked, "When will you be satisfied?"

> We can never be satisfied as long as our bodies, heavy with the fatigue of travel, cannot gain lodging in the motels of the highways and the hotels of the cities. We cannot be satisfied as long as the Negro's basic mobility is from a smaller ghetto to a larger one. We can never be satisfied as long as our children are stripped of their selfhood and robbed of their dignity by signs stating: "For Whites Only." We cannot be satisfied as long as the Negro in Mississippi cannot vote and the Negro in New York believes he has nothing for which to vote. No, no, we are not satisfied and we will not be satisfied until justice rolls down like the waters and righteousness like a mighty stream.

He appealed to the multitude: "Go back to Mississippi, go back to Alabama, go back to South Carolina, go back to Georgia, go back to Louisiana, go back to the slums and ghettos of our modern cities, knowing that somehow this situation can and will be changed."

"I still have a dream," King added extemporaneously. "It is a dream deeply rooted in the American dream," a dream of racial justice and social harmony. Rhythmically blending Amos, Isaiah, and "My Country 'Tis of Thee," King's dream rolled over the crowd, becoming more utopian and yet believable as the audience's antiphonal response rose tumultuously.

> I have a dream that one day on the red hills of Georgia the sons of former slaves and the sons of former slaveowners will be able to sit down together at the table of brotherhood.
>
> I have a dream that one day even the State of Mississippi, a state sweltering with the heat of injustice, sweltering with the heat of oppression, will be transformed into an oasis of freedom and justice. I have a dream that my four little children will one day live in a nation where they will not be judged by the color of their skin but by the content of their character. I have a dream today.
>
> I have a dream that one day down in Alabama with its vicious racists, with its Governor having his lips dripping with the words of interposition and nullification—one day right there in Alabama, little black boys and black girls will be able to join hands with little white boys and white girls as sisters and brothers.
>
> I have a dream today.

Spines tingled and eyes teared as King ended:

> When we let freedom ring, when we let it ring from every village and every hamlet, from every state and every city, we will be able to speed up that day when all God's children, black men and white men, Jews and Gentiles, Protestants and Catholics, will be able to join hands and sing in the words of that old Negro spiritual, "Free at last! Free at last! Thank God almighty, we are free at last!"

In less than fifteen minutes, King had transformed an amiable effort at lobbying Congress into the high-water mark of the black freedom struggle. "That day," James Baldwin wrote, "for a moment, it almost seemed that we stood on a height, and could see our inheritance; perhaps we could make the kingdom real, perhaps the beloved community would not forever remain that dream one dreamed in agony." King's dream had buoyed the spirit of African-Americans and touched the hearts of whites. Not all, to be sure. It changed neither votes in Congress nor the minds of those most opposed or indifferent to racial equality. Billboards in the South proclaimed: "Kennedy for King—Goldwater for President." But, for many, King's eloquence and vision offset the ugly images of black violence that the demonstrations had started to evoke, replacing them with an inspiring picture of the movement at its benevolent best. To the extent that any single public utterance could, this speech made the black revolt acceptable to white America. King's dream capped the wave of direct action starting in Birmingham which in 1964 resulted in the passage of the civil-rights act.

Some blacks, however, felt betrayed by King and those responsible for the March on Washington. As most in the crowd cried and cheered when King perorated, one young black shouted furiously: "Fuck that dream, Martin. Now goddamit, NOW!" Others mocked "De Lawd." Malcolm X called the demonstration the "Farce on Washington." Ridiculing the March as "a circus, nothing but a picnic," Malcolm wondered: "Who ever heard of angry revolutionists swinging their bare feet together with their oppressor in lily-pad park pools, with gospels and guitars and 'I Have a Dream' speeches?" James Farmer spent the day in a Louisiana jail, refusing bail. Annoyed at the moderating influence of Kennedy and King, he stayed in his cell to make the point that he did not consider the March on Washington sufficiently militant. SNCC staffers were livid that John Lewis, their chairman, had been forced to soften his words in deference to the demand of some of the white speakers. Lewis had prepared a speech describing the civil-rights bill as too little, too late, denouncing both Republicans and Democrats as hypocrites, threatening the South with a Sherman-like "scorched earth" march through the heart of Dixie, and demanding of Kennedy: "I want to know—which side is the federal government on?" The civil-rights establishment forced Lewis to launder such remarks from his address, turning the demonstration for jobs and freedom into, according to James Forman, "a victory celebration for the Kennedy Administration." But the angry reactions to the March on Washington and King's leadership, largely hidden from view that serene August afternoon, forecast the divisions and differences that would one day wreck the movement.

Nevertheless, throughout 1963, the black struggle remained outwardly united. An end to segregation appeared at hand, although Congress dawdled. In November the sudden crack of a rifle in Dallas precipitated the overdue legislation. The assassination of the President immediately stirred sympathy for the attainment of the goals Kennedy sought and an abhorrence of violent fringe politics, like those associated with the Klan and other extreme white supremacists. Many considered passage of the civil-rights bill the most fitting memorial to their slain leader.

The House of Representatives acted quickly after the 1964 session began. It considered the measure for eleven days and passed it overwhelmingly. The Senate took nearly three months to debate before voting 73 to 27 for the bill. On July 2, President Lyndon Johnson signed the act which prohibited discrimination in most places of public accommodation, authorized the government to withhold federal funds to public programs practicing discrimination, banned discrimination by employers and unions, created an Equal Employment Opportunity Commission, established a Community Relations Service, and provided technical and financial aid to communities desegregating their schools. The movement barely had time to celebrate. It was in the midst of the Mississippi Freedom Summer and a mighty effort to secure the franchise for blacks, the final item on the established civil-rights agenda.

Donna Langston

THE WOMEN OF HIGHLANDER

In this essay, Donna Langston explores the activities of women in the integrated Highlander Folk School, founded in 1932. Responsible for training union organizers, the school's progressive participants and leaders recognized the importance of the civil rights movement and expanded its activities to include training civil rights workers. White and black men and women traveled to the Tennessee school in the 1950s and 1960s and developed strategies and legal tactics to strengthen the struggle against racial oppression. In the face of state-sponsored repression and threats from terrorist organizations, the school encountered difficult challenges, eventually closing, but not before preparing many workers, particularly women like Rosa Parks, Septima Clark, and Bernice Robinson for leadership positions in the civil rights movement.

Donna Langston is a professor of women's studies at Mankato State University.

Donna Langston, "The Women of Highlander" from Vicki Crawford, Jacqueline Anne Rouse, and Barbara Woods, eds., *Women in the Civil Rights Movement: Trailblazers and Torchbearers, 1941–1965* (Brooklyn, NY: Carlson Publishing, 1990). Reprinted by permission.

Introduction

Highlander Folk School (HFS) was founded in 1932 in Monteagle, Tennessee, and served as a regional model for progressive education and politics. During the 1930s and 1940s, HFS was a training ground for labor union organizers. In the 1950s and 1960s, it was closely involved in the civil rights movement. In the 1970s and 1980s, HFS focused on environmental issues and on poverty in Appalachia. The history of HFS provides an important role model for the multi-faceted political struggles we now face.

Traditional historical accounts of HFS have not adequately stressed the role that women played in the school's struggles and successes. The school's very existence came about as a result of the donations of Dr. Lillian Johnson of Memphis. The contributions of women such as Zilphia Horton, Septima Clark, and Bernice Robinson were instrumental in the development of HFS's social, cultural, and educational programs. The school was also publicly supported during difficult times by prominent women such as Eleanor Roosevelt.

Civil rights movements have often used a variety of strategies and tactics in their struggles, including legal tactics; nonviolent direct action such as boycotts, arrests, mass marches, and sit-ins; the use of the vote; cultural programs; and education. While women in civil rights movements have played central roles in all of these strategies, their involvement in cultural programs and education has been pivotal. The women of HFS recognized the political significance of culture and education. They devoted much of their talents to shaping programs that fostered the formation of class and race identity and raised consciousness.

HFS is an exciting example of men and women from varying class and race backgrounds working together in common endeavors. Examining both the strengths and weaknesses of their efforts can provide important lessons concerning the possibility of coalition politics.

Workers' Education

HFS came into existence through the generous land and building donations of Dr. Lillian Johnson. Johnson came from a wealthy Memphis banking and merchant family. She was a graduate of

Wellesley, had a doctorate in history from Cornell, had been president of Western State College in Oxford, Ohio, was a leading suffragette, and was a member of the Women's Christian Temperance Union. Johnson had studied the cooperative movement in Italy. She returned to the South interested in spreading the idea and started a community center for the mountain people.

She bought land in Grundy County, Tennessee, one of the poorest counties in the nation, built a two-story house, and started a school. Johnson had two women from the University of Tennessee at Knoxville train two women from the mountain community, May Justus and Vera McCampbell, to teach. By 1930, she was interested in retirement and looked for others to carry on her community center work. Johnson chose HFS as her replacement. She gave them a year's probationary lease, which was extended indefinitely.

Highlander Folk School started operations in November 1932. The name of the new school was based on the popular name for an Appalachian (Highlander) and after the folk schools in Denmark that were used as a model for this adult education center. At first HFS opened along the lines of a settlement house in a rural setting, serving as a community center. The staff worked without pay.

The first activities of the school were social evenings. Social and cultural activities provided a rich resource of outreach services to the surrounding community and the women of HFS were particularly involved in this development. In the middle of a poverty-stricken community, HFS was a place where working people could check out books from a well-stocked library and send their children to take free music lessons. Residents of the community were invited to plays and weekly dancing. Zilphia Horton from Arkansas, who married Myles Horton, one of the founders of HFS, arrived at the school in 1935 and played a central role in nurturing community relations.

During its first three years, HFS established a union for WPA workers, a community cannery, a community nursery school, and a quilting cooperative set up by Myles Horton's mother. The nursery school was organized by Claudia Lewis. Later it was run by Johanna Willimetz, a graduate of Wellesley who used her personal contacts to raise money and acquire supplies for the school. By the end of 1935, HFS had become the social center of the community.

Starting its first year, four evening classes were held weekly, with an average attendance of twenty men and women between the ages of eighteen and eighty. The subjects were psychology, cultural geography, revolutionary literature, and current political and economic problems. Class discussion was based on the current situations in the South, as staff soon learned that education was most effective when it was based on people's lived experiences. For example, when asked to explain the theory of surplus value, one student, an unemployed nurse who had paid for her HFS tuition with a basket of onions, beans, and canned fruit, explained, "When I was working at the hosiery mill in Chattanooga, we were told that we would have to take a wage cut or the mill would go out of business. Of course, we took the cut. About ten weeks later, I read in the paper that the daughter of the mill owner was sailing for Europe to spend the winter. I suppose it was the surplus value we had produced that paid her way.

HFS staff were increasingly drawn into the labor struggles that affected the people they served. The school opened during a time of intense class conflicts. The South in the 1930s was extremely violent. Blacks and labor leaders were targeted as offenders against Southern white purity. One of the first attempts to bomb HFS was due to the school's support of workers during the 1933–34 Wilder coal strike. HFS provided a refuge for the struggling Southern labor movement. The early initial goals of HFS were to: (1) serve as a community center for residents in the area based on ideas of unionism and cooperation; (2) develop a workshop program in order to train hundreds of Southern labor leaders; and (3) develop a field and extension program that would enable HFS staff to teach in other communities and in strike situations whenever requested.

The school developed intensive-study residence terms lasting from four to six weeks. Classes were offered in labor history, economics, strike tactics, public speaking, current events, and parliamentary law. One- or two-week "workshops" were held, as were weekend conferences, focusing on a single subject, such as political action or race relations. . . .

Efforts at Desegregation

From its beginning in 1932, this Southern school was an integrated institution. The very first announcement produced by HFS stated that it was open to blacks and whites. It wasn't until 1944 that blacks began to attend as students, but beginning with sociologist Charles

Johnson from Fisk University during the first year, blacks were invited as speakers. Whenever HFS staff was called on to assist in organizing drives, they would set up only integrated unions, co-ops, and other groups. HFS believed that democracy in the unions should apply to both sexes and all races. The facilities had no provisions for segregation.

During the early 1930s, a few black leaders, such as J. Herman Daves of Knoxville College and Charles Johnson, visited HFS. HFS produced a filmstrip, "Of a New Day Begun," for the Race Relations Department of Fisk. In 1935, the interracial All Southern Conference for Human Rights was chased out of Chattanooga by vigilantes. They managed to elude the group of bigots and continued their proceedings at HFS that same day. HFS was a unique institution in the South where blacks and whites could meet.

The explicit policy of HFS was to operate on an integrated model not only among its students, but also among its staff and policymakers. The first black to join the HFS board was Dr. Lewis Jones, a sociologist at Fisk University, in 1942. Dr. P. A. Stephens, a physician and surgeon, and the most influential black man in Chattanooga, refused several invitations before finally joining the Board of Directors in 1947. That same year, Grace Hamilton, of the Urban League in Atlanta, joined the board, followed by Dr. B. R. Brazeal, dean of Morehouse College in Atlanta, who joined in 1949.

One of the most controversial issues during the period HFS worked primarily with unions was race. Unions were reluctant to sponsor integrated schools. Not until 1944 was an integrated session held at the school by the United Auto Workers [UAW].

HFS conducted numerous workshops for labor groups. Segregation was practiced by many unions and racism was an entrenched problem among the white working class. In 1940, HFS informed all unions it served that the school would no longer hold worker education programs for unions that discriminated against blacks. In 1944, after refusing for four years, the UAW finally accepted an invitation to attend an integrated workshop. Forty black and white members participated. Other unions followed.

In 1949, a meeting for UAW president Walter Reuther's reelection campaign invited only white leaders. When a black union leader arrived uninvited, the HFS staff interrupted the meeting with an ultimatum to integrate or leave before the next meal. The meeting proceeded on an integrated basis. This policy of nondiscrimination was viewed by Southern society as Communist-inspired and immoral.

HFS was active in union organizing years before unions were legal, and in the 1950s they became involved on the same level in the Southern black civil rights movement, well before the movement gained national prominence and support. Before the 1954 Supreme Court *Brown* decision, HFS workshops were addressing problems of desegregated schools and full citizenship.

In 1952, the HFS Board of Directors decided that race relations should become the school's primary focus. At an April 1953 session of the executive council, the governing body agreed that race relations was the most pressing Southern problem. Members of the board emphasized the immediacy of the issue as a result of *Brown:* "The next great problem is not the problem of conquering poverty, but conquering meanness, prejudice, and tradition. Highlander could become the place in which this is studied, a place where one could learn the art of practice and methods of brotherhood. The new emphasis at Highlander should be on the desegregation of the public schools in the South."

HFS prepared a curriculum for community leaders, black and white, who expected to be involved in implementing the decision. Two summer workshops were held in 1953 on "The Supreme Court Decisions and the Public Schools," and subsequent workshops on school desegregation were held in 1954, 1955, 1956, and 1957. This was the first curriculum developed in the South to assist local leaders in desegregating their schools.

The 1953 workshop group developed a guide, "Working Toward Integrated Public Schools in Your Own Community," which was widely printed and distributed. In addition to the guide, a series of recommendations for local community leaders, entitled "Basic Policies for Presentation of Local School Boards," was composed.

Both direct and indirect effects can be traced to HFS activities. For example, weeks after attending a HFS workshop in 1955, Rosa Parks refused to give up her bus seat and her arrest sparked the Montgomery bus boycott. Another example is Esau Jenkins, who after returning from the 1954 workshop to his home on Johns Island, South Carolina, attempted to integrate school leadership on the island by running as the first black candidate for school trustee since Reconstruction. He was defeated in the election, but he succeeded in raising black interest in registering to vote and in demanding improved schools.

With increased attendance of blacks at HFS, the FBI started watching the school, harassing neighbors, and asking questions about the black students. At this time attendance of black students was equated with the presence of communism. The charges of communism continued to plague the activities of the school, often leading to reduced contributions. The closure of the nursery school was attributed to such losses.

Community leaders from across the South came to the 1953 summer sessions. Until the passage of the first civil rights bill in 1963, HFS remained one of the few places available for interracial meetings. Specifically during this time, HFS brought black leadership together, provided a model of an integrated society, and developed a successful citizenship program that was later transferred to the Southern Christian Leadership Conference [SCLC]. An outgrowth of its efforts with community leaders on school desegregation, HFS next worked on literacy and the voting rights project in South Carolina.

Citizenship Schools

In 1953, HFS received a three-year grant from the Schwartzhaupt Foundation, which gave them the freedom to experiment in adult education. South Carolina legislators declared membership in the NAACP a criminal act sufficient to warrant dismissal of a public school teacher, shortly after the 1954 *Brown* decision. In 1956, eleven black teachers, members of the NAACP in Charleston, were fired. One of them was Septima Clark. In 1954, Clark had been elected vice president of the local chapter of the NAACP. Shortly thereafter, she received a letter from the South Carolina school system informing her that she could no longer teach in the system. After she was fired, Clark came to HFS as the director of education. (She subsequently turned down several teaching jobs in New York to stay in the South and continue her work at HFS.) Clark traveled across the South, setting up schools in beauty parlors, country stores, and private homes. Her work at HFS and later with the SCLC required coordinating the citizenship schools throughout the South.

In 1954, Clark attended a workshop on school desegregation at HFS. That summer she returned for another workshop, this time bringing Esau Jenkins and Bernice Robinson. Robinson was Clark's cousin, a Charleston beautician who had completed high school at night. She became the first citizenship school teacher volunteer and later an HFS staff member and member of its Board of Directors.

Esau Jenkins was a poor farmer with seven children who drove a bus between Johns Island and Charleston. He had instructed a handful of students on his route, using the bus as a classroom. His first pupil was Alice Wine, who went on to become a registered voter.

Jenkins viewed the most pressing problem in his community as illiteracy, because adults had to pass a literacy test to be eligible to vote. Jenkins persuaded HFS to set up a school in his community. The Johns Island principal was afraid to let HFS use the local school, and the preacher was afraid to let them use the church. So HFS lent Bernice Robinson $1,500 without interest to buy an old school building and paid for her transportation, materials, equipment, and supplies.

Previous adult literacy programs had been held in children's chairs and adult students had to read material that was of little practical use to them—"See the red ball." The adult literacy program formulated by Septima Clark and Bernice Robinson provided an adult setting of peers with learning based on their life experiences. The students were respected as adults and were provided with dignified reading material. They learned to read and write using practical materials, filling out, for instance, replicas of Sears mail-order forms. Students were taught how to fill out voter registration material, mail orders, driver's license exams, and how to sign checks. . . .

After three months of instruction, fourteen students took the voting test and eight of them passed and were registered. This night school for adults became the model for the citizenship schools that spread throughout the South in the 1960s and provided thousands with voter education.

The Schwartzhaupt Foundation continued to support the community leadership and citizenship school programs until 1959. By 1960, most funding came from the Marshall Field Foundation. Between 1954 and 1961, HFS had 37 programs with over 1,295 participants.

Septima Clark recruited teachers and students for the schools. By February 1961, workshops to train citizenship school teachers were being held for twenty to twenty-five persons per month. The only requirements for teachers were that they had to be from the same community as the students, be at least twenty-one, and hold a high school diploma. People of diverse ages and occupations were drawn to teaching at these schools—farmers, union members, housewives, dressmakers, and ministers. . . .

A number of great civil rights leaders, including Fannie Lou Hamer, attended the citizenship schools. Teachers returned home and became actively involved in their communities. The schools were so effective that Andrew Young thought the training program was the base upon which the whole civil rights movement was built. Septima Clark explained that the citizenship school instructors prepared a community so that they "were already prepared to listen to a black man and to know that the government of that state can be handled by blacks as well as whites. They don't know it before. We used to think everything white was right. We found out differently, though."

The citizenship school was one of the most effective organizing tools of the movement. Though education was often viewed as less militant than other strategies and tactics, these schools were a significant mobilizing factor. The Citizenship Education Program that Septima Clark and Bernice Robinson developed for HFS became the basis for future voter registration work throughout the South. By 1959, due partially to the success of the citizenship schools, HFS was investigated by the Tennessee legislature.

As HFS increased its involvement in the civil rights movement and students were drawn from predominantly black communities, the school lost its strong ties with the local community. But it was antagonism from the state, not from local residents, that eventually closed the school.

Trial

Southern public officials were always eager for opportunities to link the civil rights movement with Communist subversion. They equated integration with communism. Some focused on HFS. The governor of Georgia, Marvin Griffin, wanted to discredit Martin Luther King, Jr., and the state legislature of Tennessee wanted to discredit HFS. At HFS's twenty-fifth anniversary celebrations, King was a keynote speaker. Photographer Ed Friend was sent by Governor Griffin's

Georgia Commission on Education to the conference. (The commission was a tax-funded body the governor set up to attack desegregation.) Abner Berry, a columnist for *The Daily Worker*, registered as a free-lance writer and did not reveal his association with the Communist Party at the conference. Perhaps not by coincidence, Friend kept setting up shots into which Berry would jump with leaders such as King. The photos were used to red-bait the school and King. Friend returned, with photographs of whites and blacks dancing and swimming together and a group photo including King and Berry. Billboards shortly appeared across the South with pictures of King and Berry at the conference and the slogan "King Attended a Communist Training Center." Also, 250,000 four-page brochures and postcards featuring Ed Friend's photos were sent throughout the South.

Governor Griffin's plan backfired; a statement written by HFS and signed by Eleanor Roosevelt and other prominent Americans appeared in *The New York Times*. Still, the tactic played on the strong belief that those who favored integration must be Communist. In the next stage of harassment by government officials, the IRS revoked the school's tax-exempt status and the Tennessee legislature adopted a resolution to investigate HFS.

A resolution was introduced in the Tennessee Central Assembly in February 1959 to investigate the subversive activities of HFS. It passed both houses without opposition and was signed by Governor Buford Ellington. Five members of the legislature appointed by the governor held closed and open hearings. A two-day hearing was held on February 21 and 22. The circumstantial evidence and testimony consisted of accusations such as few people ever saw an American flag flying at the school. The committee presented a condemnatory report to the House and Senate, urging them to direct the district attorney general to bring a suit against HFS and revoke its state charter. The legislature quickly passed such a resolution, which Governor Ellington signed. The legislative committee could find no proof of Communist activity, but it directed the district attorney general, A. F. Sloan, to revoke the school's charter since integrated schools were in technical violation of state laws.

HFS survived its first decade probably only because the pro-labor Roosevelt administration was in office. In particular, Eleanor Roosevelt had lent public support when the school was attacked. Since government officials were unsuccessful in their attempts to close the school through legislative procedures, they now pursued the judicial route, beginning with a raid. The crux of the problem was that HFS had always been integrated and was increasing its focus on race relations. The literacy training program was viewed as particularly threatening to Southern white society.

On July 31, at 8:30 P.M., Attorney General Sloan and twenty state troopers and local sheriff deputies in plainclothes raided HFS. Their official purpose was to search for whiskey, as the school was located in a dry county. Myles Horton was in Europe serving as co-chair of an international conference on adult education, but Septima Clark was conducting a weekend workshop on school desegregation. Clark was arrested and charted with illegal possession and sale of whiskey and resisting arrest, the latter charge due to her request to phone a lawyer. Three others were arrested with her on charges of public drunkenness and interfering with an officer. None of them was ever brought to trial.

Initial reports contained many apparently prepackaged fabrications. First was the accusation that Horton had been drinking on the premises, which was obviously untrue since he had been in Europe at the time. Then there was the accusation that black men and white women had been having intercourse in the library, but it hadn't been built yet.

Three months later, in September, a three-day hearing in circuit court upheld Sloan's request for an injunction closing the school because it was a public nuisance. The school was padlocked and used for target practice by the Elks Club and American Legion. The raid in which HFS staff were arrested on trumped-up charges of drunkenness appeared to have accomplished what the legislative committee could not.

The trial opened on November 3 and lasted only four days. The state claimed the HFS's charter should be revoked for three reasons: it had sold beer and other items without a commercial license; Horton had received property and money from the school; and the school had permitted whites and blacks to attend together in violation of a 1901 state law. The state argued that the *Brown* decision applied only to public schools, not private ones such as HFS.

All members of the jury admitted that they opposed integration. A few enemies of HFS sat on the jury, including a cousin of the chief state witness and a cousin of the sheriff who conduced the raid. The state strategy was clear—it paraded witnesses who presented HFS as a place where illegal and immoral behavior between whites and blacks went on. The witnesses testified to having observed wild parties, drunkenness, and open sexual intercourse between whites and blacks at the school. *The Chattanooga Times* observed that HFS witnesses were as impressive as the state's were unsavory. The state had accused the school of engaging in commercial activities—the sale of soft drinks, beer, candy, gum, and razor blades. Since blacks at the school weren't allowed to go into local establishments to purchase items, HFS provided them on a rotating fund basis. Participants could take beer from a cooler and leave twenty-five cents. Selling beer without a license was the technicality that closed the school.

The state also accused Myles Horton of operating the school for personal gain. The truth of the matter was that he had worked for over twenty years at no salary. When the staff did begin receiving salaries in the 1950s, they were below those at comparable institutions. For example, in 1959, Horton earned around $5,000.

It took the jury less than one hour to arrive at a guilty verdict. On February 17, 1950, Judge C. C. Chattin ruled HFS guilty on all three counts. It was ordered that the HFS charter be revoked, and the property liquidated and put in receivership. It was the first time in Tennessee history a corporate charter had been revoked.

Two futile appeals were made. During the appeals process vandalism and a fire destroyed the original house. The school appealed to the State Supreme Court, which in April 1961 upheld the lower court's ruling, except that it threw out the integration violation. There was no constitutional issue left.

The appeal to the U.S. Supreme Court was denied a hearing on October 9, 1961 and HFS reached the end of its course of appeals. At this point HFS extension schools were serving nearly 20,000 students and about 350 teachers were working in the area of literacy and citizenship.

On November 7, HFS was placed in receivership and the school property was confiscated. It had taken the state more than two years to close HFS. On Saturday, December 16, 1961, HFS property was sold at auction. HFS had assets of about $175,000, including 200 acres of land, a dozen buildings, and a library containing several thousand volumes. The state netted $10,000 from the sale of property and an additional $43,700 from the sale of land for a total of $53,700. (Several prosecuting lawyers bought some of the land.) The state had taken over the building, land, equipment, school, library, and the director's private home. HFS never received any remuneration. The investigation, raid, hearing, trial, and conviction took place with amazing speed. The appeals process postponed closure for almost two years, but segregationists had successfully used the courts to deny the right to teach integrated classes. Horton took out a new charter for a new school the day after the first one was revoked. The Highlander Research and Education Center relocated to an urban setting in Knoxville, Tennessee. This, however, was not the end of its harassment by white vigilante groups and the state. During the 1960s, the school was investigated by Senator James Eastland's Internal Security Subcommittee, the FBI, and the IRS. Several years later, when Ellington was again governor of Tennessee, the legislature tried to investigate the new Highlander for alleged subversive activities. This time Horton and the ACLU went to federal court and got an injunction blocking the investigation.

Conclusion

It was the integrated citizenship schools that brought HFS under scrutiny of the authorities in the state of Tennessee in 1959. To ensure the survival of the schools, in late 1961 their operation was turned over to the SCLC. SCLC officials had been looking for an education program, and Clark and Robinson's Citizenship Education Program had nearly outgrown HFS capacities. Arrangements were made to give the program, funds, and staff to the SCLC.

The SCLC financed the citizenship schools with a grant from the Marshall Field Foundation. Septima Clark and Andrew Young joined the Atlanta SCLC staff to administer the schools, with Clark also serving as a consultant to the new HFS establishment. Bernice Robinson eventually left Highlander and joined the SCLC. SCLC-sponsored citizenship schools became a mass-education effort supported by foundation grants and Septima Clark had direct responsibility for these efforts. In 1963, she reported that since the program had been transferred to the SCLC, twenty-six thousand blacks in twelve Southern states had registered to vote. At this time volunteer teachers were running four hundred schools for sixty-five hundred adults.

Clark continued her work with the citizenship schools, which eventually prepared over 140,000 adults for registration tests and taught them to read and write. She was one of the few women on the SCLC board until she retired in 1970. The importance of the citizenship schools to the movement and the role that Septima Clark played cannot be adequately stressed. When Ralph Abernathy asked why Septima Clark was on the board of directors of the SCLC, Martin Luther King, Jr., replied, "Because she sets up the programs that allowed us to expand into eleven Southern states and she deserves to be on our board."

Two months after the sit-ins began at Woolworth's in Greensboro, North Carolina, students from all over the South met at HFS. For three days, April 1–3, 1960, eighty-two students (forty-seven blacks and thirty-five whites) from twenty colleges attended a workshop entitled "The New Generation Fights for Equality." Key leaders in the student movement attended, including James Bevel and John Lewis. Three weeks later, a new regional organization was founded, the Student Nonviolent Coordinating Committee (SNCC).

In 1975, Septima Clark was elected to a seat on the same board of education from which she had been fired nineteen years earlier. She was the third woman and the first black woman ever to sit on the Charleston County School Board. That same year, she also received the highest award of the National Education Association, the H. Council Trenholm Humanitarian Award.

Although Septima Clark had forty-one years of teaching service, it was twenty years before black legislators were able to reinstate her pension. In 1976, the state of South Carolina issued her a check for thirty-six hundred dollars, the sum she was entitled to annually. The governor apologized for her unfair firing. She was never reimbursed for the years between 1956 and 1976. In February 1979, Clark received the Living Legacy Award from President Jimmy Carter.

The Citizenship Education Program Septima Clark developed for HFS became the basis for the black voter registration drive throughout the South. As she observed, "Many of the achievements we made in the civil rights movement started with that Highlander program. You can see the results everywhere—in black elected officials, in voters, and now in the efforts of Indians, and Appalachian whites to get their rights. Most citizenship school projects came to an end in 1966 after passage of the Federal Voting Rights Act.

On August 28, 1961, Highlander reopened. The center carried on its work by holding workshops with students participating in the sit-in movement, actively participating in the training of civil rights workers for the Freedom Summer of 1964, and continuing training up to the time of the Poor People's March on Washington in 1967. The reorganized institution continued to train community people in leadership positions, specifically for the voter registration activities of SNCC. SNCC was one of the last black civil rights groups to continue using Highlander. Nightriders attacked one of their last meetings at the center; one of those narrowly missed by rifle shots was Stokely Carmichael. Among the participants at the annual college workshops were Bernard Lafayette, Marion Berry, James Bevel, John Lewis, Diane Nash, and Julian Bond. At the new Knoxville center Highlander ran workshops on voter registration for twenty SNCC volunteers at SNCC executive secretary James Forman's request. Highlander was then asked by John Lewis and James Forman to set up education programs for SNCC. Debate about the role of whites in the movement increased over the years, with many leaders feeling that whites should work within their own communities.

In the late 1960s, Highlander established an extension facility in the Southwest to work with Chicanos and also set up extension programs in the uptown area of Chicago. In 1971, the school moved from Knoxville to rural New Market, Tennessee. The school's projects focused on a health program, a resource and education center, and a cultural program. Once again, it worked in the field of labor education with programs for the Amalgamated Clothing and Textile Workers Union and the United Furniture Workers Union.

In the 1970s, Highlander again shifted priorities. Beginning in 1967 with the Poor People's March on Washington, HFS staff was increasingly drawn to the dream of King and others of a multiracial poor people's coalition. Highlander moved into poverty work in Appalachia, although it maintained its involvement in civil rights. For example, in 1965, SNCC held five meetings and workshops at the center. In March 1964, a workshop entitled "Appalachia People and their Problems" was held.

In the early 1980s, twelve staff members were working with Appalachian people on issues of poverty, unsafe coal mines and textile mills, and toxic waste. In 1983, Highlander was nominated for a Nobel Peace Prize by Atlanta Mayor Andrew Young and Representative Ronald Dellums of California.

Jack Bloom

THE DEFEAT OF WHITE POWER AND THE EMERGENCE OF THE "NEW NEGRO" IN THE SOUTH

The following essay by Jack Bloom is a thoughtful examination of the cultural and psychological processes that occurred in southern African-American communities during the years leading up to the modern civil rights movement. Bloom explains why the development of a new consciousness among many southern blacks in the wake of the successful Montgomery bus boycott and the *Brown v. Board* case was so significant to the movement. As he notes, the new militancy among blacks was "spurred on by white brutality and viciousness as much as by black hope." The crucial point is that white supremacy had been dealt a mortal blow in the minds and hearts of black people *before* racist laws were destroyed. Moreover, old style accommodationist leadership in the black community was resisted and supplanted by new, more aggressive forms of leadership. These events emerged in communities across the South and impacted each other, giving rise to new forms of protest.

Jack Bloom is a professor of sociology at Indiana University Northwest.

White rule was consolidated around the turn of the century. It meant terror and poverty to blacks; it meant that whites were able to shape the society and economy, to decide what would be the rules, and to change those rules at any time. It meant that even if blacks took Booker T. Washington's advice and set about to earn the respect of the whites by prospering, they would find their hopes frustrated: respect was not forthcoming in a white-controlled world. Or if it was, it would be only within the framework of black subordination and segregation.

White power meant more than whites' controlling the world within which blacks had to live. White power was able to reach into the black community itself and to shape it, to help determine the goals the black community sought, the means devised to seek those goals, the leadership the black community had, the kinds of personal options blacks often felt they had, and even the view that blacks had of themselves. As a result of the victory of white supremacy, blacks had few options. They were not in a position to confront the white-created social, political, and economic world in order to change its terms; rather, they had to find a way to survive in it, to adjust to it. Accommodation meant looking to powerful whites as benefactors, requesting "favors," accepting paternalism and subordination. It meant that whites determined the black community's leaders by deciding with whom they would communicate and to whom they would grant their "largesse." It meant that blacks failed to challenge the view of themselves as inferior.

While these patterns of action were never fully realized, they certainly became the norm. As the economic changes proceeded in the decades of the thirties and forties, these racial patterns remained largely unchanged. Blacks were growing more aggressive and impatient, but they entered the decade of the fifties with the old system basically intact. It was in the course of that decade that the old patterns were challenged and began to be broken and that the "New Negro" emerged in the South. The New Negro was first spoken of in the 1920s in the North, especially in Harlem, the most highly developed of the urban black communities. The New Negro in the North was independent of whites, aggressive, and insistent upon equality and had cast off the sense of black inferiority. These new behavioral characteristics blossomed almost immediately upon blacks' attaining independence from direct white domination.

It was another three decades until the New Negro began to appear in the South to present a significant challenge to the old style of black accommodation to white power. Southern blacks had to confront white supremacy far more directly and centrally than blacks in the North. They had to free themselves from fear and from the pervasive feelings of self-worthlessness. Instead of making requests, they had to steel themselves to make demands. They came to learn that requests to make real changes simply would not be granted without their demonstrating that the cost of not granting a demand would be greater than if it were granted. Even then, they were sometimes met with intransigence.

The new balance of power in the South made it possible to continue in the face of these circumstances. Structural changes meant that those who were determined to prevent change could no longer carry the day. Their power to affect regional and national decisions had been greatly weakened. Correspondingly, the power of the blacks had been strengthened, and part of the story of the emergence of the New Negro in the South is that blacks sensed these changes and began to act on their perceptions.

The transformation of blacks in the fifties was painful and difficult. It was spurred on by white brutality and viciousness as much as by black hope. It often took form as a struggle for leadership in the black community. In some places gradually, in others rapidly, the old style accommodationist leaders were shunted aside, and what happened in one place often had a big impact on the consciousness and organization in others. Certainly by the end of the decade there was little support for the old-style leadership in the Southern black population. Here was the death of white power *inside the black community.*

The *Brown* decision was very important in this process: it set the law clearly on the side of the blacks and thereby encouraged them to seek their rights more aggressively. By putting whites on the defense, it impelled them to organize in response, which widened the gulf between black and white and made it more necessary for the blacks to push forward.

The Montgomery bus boycott was a crucial turning point in the black struggle of the fifties—*the* crucial turning point where blacks scored an unequivocal victory over whites. A strategy, a new leadership, and a new consciousness among blacks were the product of this episode. The success in Montgomery, Little Rock, and elsewhere helped to create a new élan and leadership.

But blacks experienced more than white terror, or the victory over it, in the decade of the fifties. As they pursued their ends more aggressively, as they grew more impatient with their status, they tested the support that was forthcoming from sources many had thought to be their allies. The federal government and white liberals came to be seen as sorely lacking, and the result was more anger and frustration and the recognition that blacks had independently to set their own course. Thus, as a new decade approached, the impulse toward direct action was taking hold. . . .

Accommodation to White Power

The consolidation of power by the Southern ruling class at the beginning of the twentieth century set the terms of the Southern racial and political system for another half-century. The violence and terror that had been used to defeat Reconstruction and Populism became a normal part of the region's culture. Its use by almost any white under almost any conditions against almost any black without fear of legal reprisal was standard. Gunnar Myrdal wrote: "In the South the Negro's person and property are practically subject to the whim of any white person who wishes to take advantage of him or to punish him for any real or fancied wrongdoing or 'insult.'" Police protection was close to nonexistent and was, if anything, on the side of the blacks' tormentors. It was similar with the courts, whose judges were beholden to whites, not blacks, for their tenure in office and whose juries refused to convict when cases were brought before them. These circumstances created a generalized terror of whites that always affected blacks. John Dollard described his visit to blacks' homes accompanied by three Southern white men. "The Negroes were frightened and reluctant," he said. When he commented to his companions on how politely they were received, he was laughingly answered: "They have to be [polite]." Whites could, at any time, freely test and taunt the blacks.

Acting properly—as defined by whites—was therefore essential, though by no means a guarantee of security. One black informant told sociologist Charles Johnson in the late thirties:

> I like some white people all right I just don't want to have no trouble with them. If I did get in trouble with 'em I wouldn't do nothin'. I couldn't do nothin'. They'd kill me. White folks don't play with no colored folks. You have to do what they want you to do or else your life ain't worth nothin'.

If these grim conditions were not always sufficient to guarantee proper black acquiescence, whites had an array of other sanctions: control over jobs, credit, and mortgages. Charles Johnson pointed out in referring to school teachers and principals that "since most if not all of them hold their jobs at the will of white school officials and politicians, they are extremely careful to observe the racial etiquette as far as possible. . . ." Martin Luther King, Sr. described the situation as one where "the black man had no rights . . . that the white man was bound to respect. He wasn't nothin' but a nigger, a workhorse. He wasn't supposed to have any formal training, wasn't supposed to be bright."

This condition of virtually unchecked white power was the reality to which blacks had to adjust. There was little room for independence; they had to take great care in the presence of whites. In general, black action and consciousness were shaped by these conditions. If such was not universally the case, if there was some room for individuals to maneuver or even, in some circumstances, to ignore the expected rules of conduct, most felt resistance to be hopeless. . . .

Adjustment meant not challenging segregation in any of its manifestations: it meant not seeking to use the vote, or if voting was acceptable in individual cases, it was certainly out of the question to organize it. A black real estate operator in Atlanta told Charles Johnson: "At the Court House they have a colored elevator, but that don't bother me. It runs like the rest of them." Hylan Lewis was told by an election official in the early fifties: "We've had a few niggers voting in Kent for years. They are good niggers—know their place. And there has never been any trouble about their voting. On election day, they always come to the polls as soon as they open, vote and leave." It meant blacks' staying in their assigned "place" in the social order: "Negroes are practiced in saying 'yes, sir,' 'no, sir' to white people," reported Dollard. That place, he contended, was perhaps best portrayed by black movie actor Stepan Fetchit, who "always plays the part of a well-accommodated, lower-class Negro, whining, vacillating, shambling, stupid and moved by very simple cravings." Accepting one's place meant accepting continually demeaning behavior: not dressing well; not buying a new car or other expensive consumer items lest one appear "uppity" by challenging the status of lower-class whites; waiting in stores to be served until after the whites had been taken care of; avoiding looking whites in the eye for fear that this behavior would be interpreted as arrogance; being addressed as "boy," "girl," "aunty," "professor," but never "Mr.," "Mrs.," or "Miss"; even getting off the sidewalk and walking around to provide a respectful distance to whites. One informant told Charles Johnson: "When I see them, I let them have they side of the street, and I goes on. . . . ."

A New Beginning

The economic and sociological transformations brought to the South by the Depression and World War II prepared the basis for the emergence of the New Negro. But the war itself was the single most important catalytic event: it opened up jobs for blacks, took them off the farms, and set them in the cities; it put guns in their hands and trained them to use them; the war exposed blacks to education and to the world and made them more cosmopolitan. As a result, by the war's end blacks were becoming more self-assertive. Morton Rubin, who did a study of "Plantation County" in the late forties, noted the trend toward "a growing feeling of race consciousness and race pride. . . ."

Black veterans were to play an important part in this change. In 1946 there was a riot in Columbia, Tennessee. It was precipitated when a black veteran knocked a white radio repairman through a plate-glass window after the white had slapped his mother. The veteran was arrested, and a lynch mob began to form. Efforts to post bond in a town that had had two lynchings "by invitation" in the past two decades were blocked by raising the amount of bail. "Let me tell you one thing, sheriff," said a black businessman in response, "there won't be any more 'social' lynchings in Columbia." They got the young man released on bond, and that night a white mob came into the black part of town. It was met by a determined population that included over 150 veterans and a number of chemical workers who held membership in the CIO Mine, Mill, and Smelter Workers' union. When the shooting was over, four police officers had been wounded, one seriously. A few years later one of the participants told Carl Rowan, "Before the riot Columbia was a hellhole, but . . . we've got a good city now." Said another: "No, there ain't gonna be no more trouble. That's the one thing I learned from 1946. They know now that negroes have guts. . . . Blood was shed, but it paid off. A colored man used not to have the chance of a sheep-killing dog. But 1946 changed that."

In 1946 a black veteran arrived in Prince Edward County in Virginia to be a minister at a black church there. He had belonged to the NAACP in college, had been touched by the Wallace campaign the previous year, and "I thought religion ought to be lived up to, squared with economics, politics, all that. . . ." Leslie Griffin was to play a key role in creating the conditions that led to a student strike for better schools and ultimately to a court suit that became one of the cases consolidated into the 1954 *Brown* ruling.

The ferment suggested by these events was fueled not only by black indignation at injustice but also by blacks' sense that things were going their way. Part of this feeling involved the legal victories that the NAACP was winning against conditions that were supposed to be separate and equal but that had no pretense of equality. Under the threat of integration, cities were building better facilities for blacks. Statistics on black incomes and jobs were up, as were those on home ownership and college attendance. These characteristics, indicating the rise of a middle class, were the very phenomena later associated with increased civil rights activity. . . .

In general there was a sense that things were getting better, that perhaps the end was in sight. . . . Black sociologist Charles Johnson surveyed the period with great optimism: "We are changing from a racial society in many respects to a human relations society," he said. Looking forward to the *Brown* decision, the head of the South Carolina NAACP thought that both blacks and whites in the state would accept the Supreme Court's decision.

Brown: New Hope, New Militancy

When the *Brown* ruling was issued, its impact on the black population was electric. Louis Lomax called the day of decision a "black Monday," playing on Mississippi judge Thomas Brady's famous speech and pamphlet: "That was the day we won," he said, "and we were proud." A sixteen-year-old black student in Virginia broke into tears when told the decision by her teacher: "We went on studying history, but things weren't the same, and will never be the same again." The (black) Atlanta *Daily World* heralded that day as "one of the important days in the history of this country and the fight for freedom for all the citizens of the nation!" John Lewis recalled the impact upon him: "I was 14 and . . . as I recall we rejoiced. It was like a day of jubilee . . . that segregation would be ended . . . We thought that we would go to a better school . . . get better transportation, better buses, and that type of thing." "This decision," said Martin Luther King, Jr., "brought hope to millions of disinherited Negroes who had formerly dared only to dream of freedom."

New hope and courage appeared everywhere. Blacks were vindicated in their struggle. "Suddenly there was a voice, more impressive and resounding than that of any Negro leader, the voice of the highest court in the land, and it was saying in unmistakable language that segregation was wrong, was illegal, was intolerable, and that it must be ended," wrote Mrs. Medgar Evers. Roy Wilkins summed up the meaning of the decision for many:

> We have been subject to the whims and fancies of white persons, individually and collectively. We went to back doors. . . . We stepped off

sidewalks and removed our hats and said "Sir" to all and sundry, if they were white. . . . We could not vote. Our health and our recreation were of little or no concern to the responsible officials of government. In time of war we were called to serve, but were insulted, degraded and mistreated. . . . This school decision heralds the death of all inequality in citizenship based on race. . . .

From the black point of view, the decision changed everything, and blacks became more aggressive. In Greensboro this new mood was noted at school board meetings. Visits from the NAACP and black parents were "more frequent . . . and more assertive, but less patient. They wanted it done boom, boom, boom," Jim Crow in the department stores provoked new protests, as did segregation in other areas. In Florida, black leaders reported getting pressure from the community to communicate to whites their wish for rapid implementation of the *Brown* ruling. In South Carolina, blacks began organizing to elect to office candidates who would support their needs. And in New Orleans, the movement against segregation picked up steam after *Brown*. The NAACP planned to make sure *Brown* was implemented: the organization looked forward to gaining "complete emancipation" by January 1, 1963, the one-hundredth anniversary of the Emancipation Proclamation.

The new spirit was perhaps best illustrated in Mississippi. There, but two months after "Black Monday," the governor summoned a group of trusted (by whites) black leaders who were asked to endorse a proposal for voluntary segregation. Most denounced it; the few who did not were themselves ridiculed and denounced. Similar efforts were made elsewhere; whites simply could not believe that "their" blacks wanted it.

Blacks had played the game according to white rules. They had gone through the white courts, and they had won. Now they expected—assumed—adherence to the rules. Thurgood Marshall, who had plotted the legal strategy, said: "Once and for all, it's decided, and completely decided." It was now assumed that school boards would comply, and the NAACP optimistically prepared to be magnanimous:

It is important . . . that . . . the spirit of give and take characterize the discussions. Let it not be said of us that we took advantage of a sweeping victory to drive hard bargains or impose unnecessary hardships upon those responsible for working out the details of adjustment.

"But we were naive," said Louis Lomax. And indeed, looking back, these expressions of optimism certainly appear naive. Looking down the road, those standing on the crest of the Supreme Court ruling could see the end. They could not perceive the obstacles that yet lay before them. The next years would be a time of education, and the naivete would give way to bitterness, anger, determination, and organization. If the Southern ruling class would not give up the ground that it had legally lost, that ground would have to be wrested from it. The remainder of the decade prepared the black population to do just that.

Brown: "The Great Silence"

When the Supreme Court ruled, it was Southern whites who made the next move; blacks awaited the improvements they expected to be forthcoming. . . . [T]hey attempted to undermine its legitimacy, to establish a higher authority—the south's (white) people and their customs—and to create the solid white South to confront blacks and the federal government.

They drew a hard line between white and black. Crossing that line was made very difficult, lest the line itself disappear; white solidarity had to mean increased hostility to blacks. Black-white associations suddenly became taboo. Race relations, with which moderates had been pleased, suddenly deteriorated. This change was felt in small ways: black college chorus performances before white audiences were dropped; black groups were excluded from holiday parades and festivities; proposals for intramural sports activities between blacks and whites, which had sometimes occurred in the past without anyone's taking notice, were now viewed with suspicion as efforts to begin compliance with the *Brown* ruling. In Orangeburg, South Carolina, the white ministerial alliance refused to organize joint prayer services with blacks.

White paternalism, which was premised on unquestioned white superiority, began to disappear. Carl Rowan was told by a southern moderate in Mississippi that at Christmas time wealthy whites would no longer make contributions to buy presents for poor black children. The Urban League was excluded from Community Chest fundraising efforts in several Southern cities where it had previously participated, including Little Rock, Richmond, New Orleans, Jacksonville, and Forth Worth. . . .

These actions hardened attitudes among the blacks. Those who might still be pulled by lingering ties of affection for or dependence on whites had their channels of communication shut off. White paternalism was severely curtailed, and with it went some of the whites' ability to shape black action. Perhaps most important was that the black accommodationist leadership was undermined by the new turn. The base of these "leaders" in the black community was their ability to produce, to bring home the bacon, to make gains. In an era when most blacks' backs were bent from stooping, their own bent backs were not out of place. But when the whites drew back and in effect labeled all blacks alike, as dissenters, and would grant no concessions, the white removed the basis of the old leadership's predominance in the black community. They did so even as black sentiment was shifting away from the approach that many characterized as begging for crumbs, and as an alternative leadership began to appear. The hardening line of whites served only to stiffen the backs of blacks and to hasten the process of changing leadership.

Brown: White Terror and a New Leadership

The white response included economic coercion, violence, and terror, even murder. In four years a survey found forty-five people beaten, twenty-nine shot, and wounded, six killed. A compilation over the same period found 225 acts against "private liberties and public peace." Over time, as the campaign continued, a self-selective process took place in which those blacks who had the courage, the conviction, the inner strength, the independence, (especially economic), and the ability to stand up to the terror no matter what the cost—even possibly death—came to the fore and reshaped the attitudes of the black population. The process by which new leaders were tested and proven for leadership so different from the accommodationist leaders of the past, trained them for a wholly different approach to whites and white supremacy. "Medgar [Evers] . . . came to have . . . respect for the Negroes who dared to accept positions of leadership throughout the state," wrote Evers's wife. Far from looking for white paternalism, this new leadership was selected and trained by defying the most vicious and sometimes brutal actions of the whites. . . .

The *Brown* decision, which put right and law on the side of blacks, pushed it forward. They were no longer asking for favors or seeking the benevolence of a "friend." They now demanded their due; it was the whites who were the lawbreakers. And with the change, those blacks who persisted in the old patterns came increasingly to be viewed as traitors. Repeated efforts by whites in Montgomery to divide the blacks finally persuaded one of their number to collaborate with the whites. But he was frozen out by the black community. In Durham, the first black city councilman, elected only a year before with the support of all black community organizations, responded cautiously to the court ruling. Implementation would take time, he said, and most black pupils would not go to white schools. Other black leaders disapproved of this statement; the councilman lost influence, and by the 1957 election he was replaced.

But as a group, the old-style black leaders did not just disappear. They sometimes fought openly for their stance. The publisher of a black newspaper in Mississippi wrote almost a year after *Brown:*

> It can be safely stated as a fact that 85 per cent of the Negro school patrons in Mississippi, and the South generally, are hoping and praying that no attempt will be made to enforce the Supreme Court decision. . . . Insofar as Negroes in the South are concerned, the NAACP is an enemy of the Negro race.

A black college president told a meeting of blacks: "I don't believe you are going to throw away your churches, schools, hospitals, businesses, insurances, newspapers . . . just to sit, eat, and ride with a white person." A school principal in South Carolina warned that the *Brown* decision would create "many perplexing problems and grave consequences" for black students and teachers and that educational opportunities for black children would "suffer for the next fifty years." There were blacks with livings dependent upon separate institutions who defended segregation.

Nonetheless, more and more frequently blacks were refusing to be intimidated, were standing up to the white terror and facing it down. A seven-year-old boy asked to be sent to an all-white school. His mother: "If you got the guts to go I've got the guts to send you." An Alabama preacher had been threatened by a white gang with being beaten and thrown in the river: "I wouldn't advise you to do that," he warned. They didn't. In Greensboro, parents who were economically vulnerable applied for permits for their children to attend white schools. In Montgomery, over one hundred blacks were indicted during the boycott. One of the participants wrote:

> For the first time police . . . were confronted by Negroes who acted like men. . . . Many . . . reported to the jail voluntarily. Others . . . sat chatting leisurely in the cells long after bonds had been arranged. . . . All the threats which had been used to suppress the Negro had lost their potency. Iron bars and the prison cell would be a pleasant sight if such meant freedom and first-class citizenship for all unborn generations. . . . The thirst for freedom had pushed all fears into the background. . . .

Montgomery: Martin Luther King, Jr. and the Strategy of Nonviolent Direct Action

The actual changes emerged in counterpoint to the activities of the white supremacists, who themselves responded to challenges to their system. That was evident in the emergence of the White Citizens' Council as an immediate response to the *Brown* ruling. The organization languished in the early months of 1955. But, subsequent to the second *Brown* ruling when it was clear that all the voluntary compliance there was to be had already taken place, the NAACP began to act. The organization prepared a petition campaign calling for integrated schools. Once again the White Citizens' Councils grew.

The summer of 1955 was the most violent of the decade. The murder of Emmett Till became a cause celebre and inflamed black consciousness. Blacks in Mississippi were being told to "agree and knuckle under, or flee, or die," said Roy Wilkins. Faced with such choices, blacks had little alternative but to push forward. Angered at being unlawfully denied their rights, confident that they had some backing in Washington, D. C., blacks grew in determination. "Toward the end of 1955," wrote one observer, "the spirit of rebellion and resistance was spreading among black people in every corner of the South." Confrontation was becoming inevitable. The questions were where would be, what form it would take, and what its outcome would be.

In Montgomery, Alabama blacks had made gains as they had elsewhere in the South: merchants had been pressured to eliminate separate drinking fountains and to begin addressing black customers as Mr., Miss, or Mrs.; the city had been induced to hire four black policemen; and efforts had already begun to gain equal recreational facilities for blacks. Martin Luther King's church had been conducting a voter registration drive to increase the political power of blacks in the city.

But the structure of segregation remained solid, and the indignities continued. As elsewhere, blacks were becoming increasingly unwilling to tolerate such conditions. In the year before the bus boycott began, five black women and two black children had been arrested for disobeying the segregation laws on the buses. One black man was shot; others were threatened with pistols by bus drivers; a blind man had his leg caught in the door and was dragged down the street. King had served on a committee formed in 1955 after a fifteen-year-old high-school girl had been arrested for failing to give up her seat to a white. The committee met with the bus company and with the police but won no concessions.

A boycott had been considered for a year, but a defendant whose character could not be impugned had not been found. Six days before Rosa Parks refused to give up her seat to a white, the Interstate Commerce Commission outlawed segregation in interstate travel. Though unplanned, Parks's act was no accident. A long-time outspoken activist and secretary of the state office of the NAACP, "I had almost a life history of being rebellious about being mistreated because of my color." Mrs. Parks's arrest in December 1955 sparked the Montgomery bus boycott. Speaking of her action, Parks said, "This is what I wanted to know: when and how would we ever determine our rights as human beings?"

Parks described the ad hoc character of the action that brought about her arrest:

> At the time when I refused to move from this seat and stand up I didn't feel that I was breaking any law because the ordinances as far as I could recall didn't say a driver would have a person to leave a seat and stand. . . . When I was ordered by the driver to leave the seat, there was nothing I could do but either stand up and get off the bus, or stand up over this same seat that I had vacated because there was no where even to move back. The back of the bus was already crowded with passengers: people were standing in the aisles up to where I was sitting, and I didn't feel I was even violating the segregation law. Only thing I did was just refuse to obey the driver when

he said, "stand up." So there were four people involved: a man in the seat with me . . . and two women across the aisle. So that meant four of us would stand for one person to occupy a seat and leave three vacancies unless another white person got on.

The Montgomery effort was as important as the *Brown* decision itself in pushing the black movement forward. It was a long and difficult struggle in which the black population of the city took on the entire white power structure in a year-long battle, and won. That battle encouraged a rising tide of black militancy. It was the most important confrontation of the decade, in which blacks demonstrated to the world and to themselves the unity and the sacrifices of which they were capable. It inspired blacks to challenge white supremacy elsewhere and was a crucial turning point in the emergence of the New Negro and the eclipse of the old. It became a unifying point not only for blacks in Montgomery, Alabama but for blacks across the nation. Thousands of dollars were sent in to aid the boycott from many sources. In New York in the summer of 1956, a giant rally was held to build support and raise money. Those attending included Eleanor Roosevelt, Sammy Davis, Jr., Congressman Adam Clayton Powell, and A. Philip Randolph. Montgomery had come to occupy center stage in the struggle for black liberation.

Out of the crucible of struggle in that city, Martin Luther King, Jr. emerged. As Montgomery rose to national attention, so did the leader of the struggle. Invitations for him to speak proliferated. In 1956, King appeared before the Democratic party platform committee. *Time* and *Jet* magazines ran cover stories on him, as did many other newspapers and periodicals. By the late fifties, King was emerging as the most important black leader in America. He became a symbol of the new black spirit and came to be generally acknowledged as *the* black leader—no one approached the prestige King enjoyed.

King was a product of the new mood. The changing attitudes on the part of blacks and their newly developing sense of power encouraged his own proclivity to seek change. He, in his turn, helped to inspire blacks to reach for greater heights, to demand racial justice, and to do so with dignity and self-respect. The hastening pace of events that resulted from Montgomery, and King's self-conscious efforts helped to create a new stratum of leaders to push the struggle further. The formation of the Southern Christian Leadership Conference served both to build on this emerging new leadership and to extend it. Its establishment was very important, because it meant that now the new trend became organized.

When King came to Montgomery, he was not fully formed as the leader he would become. He was concerned about the matters that would soon come to dominate his life; that was why he had chosen "in spite of the disadvantages and inevitable sacrifices" to return to the South, "at least for a few years." He was shaped by the struggle in Montgomery as much as he shaped it. Andrew Young asserted as much: "I'm convinced that Martin never wanted to be a leader. I mean, everything he did, he was pushed into." Coretta King recalled King himself saying much the same:

> If anybody had told me a couple of years ago, when I accepted the presidency of the MIA [Montgomery Improvement Association, the organization that led the boycott], that I would be in this position, I would have avoided it with all my strength. This is not the life I expected to lead, but gradually you take some responsibility, then a little more, until finally you are not in control anymore. You have to give yourself entirely. . . .

King tried to reach out to broaden the base of the movement, to bring others, including whites, into it. He felt that those who would fight to retain racism were a minority, and he looked to winning the support of the white majority. He reminded Northern whites that no matter where one lived, "the problem of injustice is his problem; it is his problem because it is America's problem." In particular, he looked to the "millions of people of good will [in the white south] whose voices are yet unheard . . . and whose courageous acts are yet unseen." To these he held out the prospect of joining with the blacks "who yearn for brotherhood and respect, who want to join hands with their fellow Southerners to built a freer, happier land for all." Nonviolent action was central to his strategy:

> It was in this Gandhian emphasis on love and nonviolence that I discovered the method for social reform that I had been seeking for so many months. . . . I came to feel that this was the only morally and practically sound method open to oppressed people in their struggle for freedom.

Its practicality was based on King's perception that in a violent conflict, blacks must lose: it would "place them as a minority in a position where they confront a far larger adversary than it is possible to defeat in this form of combat." This approach enabled King to make an approach to whites on a new basis. No longer hat-in-hand, King rejected also what he called "corroding hatred" toward whites. Nonviolent resistance offered the possibility of reconciliation. "We are out to defeat injustice and not white persons who may be unjust," was how he put it. King recognized that whites feared blacks, and he feared that with black shackles removed, blacks would wish to turn the tables and abuse, oppress, and humiliate the whites. For that reason, he sought to reassure whites. That would make it much easier to end the system of oppression. "The job of the Negro," he exhorted, "is to show them [the whites] that they have nothing to fear. . . ." When the body that became the Southern Christian Leadership Conference first met, it adopted as its slogan "Not one hair of one head of one white person shall be harmed in the campaign for integration."

King was not simply trying to avoid the losing bloodbath that he felt would inevitably follow from an armed conflict. He was seeking to broaden the ranks of the movement: "By nonviolent resistance, the Negro can also enlist all men of good will in his struggle for equality. . . . Nonviolent resistance is not aimed against oppressors but against oppression. Under its banner consciences, not racial groups are enlisted."

King stressed that if there was suffering to be done, it would be by the blacks, that they were prepared to take whatever the whites could dish out—they still could not be stopped:

> We will match your capacity to inflict suffering with our capacity to endure suffering. . . . We will soon wear you down by our capacity to suffer.

> Rivers of blood may have to flow before we gain our freedom, but it must be our blood.

These expressions were meant to provide a bridge to reassure whites. But they had a deeper meaning, as well. They were meant to encourage a black population that had been terrorized to feel that white terror could no longer stop and intimidate them. No matter what the whites sought to do to them, blacks would stand up, take it, and not be deterred. That was the central focus of King's approach. What was most important about nonviolent direct action was its impact upon the blacks themselves:

> The nonviolent approach does not immediately change the heart of the oppressor. It first does something to the hearts and souls of these

committed to it. It gives them new self-respect; it calls up resources of strength and courage that they did not know they had.

Nonviolent resistance makes it possible for the Negro to remain in the South and struggle for his rights. The Negro's problem will not be solved by running away. . . .

King succeeded in casting the black struggle with an ideology that left little to the other side but tyranny and naked racist aggression. The old justifications of "niggers" and "black apes" wore thin in the face of the human courage and dignity displayed by blacks. King was thus well grounded to appeal for "strong and aggressive leadership from the federal government." And the government had little justification for shrinking from the task except its own powerlessness or the complaint that blacks were asking for too much, too fast.

King did not invent all of these ideas. This discussion has not been an effort to delve into their origins. King emerged from Montgomery with a synthesis of these ideas, a remarkable ability to articulate them to both black and white audiences, and the stature that enabled him to command a hearing based on his baptism and conduct under fire in the city of Montgomery. . . .

Toward Black Independence

If these events created a self-confident, though embattled, black population and leadership, their feelings were tempered by disappointment, cynicism, and anger, as the allies to whom blacks had looked demonstrated their unreliability. That was particularly true of the federal government and white liberals.

Blacks had looked to the federal government since the thirties. First the New Deal and later President Truman's concessions had encouraged them. And they had gained much from the federal judiciary. However, the government showed increasing reluctance to act. If the election of 1948 provided the lesson that it was possible for a Democrat to win by courting the black vote and ignoring the white South, it was a lesson that the Democratic candidate, Adlai Stevenson, failed to apply in the 1952 and 1956 elections, as he sought to appease white Southerners. That was why many blacks deserted the party of Roosevelt in 1956 and voted for Eisenhower. Eisenhower, however, did little more.

King and the SCLC were aware of the difficulty of prodding the federal government to act in their favor. King stated at a conference called by the Montgomery Improvement Association two weeks after the boycott victory:

> We must face the appalling fact that we have been betrayed by both the Democratic and Republican parties. The Democrats have betrayed us by capitulating to the whims and caprices of the Southern Dixiecrats. The Republicans have betrayed us by capitulating to the blatant hypocrisy of right-wing reactionary Northerners.

The SCLC sought continually to pressure the federal government to support its struggles. It sent telegrams nine months before Little Rock that urged that President Eisenhower deliver a speech in the South urging Southerners to abide by the Supreme Court decisions as the law of the land, and that Vice-President Nixon tour the South "observing and reporting on the terror to which blacks were subject." The president refused the request; the vice-president ignored it.

When the SCLC leaders met again a month later, they repeated their request to Eisenhower to speak out. "We are confronted with a breakdown of law, order and morality," they warned. "This is a sinister challenge and threat to our government of laws. . . ." They asked the president to call a conference on civil rights and again suggested that Nixon take a "fact-finding trip." When no answer came forth, King approached Roy Wilkins, head of the NAACP, and A. Philip Randolph, leader of the March on Washington movement of the 1940s, to discuss the SCLC's proposal of a pilgrimage to Washington, D.C. On the third anniversary of the *Brown* decision, some 15,000 to 20,000 people, 90 percent black, assembled at the capital "because . . . the Eisenhower Administration was dragging its heels in the matter of voting rights," explained Coretta King. Less than a month later, King and Abernathy met with Vice-President Nixon, but nothing came of that. In his writing and speaking, King continued to stress the necessity of federal government intervention in the increasingly serious struggle in the South.

In June 1958, King, Randolph, Wilkins, and Lester Granger, head of the Urban League, met with the president to discuss what he might do on their behalf. The president responded vaguely and committed himself to nothing. When the group broke up, he said to King, indicating his frame of mind: "Reverend, there are so many problems . . . Lebanon . . . Algeria." So even after the Little Rock confrontation, with the school closing in Little Rock and Virginia yet to come, with the terror operating, with suppression of black voting rights in full swing, there was little the federal government had to offer. King summed up his perceptions of the experience:

> His personal sincerity on the issue was pronounced. . . . However . . . President Eisenhower could not be committed to anything which involved a structural change in the architecture of American society. His conservatism was fixed and rigid, and any evil defacing the nation had to be extracted bit by bit with a tweezer because the surgeon's knife was an instrument too radical to touch his best of all possible societies.

When King complained of "the relatively slow progress being made in ending racial discrimination" and tied that slow progress to "the undue cautiousness of the federal government," he was expressing a growing sentiment. In June 1958, Medgar Evers, leader of the NAACP in Mississippi, wrote the president, requesting that he publicly support compliance with *Brown*. He received a vague reply from the White House staff, which, said Evers's wife, "was no answer at all."

It was not the executive and legislative branches of the government alone that were disappointing in their actions. The judiciary, which had in recent times been the strongest supporter of the black drive for equal rights, now recoiled in response to the aggressive drive of the segregationists. In June 1958, the Supreme Court made a decision that, at the time, was little noticed but came to be very important. The Court upheld Alabama's Pupil Placement Act, which entitled school administrators to place students in schools based on a variety of criteria, including behavior, physical facilities, sociological and psychological factors, and academic background. Race was not formally listed among these, though there was little question that their purpose was to disguise continuing racial discrimination. Complicated and lengthy administrative appeals were required before a plaintiff had the right to seek legal remedies. This law permitted the maintenance of segregation by allowing very minimal token integration. "Tokenism" became the white South's next stand.

Tokenism was an effective stance. By June 1961, Alabama, Georgia, Mississippi, and South Carolina still had no blacks in desegregated schools. Florida, Louisiana, North Carolina, and Virginia had less than .1 percent of their pupils in desegregated schools. Arkansas and Tennessee had less than 1 percent; Texas had 1.2 percent in desegregated schools. After advances in the fall of 1958, progress came virtually to a halt. In Greensboro, North Carolina, where the sit-ins began, token desegregation held the line. A Little Rock school official wrote to an acquaintance in Greensboro: "You North Carolinians have devised one of the cleverest techniques of perpetuating segregation that we have seen." King assessed the disappointing trend the court ruling seemed to portend:

> It raises the prospect of long, slow change without a predictable end.
> . . . This . . . is the danger. Full integration can easily become a distant
> or mythical goal—major integration may be long postponed, and in
> the quest for social calm a compromise firmly implanted in which the
> real goals are merely token integration for a long period to come.

Disappointment was even greater with the white liberals who collapsed before the onslaught of the Southern establishments. They were silent, or worse. They ceased urging better conditions for blacks or affirmed their devotion to segregation. They asked blacks to modify their goals, for they were pushing too fast for the white supremacists, who, said William Faulkner, "will go to any length and against any odds at this moment to justify and, if necessary defend that condition [segregation and white supremacy] and its right to it." The truculence of white supremacy unnerved the moderates and brought them to seek calm the only way they knew how—by prevailing upon the blacks to return, only temporarily, of course (Faulkner urged the NAACP to "stop now for a moment"), to the quiet that had prevailed before *Brown* and before Montgomery.

King spoke to this issue and rejected the pleas of white liberals, refusing to allow them to set the pace of the struggle. He affirmed that blacks would set their own pace:

> The enlightened white Southerners, who for years have preached
> gradualism, now see that even the slow approach finally has revolu-
> tionary implications. This realization has immobilized the liberals and
> most of the white church leaders. They have no answer for dealing
> with or absorbing violence. They end in begging for retreat, lest
> things get out of hand and lead to violence.

King alluded to Faulkner's request to "stop now for a moment" and pointed out in response that "it is hardly a moral act to encourage others patiently to accept injustice which he himself does not endure."

Rather, he asserted: "We Southern Negroes believe that it is essential to defend the right of equality now. From this position we will not and cannot retreat."

It was clear that others were feeling the frustration. Louis Lomax expressed the reaction:

> We . . . had faith in a class of white people . . . who were pillars of the Southern community and who appeared to be the power structure of the community. . . . It was incredible to a Negro woman who had been a servant in a white home for twenty years that her employers would cringe and hide while white trash threw bricks at her grandson on his way to school.

Journalist Carl Rowan bitterly characterized the moderate response: " 'When in doubt do nothing' was rationalizing its way into believing that we would not face a racial crisis today if only we had thought to do more of nothing sooner." In Durham, North Carolina, Elaine Burgess caught the trend in one leader's frustration: "We'll have to keep pushing, pushing, pushing to get what we want." Daniel Thompson discovered the same sentiments. Speaking of white moderates, one black leader said: "They have talked a lot but never about the real issue—segregation. They have agreed with everything the White Citizens' Council advocates except closing schools. I think they are the Negro's worst enemy." And another: "We see them now as they have always been—segregationists, who want us to continue to be satisfied with the crumbs that might fall from their weighty, segregated tables." In Memphis blacks were becoming disillusioned with the policy of supporting white liberals, who became increasingly segregationist as the White Citizens' Council pressure was applied.

By the end of the decade, blacks were disabused of their illusions about white liberals and the federal government. These lessons helped to define the course of action blacks would take in the 1960s. More and more, they came to see that they could not rely on anyone to carry their torch for them, and that if others were to act on their behalf, they would have to be pushed into it. In the fall of 1958, Bayard Rustin organized a youth march on Washington for integrated schools, with King's support. Ten thousand attended. Some six months later, another such march brought out twenty-five thousand. In Richmond, Virginia, two thousand participated in a demonstration for integrated schools, the first such in the South. . . .

By the end of the decade, blacks, especially students, had begun experimenting with what would become the hallmark of the sixties—direct action. In August 1958, the youth group of the NAACP in Oklahoma City organized a sit-in. This action spread to Enid, Tulsa, and Stillwater, Oklahoma and to Wichita and Kansas City, Kansas. There were sit-ins at Miami department store lunch counters, which included three arrests, and in Nashville just two months before the Greensboro sit-ins, this time without arrests. Neither succeeded. In Louisville the NAACP tried sit-ins in 1959, as did the Charleston, West Virginia and Lexington chapters of CORE, the latter two successfully. And in Atlanta a boycott ended segregated busing in 1959.

By 1960, élan and momentum, which had been broken among the advocates of white supremacy by the defeats in Little Rock and in Virginia, were with the black movement. This momentum was not to leave until the Southern political system was transformed. The stage was now set for the rapid escalation of the pace of struggle that was to begin in Greensboro.

August Meier and Elliot Rudwick

DIRECT ACTION: HIGH TIDE AND DECLINE

August Meier and Elliot Rudwick's essay is an insightful analysis of the rise and decline of the Congress of Racial Equality (CORE). The essay surveys the role that CORE played in contributing important elements to the civil rights movement with the 1961 Freedom Ride and the manner in which the organization assumed an important supporting role in major demonstrations and events in the early 1960s. Meier and Rudwick argue that the nonviolent Freedom Rides represented the pinnacle of CORE's visibility and simultaneously demonstrated the effectiveness and power of nonviolent protest and the depravity of those who fought it. CORE members were mostly middle-class whites and black northerners until the mid-1960s. The organization worked in coalitions with other civil rights organizations and developed unique roles in different cities. In some cases, rivalry erupted between local chapters of CORE and the NAACP. An essential point here, is that CORE varied nationally. It was not a monolithic organization in a state of ideological stasis, but highly adaptable.

August Meier and Elliot Rudwick are the authors of several books on the civil rights movement, including *CORE: A Study in the Civil Rights Movement, 1942–1968,* originally published in 1975. Rudwick taught sociology at Kent State University for many years. Meier is emeritus professor of history at Kent State University.

In 1961, CORE's Freedom Ride had been the great symbolic event that set the tone of the entire black protest movement for months. In contrast, during the period of CORE's greatest activity the important symbolic events—the Birmingham demonstrations of May 1963, the March on Washington a few months later, and the Mississippi Freedom Democratic Party's Challenge to the seating of the state's "regular" delegation at the Democratic National Convention in August 1964—were all occasions in which CORE played only a supporting role. The sixteen-month period between the Birmingham demonstrations and the Convention Challenge delimitated a distinct phase in CORE's history during which time the entire direct-action movement crested and started to recede.

Martin Luther King's Birmingham campaign coincided with the inauguration of an extraordinarily vigorous era of direct action. In the following months CORE involved more people than ever before, heightened its demands, conducted massive and tactically more radical demonstrations in both the North and South, and mounted major voter registration campaigns against overwhelming odds in Mississippi and Louisiana. Compared to previous years, the Freedom Movement made enormous strides; yet its very successes only revealed how much more needed to be done. Consequently, there was an increasing feeling of pessimism that eroded the faith in direct action and the commitment to nonviolence and interracialism. The rejection of the demands of the Mississippi Freedom Democratic Party at the Democratic National Convention crystallized this disillusionment with CORE's traditional strategy. Although it was not fully recognized then, the events of the summer of 1964—the large-scale rioting in Rochester and New York City, and the failure of the Convention

Challenge—symbolized the end of an era both for CORE and for the civil rights movement.

In the spring of 1963, as in 1960, the Negro protest movement became suffused with a new militance. "Freedom Now!" became the slogan. Like the Greensboro sit-ins, the Birmingham demonstrations both epitomized the change in mood and became a major stimulus for direct-action campaigns across the country. As Farmer told the 1963 Convention at Dayton, "Twenty years ago there were just a few of us. Today . . . hundreds of thousands of people are now marching and [thousands are] sitting-in." Again, like the spirit behind the 1960 sit-ins the new sense of urgency reflected a revolution in expectations. For blacks the achievements of the intervening three years now seemed like mere tokenism. Wilfred Ussery of San Francisco CORE observed, "Birmingham brought a drastic revision in our thinking. You can nibble away at the surface for a thousand years and not get anywhere." A complex amalgam, the new mood in part involved what Farmer called "a spiritual emancipation"—a pride in being black, an optimism over what black bodies could accomplish through creative dislocation. Yet there was also a spirit of angry defiance, and a spreading tolerance for violence. In June 1963 Farmer insisted that CORE intended to channel the energy of discontent nonviolently, but he warned that the cities were "explosive," and predicted that "It will be a long, hot summer." As the black journalist Lerone Bennett observed, "the burning militance of the Birmingham leaders . . . pinpointed a revolutionary shift in the attitudes of the Americans called Negroes."

CORE was an active participant in the demonstrations that swept the youth during the spring and summer of 1963. There the heightened militance was evident in the numerous mass jail-ins, the involvement of all strata in the Negro community, the jeering at white policemen, and a disposition to meet violence with violence. Moreover, as Bayard Rustin observed, "The package deal is the new demand." Instead of fighting for one reform at a time, the pattern was simultaneously to make a number of demands that typically included integration of buses, public accommodations, schools, public buildings, and recreational facilities; an end to police brutality; and an equal employment policy in city halls and downtown stores. Even before Birmingham, CORE chapters in North Carolina were experiencing an upsurge in direct action. Subsequently CORE led major projects in Gadsden, Alabama; Plaquemine, Louisiana; Tallahassee, Florida; and the North Carolina Piedmont, as well as playing an important role in campaigns sponsored by SCLC in Birmingham, by SCLC and SNCC in Danville, Virginia, and by the NAACP in Jackson and Clarksdale, Mississippi.

Yet, as so often happened, these other organizations—especially SCLC—received the limelight, a situation epitomized in May 1963 by CORE's William Moore Memorial Freedom Walk. Moore, a white mailman was murdered in Alabama on April 24 while on a one-man walk from Chattanooga to Jackson protesting southern segregation. CORE leaders had advised Moore, a member of the Binghamton, New York, chapter, against this demonstration, but in the atmosphere of crisis that followed his death the Steering Committee immediately planned a Freedom Walk along the route he had planned to take. SNNC also rushed to the scene, and a small interracial band led by Richard Haley left Chattanooga on May 1. As they proceeded along the highway, hostile whites threw stones and bottles, and upon reaching the Alabama state line the marchers were arrested. When Eric Weinberger went limp, state troopers repeatedly shocked him with electric cattle prods. Refusing to accept bail the walkers spent a month in Kilby State Prison. For a brief moment CORE leaders hoped that this project would become another mass movement like the Freedom Ride bringing federal intervention and spotlighting the organization's contribution. But even though a second group was arrested, Birmingham seized the national headlines aborting the impact of the arrests and jail-in sponsored by CORE.

Because the Freedom Walkers had been first detained in the county jail at Gadsden, CORE had established useful contacts there which enabled the organization to mount a major campaign in the city. Mary Hamilton, who had coordinated the Walk and then was jailed in the Birmingham demonstrations, returned to Gadsden, where she was soon joined by three other CORE workers. Organizing local protest groups and the SNCC and SCLC staffers assigned to the city into a coalition known as the Gadsden Freedom Movement, they announced a broad-ranging package of demands including complete desegregation of buses, hotels, restaurants, schools, and parks, and merit employment in downtown stores. There followed a series of demonstrations notable for the use of radically new tactics and civil disobedience, followed by savage police repression.

Direct action involving sit-ins, picketing, and daily marches began on June 10. With as many as 700 participating, demonstrators blocked entrances of business establishments, conducted "snake dances" through downtown stores, and held a lie-in that completely covered the sidewalk in front of a drug store. A week after the direct action began, CORE field worker Marvin Robinson, addressing hundreds of protesters on the police headquarters lawn, vowed a campaign of massive civil disobedience in defiance of a court injunction against disruptive demonstrations. Next day, over 450 persons, headed by Robinson, marched into the courthouse, where they were all arrested. That night as 300 blacks held a vigil on the courthouse lawn, state troopers dispersed them with clubs and electric cattle prods. In the course of the following week Martin Luther King arrived in town, urging an overflow crowd to sustain the drive, and another 100 people were arrested for violating the injunction. Yet the firmness of the authorities, and the trials of the hundreds who had been jailed, sapped the movement's energy, and on July 1, following desegregation of the local buses and a pledge by the white officials to negotiate the other issues, the blacks suspended direct action. Further negotiations failed, and despite the reluctance of some of the civil rights staffers in Gadsden, who feared more police violence which would only crush the movement, another campaign was organized. To help revive the protest, Farmer flew in for a mass rally. But on August 3, when marches were resumed, state troopers with cattle prods moved in before the demonstrators even reached downtown, beating them and arresting 700.

As in other places this kind of determined repression completely exhausted the protesters. CORE had neither gained the publicity that King had found in Birmingham nor moved the blacks of Gadsden much closer to freedom. The campaign was a failure and tied up the local movement in litigation for two years. The most celebrated case was that of Mary Hamilton, whose contempt citation for refusing to answer the prosecutor when he addressed her as "Mary" was reversed by the U. S. Supreme Court. By the time the charges against the others were overturned, the 1964 Civil Rights Act had desegregated the city's public accommodations. . . .

In the North the Birmingham crisis, coming, as Rich observed, at a time of "new ferment in the entire civil rights movement," precipitated an enormous outpouring of direct action and fiscal support.

Many northerners, blacks and whites, flocked to join CORE both as active and associate members. Others, already in CORE, became more deeply involved than before. For example, Ruth Turner, a black Cleveland school teacher who had first become active in CORE while a graduate student at Harvard in 1961, gave up her job to devote full-time to the Cleveland chapter because "Birmingham brought about the rather sudden decision" that she "could no longer continue teaching German in a time like this." Not long afterward, her future husband, Antoine Perot, found himself "hooked" by the March on Washington, and switched from the NAACP in which he had been active, to CORE, which he felt was the organization directly confronting issues in Cleveland.

Since the chapters continued to give National little money—only $11,000 during fiscal 1964—the heart of CORE's fund-raising remained the mailing list of "associate members," which jumped from 61,000 in June 1963 to 70,000 less than three months later. About 95 per cent of these contributors were white, and they were disproportionately Jewish. On a list of the largest contributors—"The Extra Special Specials," and on another list of substantial donors, "Tip-top contributors in New York City area," the majority of names were also Jewish. In addition, special projects swelled the total. Celebrities like Odetta, Nat "King" Cole, Frank Sinatra, Dean Martin, Sammy Davis, Jr., and Dick Gregory gave benefit performances, while the third annual Artists for CORE exhibition cleared over $40,000. Thus the crescendo of activity during the spring and summer of 1963 had an impact similar to the Freedom Ride. Receipts for six months ending November 30, 1963, were $502,000—almost as much as was raised in the preceding twelve, and for the fiscal year 1964 CORE's income reached $886,000. In turn this improvement in CORE's financial picture permitted a dramatic growth in the size of the staff, from forty-nine in June 1963 to somewhat over ninety by the spring of 1964. This figure encompassed about thirty clerical workers, twenty-five administrative and professional staff, including field secretaries, and forty full-time task force workers. The most notable single staff addition in this period was Carl Rachlin, who in January 1964 resigned from his law firm to become full-time CORE counsel.

Simultaneously, there was an explosive increase in the number and size of CORE chapters. Field secretary Chet Duncan wrote exuberantly to McCain in July 1963, "The entire western region has come to LIFE!" Located overwhelmingly outside the South, and as earlier, most numerous in the New York metropolitan area and California, the new CORE groups generally sprang up spontaneously. Between June and October, twenty-six affiliates were added, making a total of ninety-four, or about a 40 per cent increase since Birmingham. By the 1964 Convention the total had reached 114. Equally dramatic was the expansion of individual chapters. A Los Angeles CORE leader noted, "Birmingham has done the recruiting for us," and not long after another elated member exclaimed, "The Action Committee meeting which was held last Monday was so huge, it looked like a membership meeting." Across the country, in Brooklyn, membership soared from thirty-five to one hundred over the summer of 1963. . . .

Interrelated with the growth of northern CORE activity was the deepening CORE commitment to move beyond the issue of racial integration to the problems of the black poor. As Farmer observed, "We are fighting on two fronts. We are trying to break down segregation and we are trying to make facilities in segregated areas as good as possible." Harlem, he said, would not soon disappear, and, while CORE should help those blacks who wished to move into white neighborhoods, the organization should also work to make the ghetto "a decent place to live." CORE, Farmer maintained, needed to "broaden our base" by making special efforts to recruit among the masses, both "to provide CORE with roots in the community" and to "cope with the specific problems in the ghetto." Norman Hill, who became Program Director in September 1963, continued to promote a "ghetto-orientation" among the chapters; during the winter of 1963–64 he held numerous regional conferences to provide the affiliates with the philosophical perspectives and practical tactics for helping the slumdwellers. In addition to this encouragement from the national staff, the affiliates also were motivated strongly by the dynamics of the movement itself. Spurred on both by the successes that had thus far been achieved and by the enormity of the problems still unsolved, the chapters ambitiously plunged forward. They launched dramatic demonstrations against job discrimination, fostered rent strikes against slumlords, worked with other groups in school boycotts, and initiated action against police brutality. And while many affiliates stayed within the traditional style of CORE activism, eschewing disorderly conduct and civil disobedience, others were characterized by an unprecedented and escalating militance.

During the post-Birmingham era, campaigns against job bias were the most common projects among the northern and western chapters—and generally the most successful. Although CORE groups were concentrating principally on retail stores, banks, and the construction trades, they were attacking a broader range of targets than ever. And in these projects the radicalization of both goals and tactics was readily apparent. Compensatory, "preferential" employment had become a universal demand; the employer, Farmer told the 1963 Convention, "is now obligated to find a qualified Negro." Impatience among the chapters was pervasive. For example, Dayton CORE's deadline in negotiating with downtown merchants during the spring of 1963 was "a maximum of 30 days," its leaders declaring, "We don't intend to spend weeks negotiating." Letters from St. Louis CORE to businessmen explicitly threatened speedy direct action, and chairman Robert Curtis announced that his group would meet with several bankers to inform them "exactly how many Negroes we want hired immediately." Calling for a Christmas boycott of downtown stores, San Francisco CORE in November declared, "We in the Congress of Racial Equality know that the Negro community is fed up with the scraps and crumbs the power structure has heretofore been willing to dole out with respect to jobs. . . . Stores that are unwilling to meet with CORE and reach agreement by Thanksgiving, "will be subject to a wide range of direct action, designed to obtain immediate concessions for the Christmas season."

Syracuse CORE epitomized the changing stance of the affiliates in mid-1963. In June, a chapter leader requesting information on how to conduct employment projects, confessed to the national office that past complaints of job discrimination had not been pursued because of ignorance about ways to proceed. Yet only weeks later the affiliate had successfully completed the Hotel Syracuse employment project, using tactics that previously would have been summarily rejected: "marching through the hotel singing [and] sitting down in the lobby . . . [for] a general CORE meeting." Such tactics caused "great public resentment. . . . This has come as a mild shock, since we previously have counted on public support. . . . But one wonderful accomplishment: last year, when we picketed the school board on de facto segregation, everyone though this was terrible.

Now, everyone talks in terms of 'why don't you *just picket*, why do you have to SING, SIT-IN, and DO ALL THOSE HORRIBLE THINGS?'" The hotel settlement upstaged the local NAACP branch, and a delighted CORE member crowed, "CORE is THE civil rights group now."

From Long Island and Baltimore to Seattle and San Francisco retail stores were still an especially popular object of attack. Some chapters, caught up in the zeitgeist, thought they had the power to tackle an entire downtown commercial district. Affiliates in Dayton, San Francisco, and Lexington, Kentucky, saw nothing extraordinary about negotiating with representatives of twenty to thirty important stores, while Berkeley CORE demanded speedy agreements from nearly two hundred stores in an eight-block stretch of Shattuck Avenue. CORE members in Dayton, Lexington, and St. Louis, after fruitless picketing on the sidewalks, began parading through major department stores. . . . Although CORE leaders in these communities accordingly dismissed the results of their campaigns as unacceptable tokenism, they had actually secured gains which a year earlier would have been viewed as major accomplishments. For example, in Berkeley fourteen businesses signed with CORE, including Hinks Department Store, which the chapter would later point to as a model example of an equal opportunity employer.

Indeed job settlements were typically greater than before. Chapters returning to companies with whom they had dealt in earlier years often made striking gains. In the spring of 1963 Berkeley CORE, charging that Montgomery Ward had not progressed beyond tokenism, demanded the hiring of thirty-five Negroes within a month and eight-five more within the next four months. Ward's lawyers tried to secure an injunction against the mass picketing, but the judge proved sympathetic to CORE. In compliance with a precedent-setting court-supervised agreement which provided for regular reports and special recruitment policies, Ward hired about seventy-five blacks within several weeks, about half in sales positions. Denver CORE's month-long picketing at Safeway brought twenty jobs—four times the number gained in its previous timid encounter with the company. Detroit CORE, which in its 1962 campaign against Kroger supermarkets won only vague promises, found in July 1963 that several Saturdays of picketing brought thirty-one jobs, including management trainees, truck drivers, and office workers. By the following spring Kroger and another local chain had together hired over two hundred blacks. The mid-1963 Seattle CORE-NAACP boycott of the Bon Marche ended with the hiring of fifteen full-time and part-time blacks; within two months the total had risen to forty, while nearly fifty had been hired at several other department stores. With pride Seattle CORE leaders announced that in its two years of existence, the chapter had opened 250 white-collar jobs to Negroes. Equally impressive was Baltimore CORE's campaign against Stewart's Department Store which, after three months of picketing, agreed to increase black sales personnel from five to forty and to upgrade two Negroes to executive positions. And as often happened, other downtown Baltimore firms, wishing to avoid CORE picket lines, had meanwhile rushed to modify their employment practices, which resulted in an estimated two hundred new clerical and sales jobs. Long Island CORE negotiated substantial settlements with three local shopping centers; merchants at the Mid-Island Plaza in Hicksville, for example, promised in March 1964 to increase their nonwhite employment by one hundred within three months. The most outstanding victory against a retail chain occurred in New York—in a case where direct action was not used at all. In late 1963 National CORE and a committee representing local CORE chapters, NAACP branches, and Puerto Rican groups won a preferential agreement from A & P to hire four hundred blacks and Puerto Ricans over the next two years, virtually filling all their turnover needs in the clerk category. . . .

The attacks on bank discrimination, although not always as successful as CORE chapters hoped, nevertheless obtained significant results. These projects, which all aimed at achieving a substantial black presence in white-collar positions, ranged tactically from the staid picketing in Boston to flamboyant techniques used in St. Louis. Taking their cue from the successful employment of obstructive tactics in an NAACP-sponsored bank project at East St. Louis, St. Louis CORE decided to disrupt business at the Jefferson Bank, long under attack by civil rights groups. In late August 1963 when the financial institution rejected CORE's demand of four jobs within fourteen days, many demonstrators, defying a restraining court order, blocked the main entrance, sat on the floor, and obstructed the tellers' windows. During the following weeks over one hundred were arrested. Fifteen were sentenced to jail terms of sixty days to one year. Alderman William Clay, for example, spent nearly four months behind bars. Yet in the months after CORE's campaign, eighty-four blacks obtained white-collar jobs in fifteen St. Louis financial institutions, including Jefferson Bank. Boston had even greater success, though it used none of these tactics. In February 1964, after several months of negotiations, agreements were reached with the Merchants National and Shawmut National banks which brought 150 white-collar positions. A few days later, over one-hundred pickets appeared at the First National Bank, which had rejected CORE's demands. Picketing ended after nearly two months, when the institution employed forty-three blacks, bringing to nearly two hundred the total hired by fiduciary institutions since September 1963—the time that Boston CORE first began this project.

Even more ambitious was the campaign conducted by the California Chapters during the spring and summer of 1964 against the Bank of America, the world's largest privately owned bank. With its statewide system of nearly nine hundred branches and 29,000 employees, few of them black, the Bank of America was an ideal candidate for coordinated action on the part of the California affiliates. The company refused to supply racial employment statistics to the chapters' Bank of America Negotiating Committee headed by William Bradley, chairman of San Francisco CORE, or to accede to CORE's demand that it hire 3600 nonwhites during the next year. Picketing began toward the end of May, but probably because of the demoralization stemming from punitive court action in recent Bay-area demonstrations the project lacked the enthusiasm which had marked earlier job campaigns. Picket lines around the state typically did not exceed thirty to fifty people and petered out after a few weeks, and tactics were usually nondisruptive. However, in San Diego, CORE members, defying a court injunction, were arrested after sitting-down in the bank lobby and blocking the front entrance, and ultimately chapter chairman Harold Brown served nearly sixty days in jail. In late summer Bradley announced a "suspension" of the project, stating that CORE had to accept less than its original demands because of chapter apathy. Yet, although the bank would not concede the validity of CORE's accusations, nearly 240 blacks had been hired in white-collar categories between May and July. . . .

While employment had replaced housing as the most salient activity among CORE affiliates, the actual amount of effort devoted to the latter also rose substantially. Housing projects exhibited clear regional variations: the western chapters continued to emphasize breaking down of discrimination in white neighborhoods, an effort in which they were joined by activists in the Washington, D. C. metropolitan area, while northeastern affiliates began concentrating on upgrading tenements in the black ghetto. The drama of the demonstrations, the creative innovations in tactics, and the tenacity of CORE groups notwithstanding, the results proved to be limited.

No chapter received more publicity from its housing efforts than the Los Angeles affiliate, which continued its major campaign against a builder of upper-middle-class residential tracts. Enthusiasm for this project, which received warm support from the NAACP and other groups, reached a high pitch during the summer of 1963. Two hundred were arrested during a two-week period, and on one Saturday a thousand people participated in a mass march to one of the suburban tracts. Despite this pressure and an injunction which the state attorney-general secured against the builder, the case ended in inconclusive litigation in the courts. In Seattle there was also a protracted campaign against a racist real estate firm. In March 1964, after the chapter had conducted windowshops and unsuccessfully lobbied for a fair-housing ordinance, it began sit-ins at the Picture Floor Plans Company. Tactics escalated with each passing weekend. For the first time in Seattle CORE's history, youthful activists chanted and sang, shouted insults, and pushed and shoved when the locked door was opened to admit a customer. The salesmen grew more hostile and when one struck a demonstrator, the affiliate suspended the project. The day after a court injunction halted all picketing against realtors. Meanwhile, beginning in the summer of 1963, Prince George's County, Maryland, CORE, a new chapter outside the District of Columbia, had been conducting massive picketing and sit-ins at the Levittown development in Belair. This series of demonstrations ended after those who were arrested while sitting-in were convicted and fined on trespassing charges and the management secured a permanent injunction restricting the demonstrators' access to the Levitt properties. Although a few home owners privately sold their properties to blacks, the Levittown management adamantly retained its "white only" policy. Nearby, the Washington CORE chapter was only slightly more successful after it stepped up its direct-action tactics against apartment developers. Several dwell-ins during the summer of 1963 at buildings managed by the Cafritz company proved fruitless. But a year later CORE sit-ins at the Trenton Park apartments produced seven arrests, an agreement to rent to two black families who had previously been rejected by the management, and the promise of a nondiscriminatory policy in the future.

In the summer of 1963, at least four affiliates mounted major direct-action campaigns to support the struggle for fair-housing legislation. Two were successful, although in the case of California the law was subsequently overturned by a referendum. In Ann Arbor many organizations supported the proposed municipal ordinance, but without the pressure of the demonstrations led by CORE, it probably would not have been enacted. Protests from May through September 1963, with picket lines numbering as many as eight hundred participants, culminated in a series of City Hall sit-ins that produced sixty-eight arrests. Dissatisfied with the weak ordinance that resulted from these endeavors CORE would subsequently resort to further direct action until a new law was passed early in 1966 covering nearly all of the city's housing.

Elsewhere in Ohio, California, and Colorado, attention focused on the state house. In Columbus during June and July 1963, CORE and other organizations held sit-ins in the governor's office and the House chamber. Rev. Arthur Zebbs, the black Columbus chapter leader who directed the action, chained himself to a seat in the House gallery for over eight hours. A few days later, demonstrators, including chairman Ruth Turner of Cleveland CORE, staged an all-night vigil at the governor's office, while Bruce Klunder, a young white minister and Cleveland CORE's vice-chairman, conducted a one-man sit-in at the House chamber. After the legislature killed the fair-housing bill, Columbus CORE conducted more sit-ins at the capitol, and held nightly picket lines outside the executive mansion in a futile effort to revive the legislation. . . .

In the Northeast, CORE chapters were turning from housing campaigns benefiting middle-class blacks to projects serving lower-class people. The New Haven affiliate explained in September 1963: "CORE recognizes the necessity of pressure to obtain homes in decent areas for those Negroes who, in a sense, have 'got it made.' . . . But the true housing problem is the problem of the slum tenant, the poorest paid worker, the family on welfare, the family on ADC." In New Haven, Boston, New York, Philadelphia, and other cities, CORE sent inspection teams into slum buildings to document and publicize complaints of inadequate heating, broken plumbing, vermin, and other health and safety violations. At first, direct action was confined to picketing landlords' offices or homes, but with progress slow or nonexistent, several chapters over the course of the year turned to a variety of other tactics. Philadelphia CORE dramatized conditions by unloading debris near a slumlord's suburban home. New York University CORE members, angered by lenient housing inspectors and judges, were arrested when they dumped on City Hall plaza a truckful of junk found outside rat-infested tenements. The Long Island chapter, battling on behalf of migratory farm workers living in shacks, dumped garbage at the Riverhead City Hall and staged a mass protest march downtown. New Haven CORE members held a sit-in at a grocery owned by a slumlord, and when evicted by the police they blocked traffic for two hours on a heavily traveled thoroughfare. On another occasion five members of the chapter were arrested in an unsuccessful effort to prevent the eviction of a black family. The protesters then brought the household effects to the Green in downtown New Haven, where seven more were arrested in a scuffle with the police. . . .

A few other affiliates, particularly in New York City, used a more militant tactic—the rent strike. Once widely employed in the 1930's but only sporadically thereafter, use of the rent strike reached a feverish pitch in late 1963 and early 1964. Following the initial enthusiasm, however, it proved to be only a palliative. During the spring and summer of 1963, the New York University, Columbia University, and Brooklyn CORE chapters had helped tenants file complaints with the city's Buildings Department, and in the summer Norman Hill directed "pilot projects" in Newark and Brooklyn which sought to organize tenants for possible strikes. Although the New York Buildings Department had in some instances reduced the rents, and the Sanitation Department had cleaned up outside the Eldridge Street tenements after NYU CORE's trash-dumping episode, for the most part, CORE's efforts were stymied. Even after Farmer personally protested to city officials about the numerous violations of a particular slumlord, the man received only a token fine. With CORE groups still merely talking about the possibilities of rent strikes, the Northern Student Movement, an interracial organization of college and university youth, inaugurated one in Harlem during September. Inspired, the affiliates quickly followed this example. On

October 1, 1963, NYU CORE announced that the East Side Tenants Council on Eldridge Street had started a strike, and a month later it proudly claimed that 110 tenants were giving National CORE their rent to hold in escrow. Enthusiastically backing the tactic, Farmer warned of a citywide strike of 10,000 families. Brooklyn CORE began rent strikes early in December, and soon after came the explosion of rent strikes in Harlem, under the leadership of long-time organizer of tenant protests, Jesse Gray.

CORE's cooperation with Gray was slight, but with the "rent strike fever" getting front page attention, "an extraordinary sense of exhilaration and even of historic destiny" gripped young CORE activists, as they moved rapidly to expand their activities. As one student CORE leader said, "everyone caught the fever—Rent Strike. No one knew about the legal consequences, or the amount of work involved. It seemed like the thing to do . . . the only way to beat the landlord." Brooklyn CORE claimed scores of buildings on strike; and soon Columbia University, CCNY, Bronx, and the East River chapters were involved. During the height of the enthusiasm political leaders and public agencies improved some conditions in a number of tenements. Brooklyn CORE in particular remedied many tenant grievances, largely because a sympathetic judiciary ruled that those in uninhabitable buildings need not pay rent. Yet the euphoria was short-lived. The mass media lost interest after newsmen discovered that the tenant movement was not as large and powerful as its leaders had publicly proclaimed. The courts quickly reverted to old legal evasions, which destroyed the morale of the tenants. In the words of a careful student of the subject, one CORE group after another dropped the rent strikes, "exhausted by the endless routine of court appearances, frustrated by the impossibility of actively involving slum tenants in complex legal procedures, [and] unable to sustain the militant atmosphere of the early days." Two professors at the Columbia University School of Social Work, who were close observers of the rent strike movement, later recalled: "When CORE organizers failed to resist the eviction of a family on the Lower East Side, other striking tenants, fearing that they also would be turned out, hysterically demanded the rent money from their escrow accounts. That event broke the strike in the CORE stronghold on Eldridge Street." By the autumn of 1964 the New York rent strike movement had practically disappeared. . . .

At the very time that housing and employment campaigns were reaching their zenith, de facto school segregation also became a paramount issue for many chapters in the North. As Farmer told the 1964 Convention, "Our demand, categorically, must be quality integrated schools." Struggles on this issue were conducted from coast to coast and involved tactics ranging from picketing through sit-ins to mammoth boycotts. Rather than proceeding on their own, the affiliates almost everywhere worked together with other organizations. Such coalitions in school campaigns were probably a necessity, given the fact that indifferent or recalcitrant school boards, subjected to intense counterpressure from northern segregationists, would not even vaguely consider policy changes without a unified front among the civil rights organizations. Moreover, the effectiveness of the most dramatic tactic used—the school boycott—required massive pupil participation, which a small group like CORE could not obtain by itself.

CORE often provided the "cutting edge" in the use of direct-action against school segregation. At St. Louis it was CORE leaders like Charles Oldham and William Clay who, by blocking the buses, protested against the segregation of black pupils in the receiving schools to which they were being transported. CORE thus pushed the local umbrella group into demonstrations. Within weeks the coalition's attack broadened to include the whole system of de facto school segregation, and the campaign culminated in the early summer of 1963 with a mass march on the school board. In Los Angeles in September, CORE was the spearhead for direct action by the broad-based coalition of seventy-six organizations, when eight chapter members conducted a sit-in and hunger strike for several days at the Board of Education building. Subsequently, vigils and "study-ins" were conducted, with hundreds of youths sitting-in the corridors during board meetings, and in November, CORE held a "sing-in" that broke up the session. Meanwhile the Long Island and Brooklyn chapters escalated tactics in campaigns started earlier. In June and July Brooklyn CORE held a marathon three-week sit-in at the State Commission for Human Rights, which culminated in a blockade of the main entrance of the Board of Education. These actions finally won permission for two more black children to transfer to predominantly white schools outside their neighborhoods. In Malverne,

Long Island, at the end of the summer, police arrested half a dozen CORE members for sitting-in at a predominantly white elementary school, and on the first day of classes the chapter led a boycott of a black elementary school.

CORE's most important demonstrations on the school issue during 1963 occurred in Chicago, bringing to a climax a concern that went back to the first Chicago CORE's poster walk for integrated education twenty years before. Now dramatic actions resulted in nearly two hundred arrests. In July the chapter began a week-long sit-in at the office of the school board president, threatening to hold massive demonstrations at all-white schools if the board failed to redraw boundary lines. Several days later, when police attempted to prevent some protesters from reentering the building, a pushing, shoving, and kicking melee resulted, injuring a number of demonstrators and policemen. Veteran CORE people regarded these techniques as unnecessarily extreme, and the chapter chairman, Sam Riley, publicly apologized for the violence and resigned his post, saying, "I believe there should be more discipline among the demonstrators." Nevertheless, even more disorder accompanied CORE's renewed action in August—this time in cooperation with a black neighborhood group at a ghetto construction site where mobile classrooms were being installed. The protesters demanded that the Board of Education transport black children to available classroom space in predominantly white schools rather than add "portables" to segregated schools. On August 2, in a driving thunderstorm dozens were arrested during a muddy "lay-down," blocking trucks, earth-moving equipment, and police cars. Tactics were escalated as demonstrators chained themselves to construction equipment, and reached a climax a few days afterward when one hundred more were arrested. Some protesters threw stones at police; others kicked and cursed while being carried to patrol wagons. The publicity thus generated forced the board to dismantle the mobile classrooms at the disputed site. However, they were simply moved to other locations where CORE mounted short-lived protests that quickly spent themselves. The chapter's pre-eminent role in direct action against the school administration had now ended. Nevertheless, CORE had made the de facto segregation issue salient and paved the way for the famous Chicago school boycotts that followed.

CORE chapters participated in the school boycotts in at least seven cities. Involving nearly the entire Negro school population in their respective communities, these demonstrations were quite different from the single-school boycotts carried out previously in the smaller cities of Syracuse and Englewood. Boston, in June 1963, was the first place to have a citywide boycott. Chicago, in November, gave the tactic nationwide publicity. The movement crested in February 1964, with a second boycott in both Chicago and Boston, and similar demonstrations in New York and Cincinnati. There followed another New York school boycott in March, two more in Kansas City, Kansas, and Cleveland in April, and one in Milwaukee in May. All were sponsored by broad-based coalitions which varied greatly in their stability and in the role that CORE played. . . .

In [most cities], the school campaigns failed. St. Louis, where the school board did move to increase integration, was an exception, although even there CORE militants were dissatisfied. In Cincinnati, Los Angeles, and New York, the direct-action campaigns ended in inconclusive negotiations with the school boards. In Boston the movement's failure was symbolized in 1965 by the re-election of Louise Day Hicks, the flamboyant leader of the Board's antibusing faction. Several factors contributed to these disappointing results. Not only did the protests generate intense white counterpressure, but there were also key factors at work in the black community and the nature of the protest itself. Grass-roots blacks were more interested in improving ghetto schools than in sending their children to distant integrated ones. The boycotts themselves, limited to symbolic one-day stay-outs, lacked the sustained pressure needed to change basic policy. Finally, the coalitions, which included highly diverse organizations, proved unstable. A boycott required enormous planning and neighborhood work, yet when it was over the effects were miniscule.

If CORE found it difficult to grapple effectively with school segregation, the organization faced even greater recalcitrance when it tackled police brutality. Although the frequent abuse of police power had always been present in black neighborhoods, the issue, which became a major one for some affiliates by 1964, grew in salience for several reasons. The use of police dogs in the Birmingham demonstrations had aroused enormous concern. As CORE became more involved with the problems of the black poor, it recognized the importance of police brutality and its usefulness as a grievance around which to organize the slumdwellers. Finally, the northern chapters' use of civil disobedience and going limp placed them in direct confrontation with law-enforcement agencies. Uncooperative demonstrators were dragged to the patrol wagons and in some cases they even tussled with the arresting officers. This created situations which reinforced the policemen's reputation for brutality already rooted in the facts of ghetto life. Beginning with the large-scale direct-action projects of the summer of 1963, CORE affiliates increasingly charged police with violence against demonstrators. At the Downstate Medical Center in Brooklyn, pickets complained of unnecessary roughness and beatings. In Manhattan, mounted policemen were accused of riding their horses over demonstrators who sat down on the sidewalk. New York CORE chairman Gladys Harrington declared that "horses in New York are no different than police dogs in Birmingham." Pickets at the Jefferson Bank in St. Louis were pushed and dragged into patrol wagons. Demonstrators in Chicago were shoved down the stairs at the Board of Education Building. In the Los Angeles housing protests, arrested activists were handcuffed, taken to an overcrowded jail, and forced to sleep on benches or on the concrete floor.

Affiliates employed various tactics to spotlight the problem. In October 1963 San Francisco CORE members participated with other organizations in a mass march on city hall, consisting of two hundred people, in protest against a recent egregious incident of police brutality. Early in 1964 several members of Syracuse CORE were arrested for sitting-in at the police chief's outer office. About the same time Cleveland CORE picketed police headquarters, and in the summer it demonstrated at City Hall demanding a civilian review board. In March, Brooklyn chapter chairman Isaiah Brunson and Bronx chairman Herbert Callender handcuffed themselves to a grill outside the office of the police commissioner. A few weeks later these men and others were removed by police after they sat down in the corridor outside Mayor Wagner's office, protesting police brutality and other issues. They were removed by the police. National CORE, in assigning a full-time field secretary to the task, played a key role in helping mobilize support for a bill to establish a New York City civilian review board. After the Harlem riot of July 1964, which erupted following a CORE demonstration at a precinct station in protest against the police slaying of a black youth, CORE pressed even harder for such a board.

CORE's use of direct-action tactics was at its zenith for almost a year following Birmingham. Street demonstrations for desegregated public accommodations, compensatory employment, and integrated suburban housing reached their peak during the summer and early autumn of 1963, while the rent strike and school boycott movements came to a climax over the winter of 1963–64. There were, it is true, local exceptions as well as important regional variations. The western chapters, which often lagged behind the eastern affiliates, did not embark upon their most ambitious employment demonstrations until 1964, and failed to sponsor rent strikes or school boycotts. Yet for the relatively brief span of ten to eleven months, CORE groups energetically carried on a veritable cascade of campaigns against a broad range of discriminatory practices. And as they did, the militance of their tactics escalated.

These tactical changes were especially well illustrated by the succession of projects in the San Francisco Bay area. In the pre-Birmingham era, a leader of the University of California chapter recalled, "Image was all-important. Suit and tie was the standard direct action costume. Talking and smoking were forbidden on picket lines."* In the autumn of 1963 "a significant turning point" came with the job campaign at Mel's Drive-In restaurants in Berkeley and San Francisco. Not only were the picket lines manned by CORE and other organizations of unprecedented size, but "The notion of trying to maintain a respectable image was almost entirely demolished. . . . There was singing, shouting, clapping, smoking, talking, walking two abreast, dancing, and all types of dress on the line." Scuffles broke out as police officers forced the demonstrators, who had linked arms and gone limp, into the paddy wagons. Victory came following "two large waves of sit-ins and arrests," described proudly as "civil disobedience." Thereafter Bay-area demonstrators "put increasing pressure on their leaders for escalation of tactics," and in

---

*Certain chapters were still insisting on proper decorum as late as 1964. Milwaukee CORE directed demonstrators that there would be "no talking whatsoever" on picket lines and that participants should dress "comfortably but neatly." Women were specifically forbidden to wear slacks or shorts. (Milwaukee CORE, "CORE Demonstration Rules" [1964], Milwaukee CORE Prs.)

February 1964, CORE introduced the supermarket shop-ins, to the consternation of the black Baptist ministers who were San Francisco CORE's close allies. When this campaign had been won, chapter chairman Bill Bradley announced that in the future such "civil disobedience would be resorted to when other tactics failed." To him the lesson of the supermarket shop-ins was clear: because CORE's new strategy had "forced" shoppers and community leaders alike "to assume a positive role . . . a solution which formerly did not exist . . . was suddenly brought into being." Such tactics, as already seen, came to a climax with massive civil disobedience at the Sheraton-Palace Hotel and Auto Row demonstrations.

Meanwhile CORE chapters from Gadsden and Chapel Hill to Syracuse and Chicago had also resorted to obstructive methods in the name of civil disobedience. Among other techniques there had been increasing experimentation with the blocking of traffic arteries—at Greensboro and Jones Beach during the summer, twice at New Haven in the autumn, and at Chapel Hill in February 1964. More famous was the Triborough Bridge demonstration held by New York's East River CORE chapter in March 1964. To call attention to the unsafe and overcrowded East Harlem schools, chairman Blyden Jackson and several other members sat down on the bridge, halting traffic during the late afternoon rush hour. A month later came the debate over the most controversial tactic ever proposed by a chapter—Brooklyn CORE's threatened stall-in on the opening day of the New York World's Fair. . . .

CORE was in flux, torn between attachment to its traditional style and the imperatives of a changing movement. As the somewhat millenarian expectations surrounding Birmingham and the March on Washington started to fade, the stress CORE leaders were under became evident. For example, shocked by the persistence of repressive violence in the South, NAC member Mark Dodson, former chairman of Long Island CORE, wrote in the autumn of 1963, "The whole approach of nonviolence . . . and of civil disobedience, needs to be worked on and evaluated and expanded. . . . We need new and/or modified approaches to put to rout the insipid idea of waiting on and for laws. . . . We . . . thought that the Birmingham demonstrations would certainly do something. . . . Just where are we now? Waiting for 'mass violence' and 'mass death?'" CORE people debated the legitimacy of some of the more extreme tactics, even as they welcomed strategies that might do for the North what the Freedom Ride had done for the South. Thus some veteran members of the organization had misgivings about methods which they believed would antagonize the public and damage rather than advance the cause. A one-time Freedom Rider, who recalled the "different spirit in 1961" when picket lines "were marked by a sense of dignity and [when] the spirit was one of non-violence" complained to Farmer that many New York demonstrations in which she had participated during the summer of 1963 "are undignified both in dress and demeanor, and the underlying feeling is one of hostility." When the new style of protesting emerged on the Mel's Drive-In restaurant project, "'Experienced' civil rights demonstrators didn't know what to think. Some stayed away; some tried to instruct the line in [what they regarded as] proper conduct; some joined in." Western field secretary Fredricka Teer urged the California chapters against disruptive tactics on behalf of the Rumford Fair-Housing Bill. She, like the bill's black sponsor himself, thought that sit-ins at the Capitol could only hurt its chances. When the demonstrations took place anyway, Teer observed, CORE "got a lot of publicity . . . and that seems at this stage of the game to determine effectiveness." As B. Elton Cox noted at the time Chicago CORE members were disorderly in the Board of Education campaign, many activists were no longer abiding by the Rules for Action.

National officials, attributing the changes to the influx of new members who were attracted as Farmer often said, "by CORE's militance rather than its non-violent philosophy," were divided in their responses to the changing style of demonstrations. McCain, upon returning from a western tour in the autumn of 1963, was disturbed about the new CORE groups who "have not spent much time going over CORE's philosophy, history, and techniques of nonviolence, therefore their activities have not always been in the 'CORE spirit.'" Rich also deplored certain new departures. Agreeing with the one-time Freedom Rider whose apprehension was cited earlier, he wrote, "There was a very different spirit in Mississippi in 1961. We're trying to rekindle that spirit." To a contributor who protested the Lucky store shop-ins, Rich replied, "I agree with you about the supermarket demonstrations. We do want our chapters to try new methods but with the CORE spirit." Farmer, on the other hand, believed that "the means of maintaining the discipline of nonviolence have got to be tightened," but usually justified the new tactics, as did Carey. On a visit to the West Coast, Farmer endorsed the state capitol demonstration, and in New York he defended the members who had blocked entrances and business activities. "We have had our rights blocked for 100 years. It is time for all Americans to realize how it feels to have your way blocked." Speaking on CBS-TV he insisted that this type of action violated neither the CORE constitution nor the Rules for Action. Similarly, Farmer approved of the Triborough Bridge sit-down, which he called a "classic" example of civil disobedience. Undoubtedly these varying responses of CORE's leaders reflected the different roles they played, and the essentially different publics to which they addressed themselves. Rich spoke primarily to old CORE friends and, more importantly, financial donors. As he wrote privately to a Seattle CORE leader after the shop-ins there, "I don't know how many thousands of dollars the shop-ins have cost us, but they have." Farmer, on the other hand, was basically concerned with legitimizing CORE's tactics to a broad public in order to pave the way for the acceptance of CORE's demands. He was also reflecting the outlook of an important part of his constituency in the chapters. As a symbol of CORE militance he would necessarily have to speak to that militance.

The division of opinion, the uncertainty and anguish about the newer tactics was best revealed in the debates over the proposed Brooklyn stall-in. In discussions with the New York area affiliates, Farmer first spoke against the stall-in, then reluctantly went along with the rising sentiment for it, and later in the NAC Steering Committee he reversed himself again. Even after the Committee's unanimous decision to suspend Brooklyn CORE and denounce the stall-in tactic, National CORE was attacked in New York by Bronx, New York, Columbia University, Yonkers, and the Long Island affiliates. CORE members in north Jersey were greatly divided. The Bridgeport, Connecticut, group, though publicly backing National CORE, was "split right in half" and one leader of the chapter reported, "emotionally almost all of us favor" the stall-in, believing that Brooklyn CORE represented the attitude of the black masses. From Louisiana, Mimi Feingold, a white task force worker, though entertaining reservations about the practicability of Brooklyn's project, observed: "What struck me, regardless of the advisability of the stall-in was that it challenged the thinking of people at every level of the power structure which, in itself, is a very valuable thing. . . . It is imperative, it seems to me, that precisely those people who think this country has made substantial strides toward granting Negroes civil rights (such as Pres. Johnson) be constantly made aware of the impatience of hundreds of thousands of people. . . ." Delegates to a Western CORE Regional Conference overwhelmingly endorsed the stall-in. The conference also devoted a session to civil disobedience— a technique which many participants supported vigorously. One Los Angeles delegate declared, "Civil disobedience is effective. Sometimes lesser means are not. . . . We're moving into areas where there is no more one-to-one relations with our adversary. We are dealing with bigger entities like cities, etc. . . . We're hitting institutions, not in- dividuals. We have to use harder force." In view of the substantial sentiment supporting Brooklyn, Farmer administered only a light wrist-tapping and made special efforts to win the personal loyalty of the disaffected militants. Brooklyn CORE's suspension was lifted on May 1, when the affiliate was placed on probation for ninety days. Herbert Callender, the Bronx CORE chairman who had vociferously backed Brooklyn, was appointed a field secretary in August. A short time afterward Farmer nominated Brooklyn CORE leader Ollie Leeds to the NAC.

The opposition of many CORE officials to Brooklyn's plans was rooted in pragmatic more than ideological considerations. Some Steering Committee members were ambivalent; and, indeed, the ob- jection was not based on the tactic itself, but upon the fact that the stall-in was not directed against specific targets. Brooklyn CORE, in defending its position, challenged Farmer to differentiate between the Triborough Bridge demonstration which he approved and the stall-in which he did not. Since both involved traffic stoppages and neither was directed at the specific agents responsible for discrimi- nation, clearly the only essential distinction lay in the scale of the two projects. As Alan Gartner explained, "The considerable auton- omy which CORE chapters enjoy would under normal circum- stances permit such activity. However, the scope of the [proposed stall-in] protest, and the form in which it was to take place, made it a matter for national CORE's concern." Farmer himself openly said at the time that his opposition was based not on principle but on questions of strategy and timing. In the view of CORE's national leadership, the stall-in, compared to which the Triborough Bridge demonstration was but a pinprick, would have aroused enormous resentment among many sympathetic whites and would have exacerbated CORE's financial problems, without the slightest chance of remedying any specific evils. It would have articulated CORE's militance brilliantly and made clear the growing anger and alienation in the black community, but Farmer concluded that, given the social climate of 1964, it would have produced a serious setback for CORE and the civil rights movement.

Ironically the debates over the stall-in came at the very time that direct action had passed its apogee. In fact, the World's Fair project was the last major demonstration which CORE sponsored in New York City; and in most other areas across the country the use of this technique was in precipitous decline. This was due to a paradoxical combination of achievement and failure. As had happened with the lunch-counter sit-in movement of 1960, so by the autumn of 1963, both the victories in the upper South and the dismaying failures and repression in the lower South, seemed to pretty much exhaust, temporarily at least, the potentialities for nonviolent direct action in that region. It is likely that a wave of demonstrations aimed at completing the battle against jim crow public accommodations would have subsequently arisen had it not been for the passage of the 1964 Civil Rights Act. This law was in itself a legislative milestone made possible by the wave of activism which had swept the South in the spring and summer of 1963. Meanwhile victorious job campaigns in the North also provided a significant record of accomplishment. Yet both the substantial desegregation which had occurred in southern public accommodations, and the new willingness of many northern business firms—which had learned from companies experiencing direct action—to make concessions simply through negotiations with CORE, created a vacuum that left activists searching for new situations in which to apply nonviolent techniques. On the other hand, aside from gains in employment projects, the northern CORE chapters seldom experienced substantial progress. School segregation and police brutality seemed almost immune to attack; rent strikes and urban renewal demonstrations produced at best only temporary relief; drives for suburban fair-housing, where successful, brought merely token victories for the middle class; and even in the case of jobs, the highly publicized construction-trade campaigns led only to broken promises. Moreover, in some cases where public officials were sufficiently determined, repressive actions effectively crushed even the most militant demonstrations, not only in southern communities like Gadsden, Tallahassee, Plaquemine, and Chapel Hill, but also in a number of northern cities. In situations such as Seattle's fair-housing campaign, and the Cleveland school site lie-in, court injunctions were enough to discourage continuation of disruptive tactics. In other instances, of which noted ones were the St. Louis bank project and the San Francisco Sheraton-Palace and Auto Row campaigns, punitive court action against arrested protesters broke the back of CORE's nonviolent direct-action program. Finally, it was becoming evident that even where social change had occurred, CORE's demonstrations had not significantly affected the life chances of the black poor.

For all these reasons direct action, while by no means discarded, had sharply declined by the spring of 1964. Though still emotionally committed to this technique, CORE people were by then seriously engaged in the search for new approaches that might better fulfill their quest for equality.

Radicalism and the

Decline of the

Civil Rights Movement

Uncle
Sam
wants
YOU
nigger

Become a member of the world's highest paid black mercenary army!

Support White Power — travel to Viet Nam, you might get a medal!

Fight for Freedom . . . (in Viet Nam)

Receive valuable training in the skills of killing off other oppressed people!

(Die Nigger Die — you can't die fast enough in the ghettos.)

So run to your nearest recruiting chamber!

Major shifts erupted in the civil rights struggle of 1966 when SNCC leaders called for "Black Power." The appeal of the new black militancy grew among younger African Americans and caused a fissure within the civil rights movement. The new black militants offered a bold denunciation of white supremacy while celebrating black pride and the black right to self-defense. This photo depicts Stokely Carmichael, chairman of SNCC, handing out flyers criticizing the Vietnam War outside an induction center in 1967. (Associated Press)

Timothy B. Tyson

ROBERT F. WILLIAMS, "BLACK POWER," AND THE ROOTS OF THE AFRICAN AMERICAN FREEDOM STRUGGLE

Some historians, including August Meier and Harvard Sitkoff whose work appears earlier in this book, have argued that the militancy of Black Power advocates in the late 1960s undermined the vitality of the civil rights movement, ultimately causing dissention and decline. In this essay, Timothy Tyson argues that contrary to widely held opinion, Black Power had deep roots in the indigenous civil rights struggles of the South. Tyson explores the activities of Robert F. Williams, the head of the Union County, North Carolina branch of the NAACP. Williams was a devoted advocate of civil rights, who supported the right of black people to arm themselves against racist terrorism. Williams' activities predated the Black Power rhetoric of SNCC militants by a decade. His example became the inspiration for many black militants, as well as others who formed the Black Panther Party in Oakland.

Timothy Tyson is a professor of history at the University of Wisconsin at Madison.

"The childhood of Southerners, white and colored," Lillian Smith wrote in 1949, "has been lived on trembling earth." For one black boy in Monroe, North Carolina, the earth first shook on a Saturday morning in 1936. Standing on the sidewalk on Main Street, Robert Franklin Williams witnessed the battering of an African American woman by a white policeman. The policeman, Jesse Alexander Helms, an admirer recalled, "had the sharpest shoe in town and he didn't mind using it." The police officer's son, Sen. Jesse Helms, remembered "Big Jesse" as "a six-foot, two-hundred pound gorilla. When he said, 'Smile,' I smiled." Eleven-year-old Robert Williams

"Robert F. Williams, 'Black Power,' and the Roots of the African American Freedom Struggle" by Timothy B. Tyson, *Journal of American History* 85, no. 2. Copyright © 1998. Reprinted by permission of the Organization of American Historians.

watched in terror as Big Jesse flattened the black woman with his fist and then arrested her. Years later, Williams described the scene: Helms "dragged her off to the nearby jailhouse, her dress up over her head, the same way that a cave man would club and drag his sexual prey." He recalled "her tortured screams as her flesh was ground away from the friction of the concrete." The memory of this violent spectacle and of the laughter of white bystanders haunted Williams. Perhaps the deferential way that African American men on the street responded was even more deeply troubling. "The emasculated black men hung their heads in shame and hurried silently from the cruelly bizarre sight," Williams recalled. . . .

In 1946 twenty-one-year-old Robert Williams stepped down from a segregated Greyhound in Monroe wearing the uniform of his country. Williams had moved to Detroit four years earlier to work at Ford Motor Company. Coming home from Belle Isle Amusement Park on the evening of June 11, 1943, he and his brother battled white mobs in one of the worst race riots in United States history. Williams was drafted in 1944 and endured the ironies of marching for freedom in a segregated army. When his government-issue shoe leather struck the same pavement where ten years earlier he had seen Big Jesse Helms drag the black woman off to jail, Williams was no longer a frightened eleven-year-old. Military training had given black veterans "some feeling of security and self-assurance," he recalled. "The Army indoctrination instilled in us what a virtue it was to fight for democracy and that we were fighting for democracy and upholding the Constitution. But most of all they taught us to use arms." Like thousands of other black veterans whom John Dittmer has characterized as "the shock troops of the modern civil rights movement," Robert Williams did not come home to pick cotton. . . .

Williams soon left the South for almost a decade, working briefly at Cadillac Motor Company in Detroit before using his G.I. Bill benefits to write poetry and study psychology at three different black colleges: West Virginia State College, Johnson C. Smith College, and North Carolina Central College for Negroes. "Someday," he vowed in a 1949 article for the Detroit editor of the *Daily Worker,* "I would return seasoned from the fight in the north and more efficient in the fight for the liberation of my people." In 1952, Williams wrote an essay for Paul Robeson's newspaper, *Freedom,* in which he predicted that African American college students would soon become "the most militant agitators for democracy in America today. They have nothing to lose and all to gain." At Johnson C. Smith, Williams met one of his literary heroes, Langston Hughes, who considered Williams a promising poet and sent him handwritten poems as an encouragement. In 1953, however, Williams ran out of money for college and reenlisted in the armed forces, this time in the United States Marine Corps. . . .

Upon his return to Monroe in 1955, Williams joined both the local branch of the NAACP and a mostly white Unitarian fellowship. In a Sunday sermon delivered to his fellow Unitarians in 1956, Williams hailed the Montgomery, Alabama, bus boycott and celebrated what he called "the patriots of passive revolution." . . . Invoking "the spirit of Concord, Lexington and Valley Forge," Williams declared from the pulpit that, as he put it, "the liberty bell peals once more and the Stars and Stripes shall wave forever."

The atmosphere at the Monroe NAACP was less exuberant. In the wake of the *Brown v. Board of Education* decision and the triumph at Montgomery, Ku Klux Klan rallies near Monroe began to draw crowds as big as fifteen thousand. Dynamite attacks on black activists in the area were common and lesser acts of terror routine. "The echo of shots and dynamite blasts," the editors of the freedom movement journal the *Southern Patriot* wrote in 1957, "has been almost continuous throughout the South." The Monroe NAACP dwindled to six members, who then contemplated disbanding. When the newest member objected to dissolution, the departing membership chose him to lead the chapter. "They elected me president," Robert Williams recalled, "and then they all left."

Finding himself virtually a one-man NAACP chapter, Williams turned first to the black veterans. . . . Another veteran, the physician Dr. Albert E. Perry Jr., became vice-president. Finding it "necessary to visit homes and appeal directly to individuals," Williams informed the national office, he painstakingly recruited from the beauty parlors, pool halls, and street corners, building a cadre of some two hundred members by 1959. The largest group of new recruits were African American women who worked as domestics. The Monroe branch of the NAACP became "the only one of its kind in existence," the novelist Julian Mayfield, a key supporter of Williams in Harlem's black Left, wrote in *Commentary* in 1961. "Its members and sup-porters, who are mostly workers and displaced farmers, constitute a well-armed and disciplined fighting unit." The branch became "unique in the whole NAACP because of a working class composi-tion and a leadership that was not middle class," Williams later wrote. "Most important, we had a strong representation of black veterans who didn't scare easily."

In response to the drownings of several local African American children whom segregation had forced to swim in isolated farm ponds, the Monroe NAACP launched a campaign to desegregate the local tax-supported swimming pool in 1957. Harry Golden, a prominent Jewish liberal from nearby Charlotte, observed that the specter of interracial sexuality "haunts every mention of the race question" and thought it "naive" of Williams to "experiment with the crude emotions of a small Southern agricultural community." Not surprisingly, the Ku Klux Klan blamed the affluent Dr. Perry for the resurgent black activism and a large, heavily armed Klan motor-cade attacked Dr. Perry's house one night that summer. Black vet-erans greeted the night riders with sandbag fortifications and a hail of disciplined gunfire. The Monroe Board of Aldermen immediately passed on ordinance banning Ku Klux Klan motorcades, a measure they had refused to consider before the gun battle.

When Williams and the other black veterans organized self-defense networks, black women insisted that the men teach them to shoot. But for black men as well as white men, the rhetoric of pro-tecting women was fraught with the politics of controlling women. Williams recalled that the women "had volunteered, and they wanted to fight. But we kept them out of most of it." Nevertheless, African American women who labored as domestics played crucial roles as gatherers of intelligence. They also worked the telephones and deliv-ered the weekly newsletter, Williams acknowledged. But it was not easy to confine women to these roles. When police arrested Dr. Perry on trumped-up charges of "criminal abortion on a white woman," dozens of black citizens, most of them women, armed themselves and crowded into the police station. *Jet* magazine reported that the women "surged against the doors, fingering their guns and knives until Perry was produced." In short, black women both deployed and defied gender stereotypes—demanding of black men, in effect,

"Why aren't you protecting us?"—even though they overturned such stereotypes in their daily lives.

An even more vivid local drama dragged Monroe onto the stage of international politics on October 28, 1958. Two African American boys, David E. "Fuzzy" Simpson and James Hanover Thompson, ages eight and ten, met some white children in a vacant lot. A kissing game ensued in which the ten-year-old Thompson and an eight-year-old white girl named Sissy Sutton kissed one another. Rarely in history has an incident so small opened a window so large into the life of a place and a people. The worldwide controversy that stemmed from the "kissing case" underlined the power of sexual questions in racial politics and demonstrated both the promise and the problems of Cold War politics for the African American freedom struggle.

After the kissing incident, Sissy Sutton's mother reported, "I was furious. I would have killed Hanover myself if I had the chance." Sissy's father took a shotgun and went looking for the two boys. Neighbors reported that a white mob had roared up to the Thompson home and threatened not only to kill the boys but to lynch their mothers. Later that afternoon, police officers spotted Hanover Thompson and Fuzzy Simpson pulling a red wagon loaded with soft drink bottles. "Both cops jumped out with their guns drawn," Thompson recalled. "They snatched us up and handcuffed us and threw us in the car. When we got to the jail, they drug us out of the car and started beating us." The local juvenile court judge reported to Gov. Luther H. Hodges that the police had detained the boys "for their own good, due to local feeling in the case."

Authorities held the two boys for six days without permitting them to see parents, friends, or attorneys. Passing gunmen fired dozens of shots into the Thompson home. Klan terrorists torched crosses on the lawn. Hanover's sister found his dog shot dead in the yard. For many white citizens, the case seemed to resonate with the sexual fears awakened by the prospect of school desegregation. "If [black children] get into our rural schools and ride the buses with our white children," one local woman wrote, "the Monroe 'kissing' incident is only a start of what we will have." On November 4, Judge J. Hampton Price convened what he termed "separate but equal" hearings for the white parents and the black boys. Denied the right to engage counsel or to confront their accusers, Hanover

Thompson and Fuzzy Simpson were sentenced to Morrison Training School for Negroes. If they behaved well, Judge Price told the boys, they might be released before they were twenty-one.

Robert Williams saw the "kissing case" as more than a local expression of the irrational sexual lynchpin of white supremacy; the bizarre clarity of the case and the strange politics of the Cold War suggested a larger strategy. As Martin Luther King Jr. and the Southern Christian Leadership Conference (SCLC) would do in Birmingham four years later, Williams and his friends in Monroe set out to use the international politics of the Cold War as a fulcrum to move the United States government to intervene. Determined to make the "kissing case" a global metaphor for the American racial dilemma, they fired off press releases, pestered reporters, hounded the wire services, and put in motion what *Time* magazine called "a rolling snowball" of worldwide publicity.

This publicity campaign quickly attracted the support of the Socialist Workers party (SWP), a Trotskyite group attempting to break with the American Left's tendency to subordinate race to class. Efforts for socialism and black liberation must meet as equal partners, C. L. R. James and Claude DeBruce had persuaded their SWP comrades. DeBruce, an African American, saw the need for an independent black political leadership, preferably one with ties to the NAACP, that could "project a program in the interest of the mass of Negroes." Thus when Robert Williams emerged from the black South in 1958, the SWP stood poised to assist him on his own terms. Beginning in 1958, the *Militant,* the SWP's newspaper, carried dozens of articles about Williams and Monroe—twenty-five on the "kissing case" alone. That coverage overshadowed their reports on the Cuban revolution, the anticolonial uprising in the Belgian Congo, and all the other developments in the African American freedom struggle combined. "They knew I wasn't going to join any party," he recalled, "because I had made that plain. I wasn't interested in them." The reverse, however, was not true. Robert Williams "has some audacious plans which I think are feasible," the SWP organizer George Weissman wrote. "Indeed, the more I see of him the more I think he has the possibility of becoming a *real* Negro leader."

With logistical assistance from the SWP, Williams addressed audiences at labor halls, liberal churches, and college auditoriums across the country. Soon the "kissing case" emblazoned front pages around the globe, forcing Governor Hodges to hire a team of professors from the University of North Carolina at Chapel Hill to translate the tens of thousands of letters that poured into his office. John Shure, head of the United States Information Agency (USIA) at the Hague, reported that he had received over twelve thousand letters "even though the response does not appear to have been organized." While the White House and the State Department expressed alarm at the damage to United States foreign relations, Williams had a ready answer. "It is asinine for colored people to even think of sparing the U.S. State Department embarrassment abroad," he replied. "If the U.S. government is so concerned about its image abroad, then let it create a society that will stand up under world scrutiny."

Governor Hodges soon launched a public relations campaign of his own, aiming, as an aide urged the governor, to "give the NAACP a taste of its own medicine . . . [and] place the whole Confederacy in your debt." The aide suggested to the governor that "by hitting directly at the communist connection, we might be able to convince people of the insincerity of these protests." The Federal Bureau of Investigation informed Governor Hodges that "Robert Williams has been under investigation for a considerable period of time" and that "you would have access to this information if you desire." The ensuing smear campaign asserted that the entire affair had been "a Communist-directed front," that the families of the boys were "shiftless and irresponsible," and that Hanover Thompson's mother had "a reputation for using her daughters in prostitution." The USIA and the State Department broadcast these charges around the world, winning few minds and fewer hearts. Three and a half months after Hanover and Sissy had kissed each other, Governor Hodges, under enormous political pressure, announced that "the home conditions have improved to the extent that the boys can be given conditional release."

"The kissing case," the activist lawyer Conrad Lynn observed years later, "was the case that got [Williams] in national and international attention." The case not only furnished Williams with a network of seasoned activists in the American Left but with a growing number of supporters among black nationalists in Harlem. Audley "Queen Mother" Moore, an important figure in both Communist and black nationalist circles in Harlem from the 1920s to the 1970s, organized support for Williams. He became a regular visitor to Louis

Michaux's National Memorial African Bookstore on Seventh Avenue off 125th Street, where Michaux welcomed Williams to the podium the store provided for the legendary Harlem street speakers of the day. The most important of Williams's contacts among the Harlem nationalists was Malcolm X, minister at the Nation of Islam's Temple no. 7. "Every time I used to go to New York he would invite me to speak," Williams recalled. Malcolm would tell his congregation "that 'our brother is here from North Carolina, and he is the only fighting man that we have got, and we have got to help him so he can stay down there,'" Williams recounted. Williams found ready support among Harlem intellectuals, including Julian Mayfield, John Henrik Clarke, John Oliver Killens, and other literary and political figures. "They all saw something in Monroe that did not actually exist—an immediately revolutionary situation," Harold Cruse observed. Later, in an unpublished autobiography, Julian Mayfield disclosed that "a famous black writer made contact with gangsters in New Jersey and bought me two sub-machine guns which I took to Monroe." Williams was not the best-known black leader in the United States, but he may have been the best armed.

The "kissing case" recruited new allies for Williams, but it launched him on a collision course with the NAACP hierarchy. Since the Scottsboro trials of the 1930s, the NAACP had steadfastly shunned so-called sex cases and political alliances that might leave the organization open to red-baiting. Should the NAACP "ever get identified with communism," Kelly Alexander, heard of the North Carolina Conference of Branches, told a reporter, "the Ku Klux Klan and the White Councils will pick up the charge that we are 'reds' and use it as a club to beat us to death." Differences over strategy became bitter; Alexander complained to the national office that Williams "has completely turned his back on the one organization that is responsible for him being in the spotlight today," while Williams griped that Alexander "sounds more like a *Tom* than ever." Roy Wilkins, executive secretary of the national organization, began to refer to Williams in private as "Lancelot of Monroe."

Just as the "kissing case" headlines faded in the spring of 1959, two news stories from other parts of the South gripped black America. One was the lynching of Mack Charles Parker, accused of raping a white woman in Mississippi. When Mississippi NAACP field secretary Medgar Evers heard that Parker had been dragged from his cell and murdered by a mob, he told his wife, "I'd like to get a gun and start shooting." The other was the terrifying ordeal of four young black college students at Florida Agricultural and Mechanical University. Their double date after a college dance was interrupted by four white men with guns and knives. The drunken assailants who had vowed, as one of them testified in court later, "to go out and get some nigger pussy," forced the two eighteen-year-old black men to kneel at gunpoint while they undressed the two women and decided aloud which one they would kidnap and then gang-rape. In the wake of these highly publicized outrages, Wilkins conceded in a letter marked "NOT FOR PUBLICATION" that "I know the thought of violence has been much in the minds of Negroes." By early May, Wilkins admitted, the NAACP found it "harder and harder to keep feelings from boiling over in some of our branches."

Right on the heels of the Parker lynching and the terrors of Tallahassee, two pressing local matters brought Robert Williams and a crowd of black women to the Union County courthouse. B. F. Shaw, a white railroad engineer, was charged with attacking an African American maid at the Hotel Monroe. Another inflammatory case was slated for trial the same day. Lewis Medlin, a white mechanic, was accused of having beaten and sexually assaulted Mary Ruth Reid, a pregnant black woman, in the presence of her five children. According to Williams, Reid's brothers and several of the black women of the Monroe NAACP had urged that the new machine guns be tried out on Medlin before his trial. "I told them that this matter would be handled through the law and the NAACP would help," Williams recalled, "that we would be as bad as the white people if we resorted to violence."

The proceedings against the two white men compelled Williams to reconsider his assessment. The judge dropped the charges against Shaw although he had failed even to appear in court. During the brief trial of Medlin, his attorney argued that he had been "drunk and having a little fun" at the time of the assault. Further, Medlin was married, his lawyer told the jury, "to a lovely white woman . . . the pure flower of life . . . do you think he would have left this pure flower for *that*?" He gestured toward Mary Ruth Reid, who began to cry uncontrollably. Lewis Medlin was acquitted in minutes. Robert Williams recalled that "the [black] women in the courtroom made such an outcry, the judge had to send Medlin out the rear door." The women then turned on Williams and bitterly shamed him for failing to see to their protection.

At this burning moment of anger and humiliation, Williams turned to wire service reporters and declared that it was time to "meet violence with violence." Black citizens unable to enlist the support of the courts must defend themselves. "Since the federal government will not stop lynching, and since the so-called courts lynch our people legally," he declared, "if it's necessary to stop lynching with lynching, then we must resort to that method." The next day, however, Williams disavowed the reference to lynching. "I do not mean that Negroes should go out and attempt to get revenge for mistreatments or injustice," he said, "but it is clear that there is no Fourteenth or Fifteenth Amendment nor court protection of Negroes' rights here, and Negroes have to defend themselves on the spot when they are attacked by whites."

Banner headlines flagged these words as symbols of "a new militancy among young Negroes of the South." Enemies of the NAACP blamed this "bloodthirsty remark" squarely on the national office. "High officials of the organization may speak in cultivated accents and dress like Wall Street lawyers," Thomas Waring of the *Charleston News and Courier* charged, "but they are engaged in a revolutionary enterprise." That very morning, when he read the words "meet violence with violence" in a United Press International (UPI) dispatch, Roy Wilkins telephoned Robert Williams to inform him that he had been removed from his post as president of the Monroe NAACP.

That summer of 1959, the fiftieth anniversary convention of the NAACP presented a highly public show trial whose central issue was whether the national organization would ratify Wilkins's suspension of Robert Williams. The national office printed a pamphlet, *The Single Issue in the Robert Williams Case,* and distributed it to all delegates. As part of the coordinated effort to crush Williams, Thurgood Marshall visited the New York offices of the FBI on June 4, 1959, and urged agents to investigate Williams "in connection with [Marshall's] efforts to combat communist attempts to infiltrate the NAACP," an FBI memorandum stated. Wilkins twisted every available arm. Gov. Nelson Rockefeller, in an unmistakable reference to the whisper campaign to discredit Williams, took the podium to congratulate the NAACP for "rejecting retaliation against terror" and "repulsing the threat of communism to invade your ranks." Daisy Bates, the pistol-packing heroine of Little Rock, agreed to denounce Williams for advocating self-defense—after the national office consented to buy six hundred dollars a month in "advertising" from her newspaper. "The national office not only controlled the platform," Louis Lomax wrote, but "they subjected the Williams forces to a heavy bombardment from the NAACP's big guns." Forty speakers, including Bates, King, Jackie Robinson, and dozens of distinguished lawyers, rose one after the other to denounce Williams. But when the burly ex-Marine from Monroe finally strode down the aisle to speak, he was neither intimidated nor penitent.

"There is no Fourteenth Amendment in this social jungle called Dixie," Williams declared. "There is no equal protection under the law." He had been angry, they all knew, trials had beset him, but never had he intended to advocate acts of war. Surely no one believed that. But if the black men of Poplarville, Mississippi, had banded together to guard the jail the night that Mack Parker was lynched, he said, that would not have hurt the cause of justice. If the young black men who escorted the co-ed who was raped in Tallahassee had been able to defend her, Williams reminded them, such action would have been legal and justified "even if it meant that they themselves or the white rapists were killed." "Please," he besought the assembly, "I ask you not to come crawling to these whites on your hands and knees and make me a sacrificial lamb."

And there the pleading stopped. Perhaps the spirit of his grandfather, Sikes Williams, the former slave who had fought for interracial democracy and wielded a rifle against white terrorists, rose up within him. Perhaps he heard within himself the voice of his grandmother, who had entrusted that rifle to young Robert. "We as men should stand up as men and protect our women and children," Williams declared. "I am a man and I will walk upright as a man should. I WILL NOT CRAWL." In a controversy that the *Durham Carolina Times* called "the biggest civil rights story of the year," the NAACP convention voted to uphold the suspension of Robert Williams. The day after Daisy Bates had urged the assembly to censure Robert Williams for his vow to defend his home and family, she wired the attorney general of the United States to complain about dynamite attacks on her home in Little Rock: "We have been compelled to employ private guards," she said. Williams wrote to Bates soon afterward: "I am sorry to hear that the white racists have decided to step up their campaign against you. It is obvious that if you are to remain in Little Rock you will have to resort to the method I was suspended for advocating."

Against this backdrop of white lawlessness and political stalemate in 1959 and early 1960, Robert Williams moved to strengthen the local movement in Monroe and to reach out to a national audience. Though Williams underlined the fact that "both sides in the freedom movement are bi-racial," his emerging philosophy reinvigorated many elements of the black nationalist tradition whose forceful reemergence in the mid-1960s would become known as Black Power. His militant message was neither racially separatist nor rigidly ideological. Williams stressed black economic advancement, black pride, black culture, independent black political action, and what he referred to as "armed self-reliance." He connected the southern freedom struggle with the anticolonialism of emerging Third World nations, especially in Africa. In the late 1950s, when other integrationists focused on lunch counters and voter registration, Williams insisted on addressing persistent black poverty: "We must consider that in Montgomery, where Negroes are riding in the front of buses," he said, "there are also Negroes who are starving." His approach was practical, eclectic, and improvisational. There must be "flexibility in the freedom struggle," he argued, and tactics must emerge from the confrontation itself. At the core of his appeal, however, stood his calls for absolute racial equality under a fully enforced United States Constitution, backed by an unyielding resistance to white supremacy.

In pursuit of this uncompromising vision of interracial democracy, Robert Williams became an editor and publisher like his grandfather before him. Two weeks after the 1959 NAACP convention, FBI agents reported to J. Edgar Hoover that black children were "selling a newsletter known as *The Crusader* on the streets of Monroe." Its title honored the late Cyril V. Briggs, Harlem organizer of the left-wing African Blood Brotherhood, whose newspaper of the same name had issued a "Declaration of War on the Ku Klux Klan" in 1921. The *Crusader's* self-proclaimed mission was "ADVANCING THE CAUSE OF RACE PRIDE AND FREEDOM." Soon sample mailings yielded several thousand subscribers across the country. Shortly after Williams began to spread his confrontational appeals in the *Crusader,* the first published biography of Martin

Luther King Jr. appeared, written by a member of the Southern Christian Leadership Conference's board of directors. The book was entitled *Crusader without Violence*. Whether the title was intended as a direct rejoinder to Williams or not, it situated the book within a lively and important discussion. . . .

A widely reprinted debate in the pages of *Liberation* magazine pitted Williams against Dr. Martin Luther King Jr. Again careful to endorse King's methods wherever they proved feasible, Williams advocated "armed self-reliance," explaining that among well-armed white vigilantes, "there is open defiance to law and order throughout the South today." Where law had broken down, he said, it was necessary and right to defend home and family. "Nonviolence is a very potent weapon when the opponent is civilized, but nonviolence is no repellent for a sadist," Williams noted. "Nowhere in the annals of history does the record show a people delivered from bondage by patience alone."

Dr. King conceded that white violence and white intransigeance had brought the movement to "a stage of profound crisis." African Americans were frustrated, he said, and the "current calls for violence" reflected "a confused, anger-motivated drive to strike back violently." The Supreme Court's 1954 mandate and even the triumph at Montgomery had yielded small tokens, elaborate evasions, and widespread terror. Only three responses presented themselves. Once could practice "pure nonviolence," King said, but this path "could not readily attract large masses, for it requires extraordinary discipline and courage." A position that encompassed legitimate self-defense was more practical. King pointed out that "all societies, from the most primitive to the most cultured and civilized, accept [self-defense] as moral and legal. The principle of self-defense, even involving weapons and bloodshed, has never been condemned, even by Gandhi." Here was where King the politician sensed his constituency. "When the Negro uses force in self-defense," King continued, "he does not forfeit support—he may even win it, by the courage and self-respect it reflects." This widely accepted position was, of course, precisely Williams's view—which was King's problem.

The third and most unacceptable position, King argued, was "the advocacy of violence as a tool of advancement, organized as in warfare, deliberately and consciously." Here, then, was the pale beyond which King sought to cast his adversary. "Mr. Robert Williams would have us believe that there is no collective or practical alternative," King insisted. "He argues that we must be cringing and submissive or take up arms." Essentially, Dr. King had invented his own Robert Williams, a black Geronimo plotting military strikes against the white man, and he then responded to *that* Robert Williams. Lacking theological training and combative in his manner, Williams made himself vulnerable to this caricature. But the philosophical position from which King centered his own argument—preferring nonviolence but endorsing "the principle of self-defense, even involving weapons and bloodshed"—was precisely the place where Williams had taken his stand.

The King-Williams debate resonated throughout the movement as Williams began "to symbolize the alternative to both tactical nonviolence and nonviolence as a way of life," as James Forman of SNCC wrote in his memoir, *The Making of Black Revolutionaries.* King and Williams "were supposed to present two opposed views," according to Forman, but "in my analysis, they did not seem to be at cross-purposes." Julian Bond, then a student activist in Atlanta (in 1998 he became the head of the NAACP), recalls reading the debate and "believing that Williams got the better of it" and "that Williams was not the figure King and others depicted." Bond, Forman, and most SNCC activists considered nonviolence purely a tactical stance. Nonviolence as tactics offered a way to avoid "being wiped out," SNCC's Timothy Jenkins reflected, but "if you had the capacity at any given time to defend yourself successfully with violence, there were a number of people who were prepared to use it at all times." W. E. B. Du Bois weighed in with a commentary, also entitled "Crusader without Violence," in which he discouraged applause for King's critique of Robert Williams. In Montgomery, he wrote, King had "stood firm without surrender," but Du Bois considered it "a very grave question as to whether or not the slavery and degradation of Negroes in America has not been unnecessarily prolonged by the submission to evil." . . .

The uneasy peace in Monroe would soon be broken, in large measure by followers of Dr. King. In 1961, Rev. Paul Brooks, an activist in the Nashville student movement investigating the SCLC, and James Forman, soon to become president of SNCC, came to Monroe in the company of seventeen Freedom Riders fresh out of jail in Jackson, Mississippi. The young insurgents arrived in Monroe to launch a rather incoherent nonviolent campaign in Robert Williams's backyard; some participants, including Forman, sought to support Williams, who was under enormous pressure from the Ku Klux Klan; others wanted to prove Williams wrong. . . .

Williams welcomed the Freedom Riders warmly but had a similar understanding of the stakes. "I saw it first as a challenge," he recalled, "but I also saw it as an opportunity to show that what King and them were preaching was bullshit." Two weeks of picketing at the Union County Courthouse grew progressively more perilous for the Freedom Riders. Crowds of hostile white onlookers grew larger and larger. Finally, on Sunday afternoon, August 28, a mob of several thousand furious white people attacked the approximately thirty demonstrators, badly injuring many of them; local police arrested the bleeding protesters. In his classic memoir, *The Making of Black Revolutionaries,* James Forman later called this riot his "moment of death," "a nightmare I shall never forget." To the consternation of SCLC, the nonviolent crusade swiftly deteriorated into mob violence; throughout the community, white vigilantes attacked black citizens and even fired fifteen shots into the home of the former mayor J. Ray Shute, a white moderate who had befriended Williams.

At the height of this violent chaos, a white married couple, for reasons that are unclear, entered the black community and drove straight into an angry black mob milling near Robert Williams's house. "There was hundreds of niggers there," the white woman stated, "and they were armed, they were ready for war." Black residents, under the impression that the demonstrators downtown were being beaten and perhaps slaughtered, threatened to kill the white couple. Williams, though busy preparing to defend his home, rescued the two whites from the mob and led them into his house, where they remained for about two hours. White authorities later charged Williams and several other people with kidnapping, although the white couple met two police officers on their way home and did not report their alleged abduction. The woman later conceded that "at the time, I wasn't even thinking about being kidnapped . . . the papers, the publicity and all that stuff was what brought in that kidnapping mess." During a long night of racial terror, Williams slung a machine gun over his shoulder and walked several miles with his wife and two small sons to where Julian Mayfield waited with a car. "I didn't want those racist dogs to have the satisfaction of legally lynching me," he explained to Dr. Perry.

The Williams family fled first to New York City, then Canada, then on to Cuba to escape the hordes of FBI agents who combed the countryside in search of them. Supporters of Williams gloried in the escape. Some black residents of Monroe still maintain that Fidel Castro sent helicopters for Williams. Others tell of how he got away in a hearse owned by a black funeral director from Charlotte. An agent assigned to search for Williams locally reported his frustrations to FBI director Hoover: "Subject has become something of a 'John Brown' to Negroes around Monroe and they will do anything for him."

The FBI dragnet never snared Williams, but it did not take Hoover long to hear from him. Every Friday night from eleven to midnight on Radio Havana, Williams hosted *Radio Free Dixie,* a program that from 1961 to 1964 could be heard as far away as New York and Los Angeles. KPFA Radio in Berkeley and WBAI in New York City occasionally rebroadcast the show, and bootleg tapes of the program circulated in Watts and Harlem. An activist in Watts wrote to Williams in 1962, "I am letting my other nationalist friends make copies [of the tapes] and telling each of them to let someone make a copy of theirs." During the early 1960s folk revival, Pete Seeger performed the "Ballad of Monroe" all over the country—"Robert Williams was a leader, a giant of a man," the leftist troubadour sang. From Cuba, Williams continued to edit the *Crusader,* which was distributed via Canada and sometimes Mexico, for a circulation that eventually grew to forty thousand. In 1962, his book N*egroes with Guns,* published from Cuba, became the single most important intellectual influence on Huey P. Newton, soon to found the Black Panther Party in Oakland, California. A play based on *Negroes with Guns,* Frank Greenwood's *If We Must Live,* ran in Watts from July to December of 1965 to eager crowds and enthusiastic reviews. Copies of the *Crusader* traveled down the Mississippi back roads with Student Nonviolent Coordinating Committee organizers: "this leaflet is being distributed to SNCC and COFO workers among U.S. Negroes," the Mississippi State Sovereignty Commission complained in the spring of 1964. Later that year, when SNCC began to veer away from nonviolence, members cited Williams approvingly in the fierce internal debates.

As black activists began to reject even the tactical pretense of nonviolence, the influence of Robert Williams continued to spread. By spring 1962 "the example of the North Carolina militant," August Meier and Elliott Rudwick observe, had "had a profound effect" within the Congress of Racial Equality (CORE). "Armed self-defense is a fact of life in black communities—north and south—despite the pronouncements of the 'leadership,'" a North Carolina activist wrote to Williams. Long before Stokely Carmichael and Willie Ricks led the chants of "Black Power" that riveted national media attention in the summer of 1966, most elements invoked by that ambiguous slogan were already in place. "Your doctrine of self-defense set the stage for the acceptance of the Deacons For Defense and Justice," Lawrence Henry told Williams in the spring of 1966. "As quiet as it is being kept, the Black man is swinging away from King and adopting your tit-for-tat philosophy."

Williams's influence was not limited to the South. "As I am certain you realize," Richard Gibson, editor of *Now!* magazine in New York, wrote to Williams in 1965, "Malcolm's removal from the scene makes you the senior spokesman for Afro-American militants." *Life* magazine reported in 1966 that Williams's "picture is prominently displayed in extremist haunts in the big city ghettos." Clayborne Carson names Williams as one of two central influences—the other being Malcolm X—on the 1966 formation of the Black Panther Party for Self-Defense in Oakland, "the most widely known black militant political organization of the late 1960s." The Central Intelligence Agency (CIA) exaggerated considerably in 1969 by reporting that Williams "has long been the ideological leader of the Black Panther Party." It is closer to say that the Panthers were "a logical development" from the philosophy of Williams, as Reginald Major asserted in his 1971 book, *A Panther Is a Black Cat.* According to Williams, he "talked to Bobby Seale and Mrs. [Kathleen] Cleaver by telephone when [he] was in Africa" in 1968, and the leadership "asked me to become Foreign Minister of the Panthers." At that moment, Williams had already been named president-in-exile of two of the most influential revolutionary nationalist groups: the Revolutionary Action Movement, which the CIA believed to be "the most dangerous of all the Black Power organizations," and the Detroit-based Republic of New Africa, an influential group with hundreds of members that sought to establish an independent black republic in Mississippi,

Louisiana, Alabama, Georgia, and South Carolina. "Despite his overseas activities," the CIA reported in 1969, "Williams has managed to becom[e] an outstanding figure, possibly *the* outstanding figure, in the black extremist movement in the United States."

Even though he became friends with Che Guevara and Fidel Castro himself, Williams grew uneasy in Cuba; he yearned to return home. As the Soviet strings on the Cuban revolution shortened, Williams resisted pressure to make his own politics conform to the Soviet line. As early as 1962, when Williams had been in Cuba for less than a year, an FBI informant stated that Williams had "stubbed his toes" with Cuban Communists through his "criticism of [the] Communist Party for barring Negroes from leadership" and that he "may not be able to regain his footing." "I am under constant attack by the [United States Communist Party]," Williams wrote to a friend in the mid-1960s. "They are trying to cut off my facilities here in Cuba. One would think I am Hitler and Wall Street combined." The Stalinists were "getting worse than the crackers in Monroe," Williams complained in 1964. "Things are about to the stage when I had to leave Monroe in a hurry." Williams persuaded Castro to let him travel to North Vietnam in 1964, where he swapped Harlem stories with Ho Chi Minh and wrote antiwar propaganda aimed at African American soldiers. In 1965 the Williams family relocated to Beijing, where Williams was "lionized and feted by top Peking leaders," according to CIA intelligence reports. The Williams family dined with Mao Zedong and moved in the highest circles of the Chinese government for three years. Like the Black Power movement itself, as Williams got farther away from his roots in the South, he sometimes drifted into apocalyptic fantasies; his 1967 essay, "The Potential of a Minority Revolution," for example, depicted black saboteurs and guerrilla enclaves bringing down the United States government. Though Williams had been one of the best organizers in the black freedom movement, his isolation from any local constituency made him vulnerable to the same frustrations and delusions that plagued the rest of the movement in the last half of the 1960s.

In the late 1960s, when the Nixon administration moved toward opening diplomatic relations with China, Williams bartered his almost exclusive knowledge of the Chinese government for safe passage home and a Ford Foundation–sponsored post at the Center for Chinese Studies at the University of Michigan. Not that the entire federal apparatus was happy to welcome him home: the Internal Security Division of the Department of Justice observed that "Williams could be the person to fill the role of national leader of the black extremists. We should offset attempts by him to assume such a position." Williams, however, wrote to a friend that "a lot of people are going to be surprised after my arrival not to find me fighting for leadership the way many others are doing." Returning to family ties and local activism, Robert Williams spent the last twenty-seven years of his life in the small, trout-fishing village of Baldwin in western Michigan and died on October 15, 1996.

A week after his death, Rosa Parks climbed slowly into a church pulpit in Monroe, North Carolina. Beneath her lay the body of Robert F. Williams, clad in a gray suit given to him by Mao Zedong and draped with a black, red, and green Pan-African flag. Parks told the congregation that she and those who marched with Martin Luther King Jr. in Alabama had always admired Robert Williams "for his courage and his commitment to freedom. The work that he did should go down in history and never be forgotten." Her presence in that pulpit, nearly inexplicable when placed in the traditional narrative of "the civil rights movement," demonstrates in almost poetic fashion that historians should reexamine the relationship between "civil rights" and "Black Power." Our vision of the African American freedom movement between 1945 and 1965 as characterized solely and inevitably by nonviolent civil rights protest obscures the full complexity of racial politics. It idealizes black history, downplays the oppression of Jim Crow society, and even understates the achievements of African American resistance. Worse still, our cinematic civil rights movement blurs the racial dilemmas that follow us into the twenty-first century.

The life of Robert Williams underlines many aspects of the ongoing black freedom struggle—the decisive racial significance of World War II, the impact of the Cold War on the black freedom struggle, the centrality of questions of sexuality and gender in racial politics, and the historical presence of a revolutionary Caribbean. But foremost it testifies to the extent to which, throughout World War II and the postwar years, there existed among African Americans a current of militancy—a current that included the willingness to defend home and community by force. This facet of African

American life lived in tension and in tandem with the compelling moral example of nonviolent direct action. No doubt those who began the chant "Black Power" in the mid-1960s felt that slogan with an urgency specific to their immediate circumstances. But then, as now, many aspects of its meaning endure as legacies from earlier African American struggles. Above the desk where Williams completed his memoirs just before his death, there still hangs an ancient rifle—a gift, he said, from his grandmother.

William H. Chafe

BLACK POWER

William H. Chafe provides a perceptive look at the development of Black Power in North Carolina during the late 1960s. Chafe explores the dynamics around the increasingly militant consciousness of younger activists who, as with many SNCC members, had grown intolerant of the philosophy of nonviolence that civil rights veterans promoted. Although they were virtually never proponents of offensive attacks on whites, Black Power advocates thought that self-defense was not only wise, but essential to black liberation. Chafe also examines the conflict that occurred between and within civil rights organizations in North Carolina, giving special attention to colleges and community organizations such as North Carolina A&T, the NAACP, as well as upstart organizations like the Greensboro Association of Poor People. Though confined to North Carolina, this study helps illuminate a process of ideological conflict and tactical change that swept the civil rights movement in the late 1960s.

William H. Chafe is a professor of history at Duke University and the author of several articles and books, including *The Unfinished Journey: America Since World War II.*

The late 1960's were a fiery time in America. Black Panthers and Students for a Democratic Society tried to organize ghetto dwellers into a revolutionary phalanx to overthrow capitalism. Thousands of other young people, fed up with United States hypocrisy in Vietnam and the country's failure to solve problems of poverty and race at home, condemned "the system." Millions of adults, in turn, began to suspect that everything they cared about was being undermined by dissidents from another world—people who smoked marijuana, punctuated every other sentence with "Motherfucker!" and held middle-class propriety in contempt. Violence became part of the language of political discourse. Students with automatic weapons took over a dining hall at Cornell; battle-garbed soldiers tear-gassed anti-war demonstrators at the Pentagon; and police brutalized demonstrators at the 1968 Democratic National Convention. Whether one came from the left or the right, the country seemed under siege: for radical activists it was the brutal hammer of government repression; for "middle Americans" it was the intolerance of self-righteous radicals.

In Greensboro many of the same forces were at work, nowhere more clearly than in relations between black and white. Black activists felt hemmed in and powerless before an intransigent opposition that was proficient in using sophisticated forms of obstruction to frustrate black demands. In the past, each new stage of insurgency had brought forth new modes of white control. But never before had the constraints seemed so difficult to attack, so invulnerable to conventional weapons of protest. Clearly, new approaches were needed—approaches that would address not specific instances of overt discrimination, but the structure of racism that pervaded the routines of everyday life.

Spearheading the search for these new strategies was a group of young blacks who came to maturity during the halcyon days of the civil rights struggle. For most of them, remembered history began in 1960, not in 1954 or 1945; thus the sit-ins represented a starting point, not a culmination, of protest. What had seemed radical and bold to those born ten years earlier appeared tame and ineffectual to a new generation. Attitudes, too, had changed. The initial sit-in demonstrators had believed profoundly in the goodness of America. They had trusted white people such as Ed Zane, and they had been convinced of the intrinsic workability of the system. The new generation believed none of these things. Betrayal, subterfuge, and frustration constituted their perceived experience. With no reason to trust traditional channels of authority, they set out to battle "the system" as an enemy with which they shared nothing in common.

Appropriately, the new generation of black activists began by attacking the cornerstone of white supremacy—its ground rules for racial interaction. In the past, white leaders had exerted ultimate control by shaping the pattern of dialogue between the races, dictating the terms of exchange. Now, young blacks seemed intent on overturning those modes of interaction. They would overcome the progressive mystique by operating outside of it, insisting that blacks seize control of their own lives, define their own rules, compose their own agendas, shape their own culture, language, and institutions—in short, take power for themselves, at least to the extent of determining their own priorities and methods of proceeding.

The vehicle for achieving this power was to be community organization. By mobilizing tenants around issues of slum housing, bringing workers together in unions, and "turning around the heads" of young people in high schools and colleges, the new activists hoped to establish a base of operations independent of control or influence from white Greensboro. They then would have a foundation, rooted in black institutions and controlled by black interests, from which to strike at the cultural and economic heart of white racism. In effect, the new generation of activists aspired to accomplish what Booker T. Washington had attempted eight decades earlier—to organize blacks for their own self-development and definition. But, unlike Washington, the new strategists wished total liberation from white control, not accommodation to it.

The very nature of such an approach, of course, invited bitter opposition. In part, the antagonism came from within the black community. The "young turks," as established black leaders called them, sometimes treated older activists as part of the problem, an enemy rather than an ally. The younger generation were "revolutionaries," the older generation "reformers." But the real opposition came from those white leaders whose values and control were under frontal assault. Influenced by events in the nation at large, most of Greensboro's white leaders believed that violent revolutionaries were at work in their community, too, threatening everything they had been taught to cherish. Like others in the nation, they found the thought intolerable. Their response, in turn, was to crush the incipient rebellion with massive force. The option that they had rejected in 1963 now was invoked—harshly, brutally, with neither debate nor uncertainty—a reflection perhaps of how far Greensboro's leaders would go to defend the progressive mystique from those seen to be beyond its reach.

I

Leading the new insurgency was Nelson Johnson, a native of eastern North Carolina who had entered A&T in the fall of 1965 after three years in the Air Force. Despite participating in one or two demonstrations before coming to Greensboro, Johnson had never considered himself an activist. "I had gone along with the thinking in the society that you try to do good," he noted, hoping that eventually justice would prevail. But while in the Air Force Johnson had started to question those basic assumptions. Although he defended Martin Luther King against supporters of Malcolm X, the idea of non-violence became less and less creditable. "It really got to be clear that turning the other cheek, trying to convince the enemy through moral persuasion . . . didn't really accord [with what the enemy] was about." Still, when Johnson enrolled at A&T, his primary extracurricular activity was with Youth Educational Services (YES), a white-dominated tutorial program very much in the New Frontier/Great Society tradition of helping individual blacks to "make it" within the existing system.

Gradually, however, Johnson began to question reform and integration. "A lot of the children I worked with," he remarked, "asked for white tutors, which bothered me at a time when social consciousness of our own history as [an Afro-American] people was rapidly on the rise." As he thought about the issue, Johnson began to see larger ramifications:

> The question of why we had the tutor in the first place was linked to what the school wasn't doing and what the society wasn't doing . . . like how could a kid read if the lighting in the house is not proper, and how can the light get proper if his father isn't making enough money . . . and [the questioning] went into the [social root of things]. And the more you raise those questions, the more the hypocrisy of the society starts to come out.

During the same months, Stokely Carmichael raised the cry, "Black Power," telling his audiences: "it's time we stand up and take over."

Some of Johnson's classmates were also questioning the efficacy of working through traditional channels of authority. Tom Bailey, who had taken a leave of absence from A&T to work for an anti-poverty agency in Winston-Salem in 1966, concluded after his experience there that "the system had no real intention of bringing about any appreciable change." Like other antipoverty workers, Bailey had gone to work in a poor neighborhood. After living with the people and learning their concerns, he started to organize protest groups to demand improvements in housing and recreation. But before his efforts could reach fruition, he was attacked as an "outside agitator" working for Stokely Carmichael. (He had never met Carmichael.) Forced to retreat by his superiors, Bailey, too, began to doubt the sincerity of those who preached from a distance about social reform.

Nelson Johnson, in the meantime, was moving quickly toward a more radical concept of community organizing. Although continuing his tutorial work during 1966–67, he developed much closer community ties with black Greensboro, speaking at local political and social gatherings about the problems of schooling and housing. In the summer of 1967 he went to Fayetteville, North Carolina, where an effort was under way to organize poor blacks around issues of housing, rent, redevelopment, and jobs. During these months, he and Bailey became involved with the Foundation of Community Development (FCD), a statewide organization seeking to develop political activism among the poor. The FCD was an offshoot of the North Carolina Fund, established in 1963 by Governor Terry Sanford to lead a local war against poverty. "It is not enough to have the most powerful nation in the world," Sanford had said in 1963, "and then to admit that we are powerless to give our young people training in job opportunities." The FCD was to provide part of the power that was missing, but under the direction of Howard Fuller, its chief community organizer, the FCD became more and more an advocate of Black Power as well as community mobilization.

By the fall of 1967, Johnson, Bailey, and Fuller had become convinced that white leaders would respond to black needs only if the entire black community—poor and middle class, high school and college students, average workers and professional people— joined hands to build an independent Black Power base from which to deal with the white community. The key ingredient was to be a coalition between campus and community. On the one hand, Bailey noted, "there was a lot of energy on campus that could be mobilized to assist the community-at-large in redressing its problems." On the other hand, the average black worker could teach students "what was going on in the real world as opposed to academia." The young activists sought ways of welding an alliance between the two forces against those institutions that were most oppressive, particularly housing agencies, the welfare system, and traditional political organizations. Although there appeared to be only limited support among students for protest in the winter of 1967–68, Greensboro's black newspaper warned that "things are happening a lot faster than a lot of people realize. . . . Considerable revolutionary activities are taking place in our city."

Johnson demonstrated his organizing skills with students after the Orangeburg Massacre of February 1968, when three South Carolina State students were killed by police during an attempt to desegregate a bowling alley. News of the tragedy arrived during a meeting between Johnson and FCD staffers, profoundly depressing the group but also triggering a determination to respond. "I came back here," Johnson said:

> And we asked the funeral home director to give us a coffin to carry and we went to the cemetery and took some flowers and put them on the thing, we made an effigy of the governor, and just came to the student union and started to ask people to go and without any permit or anything we just lined up and started walking and when I looked back I just couldn't see the end of the line. That was a massive activity, it was one of the biggest activities, and it was the most spontaneous, it just happened . . . nobody knew who was organizing the thing, because I was nobody, I was just somebody, I wasn't even helping carrying the casket.

That Johnson's organizing ability extended to the community-at-large became clear the following summer (1968) when black activists formed the Greensboro Association of Poor People (GAPP). Directed toward the poorest, most oppressed blacks in Greensboro, GAPP sought to build a political base by sitting down with ten or twelve people in a housing project, talking about their problems, and then mobilizing the group to act. City redevelopment plans provided one focus for organizing efforts because of inadequate relocation procedures; housing conditions offered another rallying point. GAPP quickly acquired a reputation as a community ombudsman, fighting for people's welfare money, going downtown to protest official intimidation whenever local blacks felt aggrieved. No one with a problem was turned down. The GAPP approach, Johnson noted, "was just crude pressure tactics; [but] it won the hearts of the people [because they saw] us as an organization that they were part of." By the end of the summer a viable community base existed from which to work toward a coalition with students from Bennett, A&T, and Dudley High School.

Through such activities, Johnson quickly earned the enmity, as well as the grudging respect, of his white foes. "Johnson was the master organizer," one Greensboro white leader observed. His eloquence in public, together with his effectiveness behind the scenes, made him a powerful threat to those seeking to keep the black community under control. Moreover, because Johnson acted outside the traditional parameters of racial interaction, he was impossible to deal with in customary ways. Johnson seemed to go out of his way to disturb traditional white sensibilities. "If you're trying to persuade people to see things your way," one dismayed city official commented about Johnson, "what better way to start off than to be on time and be half-way pleasant to people you're trying to persuade?" Yet Johnson would not play by those rules. Consequently, most whites believed that he was not really seeking constructive change, but rather wanted "strife" for its own sake. "He was trying to stick a pin in the whole balloon, and he didn't care."

The same radical approach, of course, created problems with older black leaders. Existing black protest organizations dealt with only a limited range of issues. Almost never would they go into the poorest areas of town and agitate around problems like welfare. Moreover, the cry of "Black Power" challenged the politics of interracialism, threatening to undercut the deepest philosophical premises of the older generation. Simple issues such as dress and hair styles could pit old against young in a cultural war. When two young girls at Dudley High School wore their hair in an "Afro," the principal suspended them. "We want to create an atmosphere which is conducive for learning," he said. The girls, on the other hand, saw the issue as one of affirming their African origins and defining their own identity. Divisions over such questions sometimes threatened to drive a wedge between the new activists and their more conventional forebears.

Yet in the end the two sides had more reason to unite than to split into opposing factions. Nelson Johnson believed in a multi-class constituency; repeatedly, he went out of his way top avoid alienating potential black supporters, working on voter registration with the NAACP, cooperating with black ministers on social welfare projects. Johnson saved his most militant rhetoric for white audiences, intentionally adopting a more moderate stance before blacks, at least in part to discredit those whites who denounced him as reckless and dangerous. More importantly, black middle-class leaders recognized the value and effectiveness of Johnson's efforts. They shared his objectives, even if they did not always endorse his style. If leaders such as George Simkins of the NAACP or B. J. Battle of American Federal Savings & Loan did not initiate the same kind of community organizing campaigns as Johnson, they inevitably supported such actions after he took the first step. Despite internal tensions, therefore, the potential existed for the kind of coalition that Johnson sought. All that was missing was a spark to move that potential toward actualization.

II

As in countless other cities, the assassination of Martin Luther King in April 1968 provided the occasion for the broad resurfacing of black anger and activism. "When the announcement came on the radio, everybody was shocked," one A&T student recalled. "Some people started crying, then all of a sudden the next thing I heard, kids were out on Market Street throwing bottles and rocks at passersby." As word of the tragedy spread, more than three hundred black students marched into downtown Greensboro. Chanting "Black Power," the students massed at the county court house for a moment of prayer, then marched on, yelling, "We shall change the white society!" After the crowd started to smash car windows and throw rocks, riot police responded, armed with tear gas and shotguns. Although the violence never got out of control, Mayor Carson Bain requested the mobilization of National Guard units.

The morning and afternoon of the next day were relatively calm. More than five hundred students, most of them from Bennett, walked peacefully to the courthouse for a noon service addressed by Nelson Johnson and others. Almost four thousand gathered for another service at the A&T gymnasium, where they heard a telegram from Jesse Jackson pleading for students "to be non-violent . . . [and] to help heal this sick nation." To defuse the situation, President Lewis Dowdy announced that the spring break would start five days early, with students returning home immediately to be with their families "during these hours of sorrow."

But at nightfall the calm ended. Shooting broke out when two white men fired into a crowd of blacks from a passing station wagon. As police and National Guardsmen arrived in Armored Personnel Carriers, students became enraged and joined the battle, throwing stones and bottles at white motorists. After sniper fire came from the A&T campus, National Guardsmen reciprocated. Three policemen were wounded by shotgun blasts, one of them seriously.

No one knew who was involved in the shooting once the first gunfire came from the station wagon. Some students said all the snipers were outsiders. Others described the campus as "gone wild," with students rushing the ROTC arsenal, grabbing guns, and organizing into platoons. Police estimated that there were no more than one to three snipers. But the shooting went on through much of the night, with five shots being fired at local firemen responding to an alarm, and repeated gunfire exchanged between Hodgins Hall—an A&T dormitory—and National Guardsmen below. Shortly after midnight, police and guardsmen used tear gas to assault what appeared to be a major source of sniper fire, and the violence came to an end. All in all, there had been six injuries.

In an act destined to become controversial, Mayor Carson Bain the next morning declared a 7 p.m. to 6 a.m. curfew and banned all marching and demonstrations. The Mayor declared his action was necessary to preserve life and safety, even though more than a thousand guardsmen were in the city and Lewis Dowdy had sent home all A&T students. That night, as an army surveillance plane circled over southeast Greensboro, National Guardsmen atop the city's tallest buildings looked down upon a deserted central city. Although some arrests were made for curfew violations, the city was eerily quiet. "What's going on right now," Councilman Jack Elam said, "illustrates that there aren't any civil rights for anyone when there is no law and order."

During the next four days peace prevailed. Conditions were described by authorities as "static" and "excellent." At white churches throughout the city, ministers pondered King's tragic death, one calling it an example of "the radical wrongness of human nature," another declaring that "we who have power in our society" must respond with "true freedom and opportunity." In the black community more than one thousand people gathered at "Big Zion," the rallying point of the 1963 Civil Rights Movement, to express their grief. Meanwhile, the Greensboro *Daily News* declared that the clearest lesson of the riots and curfew was that "the political process cannot remain free, and certainly cannot be normal, when any large group despairs of its stake in it."

To blacks, however, the way the crisis was handled exhibited just how small a "stake" they had in government. At no point did any white city leader consult black leaders about the call-up of the National Guard or the imposition of the curfew. A&T officials first learned that law enforcement officers had invaded the campus when shots were heard. Such actions, one black minister noted, displayed total contempt for the black community. Black leaders were willing to discipline dissident students; but whites bypassed them, undercutting further the channels of authority within the black community. When black leaders sought permission for a downtown march to commemorate Dr. King, city leaders rejected the request. Instead, Mayor Bain proposed that only ministers march. Cecil Bishop, the black chairman of the Human Relations Commission, could barely contain his rage. "It doesn't [sit] very well with me," he told the Mayor, "to have to always do something on someone else's terms." John Marshall Stevenson, professor at A&T and editor of the black newspaper, echoed the same theme. "Your hearts may be good," he told city officials, "but the structure is rotten to the core. You may feel you can represent all the people fairly, but the people on the other side of the tracks don't believe you can."

Predictably, the use of force to impose calm actually triggered a revitalization of protest. Most blacks questioned the necessity for the curfew, pointing out that serious violence had occurred only after the National Guard had arrived on the scene. From their point of view, the curfew functioned primarily to keep workers on the second and third shifts away from their industrial jobs. In protest against the city's indifference to their sensibilities, the blacks gathered at "Big Zion" formed a Citizens Emergency Committee (CEC). By Thursday, CEC pickets were spreading leaflets throughout the downtown area, urging blacks not to spend money where they were not given a "fair shake." As one younger activist recalled, King's death caused people "who had not been involved since the sit-ins [to be] pulled back into activity." The CEC demanded the appointment of blacks to important policy-making posts in the city, especially on the Board of Health, the Alcoholic Beverages Commission, the Draft Board, the Airport Authority, and the Housing Authority. It also requested enactment of an open-housing ordinance, stronger building-code enforcements, more enlightened police practices, enactment of a ward system, the development of a Negro history curriculum in public schools, and more frequent appointment of blacks to municipal and school administration jobs. If the agenda sounded familiar, it was. Five years earlier the same demands had appeared on the "action ideal" of black protesters. In the intervening years, nothing had been done.

On the campus, meanwhile, Nelson Johnson became the focal point for renewed efforts to build a student-community coalition. Despite the Orangeburg Massacre demonstrations, most students at A&T did not engage in sustained protest activities. To alter that pattern, a Johnson supporter later recalled, "the decision was made that the most politically expedient thing to do was to take over [the campus]." GAPP was to be "the instrument for bringing together the community and the campus," with Johnson wearing the dual hats of student leader and founder of the community-action agency. As a result of that strategy Johnson became a candidate for student-body vice president, winning election in the spring of 1969 on a platform of Black Power and community organization.

Although police subsequently portrayed Johnson as heading a revolutionary conspiracy to overthrow authority, he was—on the scale of radicalism present at A&T in 1968—a relatively moderate figure. On one extreme was the Black Liberation Front (BLF), a group described by an A&T official as "well armed and planning for armed insurgency." By most black accounts, the BLF represented a dedicated cadre committed to Black Power and violent revolution. The BLF openly allied itself with Black Panthers from near-by Winston-Salem, a group characterized by one student as "walking around with their tams and black shirts and pants—everything was black—urging students to join the Panthers." "A kind of blacker-than-thou thing was developing," Nelson Johnson recalled. "People came together around frustration and hatred for what was going on." Yet the BLF offered no program for constructive action, turning inward upon itself and ultimately becoming an alienated clique. At the other end of the scale were the traditional sororities and fraternities. Students in such organizations were willing to get stirred up about campus issues such as grades or college rules, but not to engage in prolonged social activism.

Johnson represented a third alternative, closer to one group than the other, but basically seeking to build a coalition that would draw from all the factions on campus. Although committed to community organizing and Black Power, Johnson was clearly distinct from the BLF. Most students feared the latter's potential for violence and its reckless rhetoric. Johnson, by contrast, appeared responsible. This image, in turn, enabled Johnson to build bridges to the more conservative students who, with the correct approach, and under the appropriate circumstances, might be recruited for community action on schools, housing, or wages. The problem was to find the right issues.

The tactical difficulty of harnessing campus energies to broader political concerns became manifest when Stokely Carmichael spoke on campus in December 1968. As 4000 students thronged the A&T gymnasium, Carmichael exhorted blacks not only to be willing to die for freedom but to be willing to kill for it as well. Asked who he had voted for in the recent election, Carmichael responded: "I didn't vote, I stayed at home and cleaned my guns." Carmichael's call for black revolution, however, led neither to mass demonstrations downtown nor to greater student involvement in community issues; instead, students boycotted classes to protest "unprofessional and unethical conduct" by certain of their professors whose grading practices and teaching skills were under attack. Thus, those concerned with campus questions had seized the momentum created by Carmichael's visit to generate action on behalf of their own demands. Although Johnson and his allies would rather have seen student energies devoted to community action against the city, they still lacked the clout or persuasiveness to make that happen. "We didn't know how," Johnson said. "Only later would the two focuses come together." In fact there was an inevitable cultural logic to the progression. Students had to experience a new sense of power and rebellion over questions immediate to their own lives before moving outward to issues that tied those questions to others. . . .

IV

. . . [T]he overreaction of authorities [to student protests] was rooted in a state of near-paranoia that swept state and local officials. In part, that hysteria reflected national events. In a year when blacks entered the state legislative building in Sacramento carrying guns (it was legal to do so), and students took over buildings on campuses as diverse as Antioch, Duke, and the University of North Carolina at Chapel Hill, public officials were given to seeing conspiracies. President Richard Nixon condemned "minority tyrants," and Attorney General John Mitchell called for a crackdown on extremist demagogues. It sometimes seemed that the entire country was under attack from young people who rejected the rules and values of middle-class white America.

But the near-paranoia was also a response to local circumstances. Never before had white political and economic leaders faced such a profound threat. The challenge consisted not of weapons, but of an approach to power that questioned the very ground rules by which city leaders functioned and remained in control. By organizing poor people, public-housing tenants, cafeteria workers, and high school students to reject the definition of their proper "place" handed down by white authorities, Nelson Johnson and his associates were undercutting the very foundations of white power. No longer would blacks defer; no longer would they allow someone else to set the agenda or determine the scope of possible compromise. In effect, Johnson was asking blacks to create their own base of power and solidarity, to shape their own political program, and to do so independently of what whites thought. If blacks created their own ground rules, they would cease to be vulnerable to white attempts to divide and conquer them through traditional white rules.

In this sense, the new black insurgents were rejecting the heart of North Carolina's progressive mystique. Black Power assaulted the assumption that whites should control the political agenda available to blacks. By wearing bib overalls, "Afros," or dashikis, black young people were launching a cultural attack on the right of whites to dictate black standards of dress. Whenever GAPP representatives arrived late to a meeting with white officials, or mobilized tenants to reject out-of-hand official rationales for urban redevelopment, they were defying white concern about manners and "civility." Thus, in almost every respect—their language, their cultural goals, their involvement with the poor, and their determination to build a revolutionary politics—the new insurgents posed a radical threat to the status quo. Indeed, they were striking at the very base of white control—the power to define what is real and unreal, permissible and impermissible.

Neither Greensboro's white leaders, nor those in the nation at large, proved able to deal with this political and cultural challenge on its own terms. The issues of self-definition, self-determination, and autonomy were too large, or perhaps too threatening. Instead, white leaders perceived a conspiracy—violent in nature—to commit illegal acts, to overthrow the government, to kill and maim white people. By defining the challenge in such a manner, it became easier to avoid confronting the underlying questions and yet to feel comfortable with a response to black insurgents of total rejection and hostility.

This insistence on finding a violent conspiracy, however, caused white leaders to ignore legitimate grievances and to overlook important distinctions within the black movement. In 1968 the Black Liberation Front had been dedicated to armed insurrection. But there were few vestiges of the BLF still in existence by 1969. Eric Brown and the Black Panther party had relatively little support at A&T. Furthermore, Nelson Johnson and his co-workers rejected Panther rhetoric and methods of organization. They sought to build a coalition around issues such as housing and to develop a sense of political efficacy both on campus and in the ghetto. To embrace the Panthers would automatically have sheared off large parts of that coalition. Johnson was too shrewd to engage in such self-destructive behavior. He and his associates did ally themselves with the Foundation for Community Development, and they did seek to radicalize youngsters in high school. But they were not reckless. As one member of the group later said: "The notion was to put as much pressure on as we could, but not to be insane. Let's not delude ourselves. The police, FBI included, would be very happy to pull out their pieces and blow your brains out. . . . It was always our orientation to put pressure on people but not to get innocent people into a position where they could possibly get hurt."

Although such statements are self-serving, the evidence suggests that Nelson Johnson and his associates were more committed to building the community then destroying it for the sake of armed revolution. . . . Once city officials became tied to a belief in a monolithic conspiracy, however, they overlooked the multiple constituencies among black students and imputed a set of motives to every act of protest that made it impossible to address the substantive questions at the root of the protests. Since every expression of dissent was seen as part of a subversive plot, there was no possibility—or need—to distinguish legitimate demands from violent insurrection.

The result was the irrational use of force in 1969. Despite evidence to the contrary, city officials disregarded the existence of divisions among the student protesters. It was as if they needed to see a conspiracy in order to justify their own instinct to strike out and destroy the enemy. Once Nelson Johnson and his allies had shown their contempt for the progressive mystique, they had moved beyond the pale. Thereafter, white leaders seized any evidence to radicalism to create a picture of black insurgency that would warrant all-out retaliation. . . . State Attorney General Robert Morgan insisted that the Black Panthers were so clever that one could not "distinguish between the militants with guns and the merely innocent." The implication: the Panthers melted into the population just as the Viet Cong did among the Vietnamese. When the Greensboro *Daily News* denounced black protesters for engaging in "guerrilla warfare," it was in a very real sense explaining why the use of any degree of force, however awesome, could be justified in response.

In this context, the violence of 1969 can be seen as a ritual acting out of the need to destroy an enemy who challenged one's most dearly held values, even if the exact nature of the challenge or the reasons for the reaction were never fully articulated in a conscious manner. "It was almost like watching something unfold that, once you started, it's out of everybody's control," former Mayor Jack Elam recalled. Moreover, since the enemy refused to play according to the rules of the progressive mystique, there was no need to worry about the harshness of one's response. In 1963, white leaders had chosen compromise rather than repression because making some concessions seemed the only way of preserving the city's progressive reputation. Now the rules had changed, both among the protesters and among the city's leaders. Repression had become a legitimate way of saying "never." Significantly, Captain William Jackson, who earlier had proven so adept at dealing with civil rights protest, played no role in formulating police policy. Instead, he was "pushed back" and "eased away" by superiors who wished to adopt a tough stance without encountering any opposition.

Perhaps above all, [the level of white resistance to black activism] confirmed how powerless black people in Greensboro were—despite the efforts of Johnson and others—when white authorities chose to resist change. As soon as the disturbances began at Dudley, the white superintendent of schools sent a white associate to take over. When the action moved to A&T, local officials disregarded university leaders in shaping their response. The hard reality, the *Carolina Peacemaker* editorialized, was "that when the chips are down, most so-called black power rests in the hands of whites." Whether on the school board, the city council, or other city agencies, black perceptions and priorities were either discounted or interpreted only through white eyes. Nothing could do more to give credibility to the charges of Nelson Johnson.

Clayborne Carson

INTERNAL CONFLICTS IN SNCC

Clayborne Carson's seminal study of the Student Nonviolent Coordinating Committee (SNCC) is the basis for this essay. Carson examines the complexity of nascent nationalist aspirations in a movement that extolled integration. He studies the decline of SNCC, while also giving attention to the contentious debates on Black Power and integration in the larger movement. By 1966, movement activists began to increasingly question the efficacy of nonviolence and integration. Many were influenced by the growing currents of black nationalism and had grown impatient with making appeals to the conscience of white America. In addition, a greater emphasis on class in the black community emerged with SNCC's Atlanta Project activists who doubted that the death of Jim Crow would mean the demise of black poverty. SNCC attempted to address these internal conflicts but found them difficult to reconcile. Through increasingly militant rhetoric, SNCC gravitated towards black nationalism and away from purely southern affairs. In the process of trying to appeal to the militancy in black communities nationwide, SNCC isolated many white (and black) liberals.

Clayborne Carson is a professor of history at Stanford University and the author of *The Autobiography of Martin Luther King, Jr.*

[Stokely] Carmichael and other SNCC workers roused the racial feelings of blacks through verbal attacks on the existing leadership and prevailing strategies of the civil rights movement, but their own organization was weakened in the process. Staff members expected the external attacks and undoubtedly some believed that such attacks confirmed the correctness of their actions. Yet to many SNCC workers, the organization's vulnerability was somewhat unnecessary, because it resulted from an emphasis on militant rhetoric rather than on the development of workable programs to consolidate southern civil rights gains. As Carmichael became a nationally-known figure, SNCC shifted the focus of its activities from the deep South to urban centers, prompting some staff members to question whether tangible political gains could be realized as a result of the personal following Carmichael attracted.

That the invocation of racial ideals did not always unite black communities and could even intensify conflicts among blacks became apparent within SNCC when black separatists in the Atlanta Project persisted in their demands for the expulsion of the remaining whites on the SNCC staff. The issue of white participation became a weapon in a struggle over SNCC's future direction between the separatists and other black staff members who ultimately rejected the separatists' extremism but failed to challenge their overriding belief that adherence to racial ideals should take precedence over the issues of SNCC's effectiveness and even its continued existence. Such idealism had once been an asset in SNCC's struggle to mobilize civil rights forces; it became a liability as SNCC sought to create its own bases of power in order to achieve new goals against powerful and determined opposition.

When Carmichael's involvement in the Atlanta racial violence resulted in his arrest in September 1966, a few staff members began openly to express doubts about his public activities. Executive Secretary Ruby Doris Robinson wrote that SNCC's staff had not decided, as had Carmichael, to advocate "the destruction of Western civilization." Referring to Carmichael's public image as the "architect of Black Power," she asked other staff members, "How could one individual make such a tremendous impression on so many people in such a short period of time . . . so much so that to some people SNCC is only the organization that Carmichael has at his disposal to do what he wants to get done?" Answering her own question, she asserted that Carmichael had been "the only consistent spokesman for the organization, and he has had the press not only available but seeking him out for whatever ammunition could be found—FOR OUR DESTRUCTION." She conceded that "at his best, he has said what [the masses of black people] wanted to hear," but added that "cliche after cliche has filled his orations."

A few weeks after Robinson's blast against Carmichael, similar concerns of other staff members were strengthened when a group of nine black men, carrying rifles and hand grenades, appeared at the Atlanta office claiming to be Carmichael's followers. "We had no idea they were coming down and this was the first time they had been to the Atlanta office," Fay Bellamy recalled. "Not knowing us, they were quick to let us know what equipment they had brought with them."

To an extent, the criticisms of Carmichael were based on a mixture of envy, jealousy, and understandable resentment by veteran staff members who disliked being thought of as Carmichael's followers or aides. Muriel Tillinghast recalled that SNCC had previously resisted allowing the chair to become dominant but that after Carmichael's election, "the chairman began to determine policy autonomously and the rest of us had to make a decision as to whether we were going to go with the chair or not." The staff's inability to control Carmichael's activities indicated that they had not yet found a means of reconciling their desire for discipline and democratic control.

Carmichael was aware of the need for discipline and even acknowledged his own shortcomings after they were repeatedly brought to his attention. At the October central committee meeting, he admitted that "rhetorically, there have been a lot of mistakes made." Reacting to suggestions of Robinson, Bellamy, Ralph Featherstone, and other strong figures in the Atlanta office, he agreed to stop making speaking engagements after December 10 and to spend his time "developing programs and working on internal structure."

Carmichael was probably sincere in his promise to restrict his speechmaking, but the limelight was difficult to resist. A few months later the Central Committee forbade his appearance on a television show and decided that he should always be accompanied by another staff member at his engagements. Carmichael was undoubtedly annoyed by these restrictions, since he and other staff members realized that his speeches had dramatically increased SNCC's visibility, if not its effectiveness, and were an important source of income for the financially hard-pressed organization.

SNCC's initial goals had been radical in the context of southern society, and it had once faced more fierce and immediate opposition than it confronted in 1966, but the black power controversy weakened SNCC's southern bases by discouraging many veteran organizers and prompting a movement of SNCC's personnel from long-established projects in the deep South to urban areas. SNCC was not, as some critics asserted, taken over by black militants without ties to the civil rights movement. Approximately two-thirds of the one hundred staff members in October 1966 had been on the staff at least two years. In addition, some of those who had joined the staff during 1965 and 1966 had participated in earlier civil rights efforts, though not as SNCC staff members. Nonetheless, SNCC had changed in several significant ways. The most dramatic change was the movement of personnel to urban areas. During the period from 1961 to 1966 all but a small proportion of staff members were assigned to projects in Arkansas, Mississippi, Alabama, or southwest Georgia. By October 1966 only a third of the staff were in these areas; the other two thirds were gathered near SNCC's Atlanta headquarters or scattered in cities outside the South.

A comparison of SNCC's staff in the fall of 1966 with the period prior to 1965 reveals that few of SNCC's officers and project directors in the fall of 1964 remained in SNCC. SNCC's new officers had hoped to keep Lewis in the organization to retain the appearance of continuity, but the bitterness resulting from the Kingston Springs meeting could not be overcome. Lewis initially offered his resignation on June 11, but the Central Committee refused to accept it. He became even more convinced he should resign, however, after hearing that a few SNCC workers on the Mississippi march tried to trick SCLC officials into being arrested. Although he felt no personal antagonism toward Carmichael, he was disturbed by the actions of SNCC workers who were openly hostile toward whites. When he finally announced his resignation late in June 1966, Lewis explained that he was not prepared to give up his "personal commitment to nonviolence." Consistently refusing to publicly criticize the black power concept, he later indicated that SNCC failed to provide "on-going" programs to meet the needs of blacks. "To have a program is one thing, to have a sort of speech-making public relations thing is another," he remarked.

Julian Bond, one of SNCC's founders, resigned later in the summer, shortly after the outbreak of racial violence in Atlanta. Having been re-elected in February and once again barred by the Georgia legislature from taking his seat, Bond was in the midst of his third campaign when he decided that his ties to SNCC had become too much of a liability. He explained to reporters that he did not disagree with SNCC's policies and that his resignation was in part motivated by the inadequacy of his pay ($85 a week) to support his family. Privately he was disturbed that SNCC had lost much of its effectiveness and was overly concerned with ideological matters. He later commented that SNCC did not "have a program to match its rhetoric." Unlike Lewis, however, Bond evinced little bitterness in his break with SNCC, and he continued to have close relations with SNCC workers, many of whom participated in his successful re-election campaign.

Even more damaging to SNCC's southern effectiveness than the resignations of Lewis and Bond was the deterioration of its field operations. SNCC's ability to rebuild its southern projects was hampered by the departure of its most experienced organizers. In 1966, Charles Sherrod, SNCC's first field secretary, ended his ties with SNCC when the Central Committee unanimously rejected his plan to bring northern white students to work in southwest Georgia. After resigning from SNCC, Sherrod established the Southwest Georgia Independent Voters Project, which remained active after SNCC's efforts in the area had ceased.

Several staff members in Arkansas also resigned rather than adjust to SNCC's new ideological thrust. Most Arkansas staff members ultimately accepted the validity of the black power concept, but one of them resigned after reading a particularly inflammatory field report written by a SNCC worker in New Jersey. [Cleveland] Sellers wrote that the Arkansas worker was willing to defend SNCC's actions against liberal criticisms but was not willing to "go to war with some liberal shithead over some words." Bill Hansen finally left the project, in part due to dismay over SNCC's inability to control Carmichael's public statements, as did his successor as project director, Ben Grintage, who resigned to join the Arkansas Human Relations Council.

Other projects were also weakened by resignations and declining morale among organizers. In Mississippi serious challenges from moderate black leaders who wished to create an alternative to the MFDP [Mississippi Freedom Democratic Party] exacerbated longstanding tensions between SNCC and pragmatic MFDP leader Lawrence Guyot. Although staff members were disturbed by Guyot's increasingly independent course, they were unable to refute his criticism that SNCC provided little support for the party. Sellers visited several Mississippi communities during the summer and found few SNCC staff members carrying out their responsibilities. He was particularly disturbed by the situation in Holly Springs, where he had once been project director, believing that the current director, Sid Walker, did not have the support of local blacks in his decision to retain white staff members. When Sellers summarily closed the office and recommended that most of the staff be fired, Walker defended himself by arguing that the use of white volunteers was necessary since SNCC was not able to provide funds to hire full-time black workers. Although Walker was unable to reverse Sellers' decision, this drastic action taken against allegedly nonproductive Mississippi staff members did not stem the decline in SNCC's effort in the state. In October Robinson reported that the remaining Mississippi staff members were out of touch with the Atlanta headquarters and did not feel that SNCC adequately supported their work.

Even in Lowndes County, Alabama, where SNCC leaders expected to demonstrate the potential of the black power strategy, the results of SNCC's efforts were disappointing. Carmichael's departure was followed by the gradual drifting away of other staff members, forcing the Central Committee to send Ralph Featherstone to the county in a belated attempt to revive the project. In October, however, Carmichael reported that only one of the Alabama workers, Rap Brown, planned to remain as a full-time worker after the November election. SNCC tried to remedy the situation by drawing workers from other projects in the days before the election, and this temporary influx brought the LCFO [Lowndes County Freedom Organization] tantalizingly close to victory. Carmichael returned on election eve to address an enthusiastic gathering of black residents, telling them to remember the oppression they had endured. "We remember all the dust we ate," he cried. "We say to those who don't remember: 'You better remember, because if you don't move on over, we are going to move on over you!'" Despite this last-minute effort, LCFO workers were unable to counter the efforts of whites to transport plantation workers to the polls with instructions to vote for white candidates. Without these black votes, LCFO candidates were defeated, receiving from forty-one to forty-six percent of the vote. More importantly, after the temporary additions to the staff had left, SNCC no longer could aid black residents in continuing their struggle.

SNCC organizers outside the South had little difficulty adjusting to the rhetoric of black power, but they failed to transform black support for the concept into actual political power. Los Angeles SNCC worker Cliff Vaughs announced plans during the summer of 1966 for incorporating predominantly black sections of Los Angeles into a "Freedom City," but this project never got off the ground. Early in 1967 the Central Committee concluded that Vaughs was no longer effective and asked him to hand in his resignation. Soon afterward, the Los Angeles office was closed.

SNCC workers in Washington had somewhat greater success in establishing the Free D.C. Movement (FDCM), a pioneering effort to achieve self-government for the district. These efforts were eventually successful but office director Marion Barry complained during August that SNCC was losing good organizers to the federal poverty program because it could not pay sufficient wages. Sellers reported that "there was general hostility in some [black neighborhoods] because of lack of program." Other Central Committee members criticized Barry's comparatively moderate political orientation and did not object when he quietly resigned his post in SNCC to work as an independent organizer. He soon became head of an anti-poverty organization called Pride, Inc.

Bill Hall's organizing effort in Harlem was intertwined in a bitter struggle by black residents to gain control over predominantly-black schools, and he became skeptical of SNCC's ability to deal with black urban problems. Hall recalled that many people who joined SNCC after 1965 did not recognize the need for technical skills. Determined to acquire such skills, he left New York and SNCC to return to college. After his departure, SNCC's activities in New York were largely limited to fund-raising.

SNCC's Chicago office was raided by police late in 1966, and several months later its head, Monroe Sharpe, went into exile in Tanzania to escape police and FBI harassment. In 1967 Joyce Brown and then Bob Brown tried unsuccessfully to revive SNCC's activities in the city.

SNCC's officers were overwhelmed as they tried to reinvigorate these waning projects. Sellers complained at one point that it was "a joke" to believe that he could "do an effective job when in fact everyone on the staff is an individual and has a parochial attitude." On another occasion he noted that SNCC could not accomplish its goals and implement programs "until we can discipline ourselves," mentioning specifically "the need to use resources wisely and to their full capacity." In a similar vein, Robinson reported that she had decided against describing the activities of all staff members, since that would be "in bad taste."

SNCC's declining effectiveness not only hampered its projects but also contributed to the loss of northern financial backing. Individuals who might have backed SNCC's drive for black power were unwilling to support an organization that had few promising projects. SNCC began to rely almost totally on speechmaking and its New York office, manned by professional fund-raisers and veteran staff members, to provide funds for payroll expenses. When these sources proved insufficient, staff members were forced to skip paychecks, prompting some to leave the organization in order to support themselves and their families.

SNCC's problems were by no means solely caused by its own militancy and lack of discipline. SCLC and CORE also had difficulty in adjusting to a new political context in which their previous tactics and strategies were often inappropriate. One of SNCC's strengths had always been its ability to change and to attract new personnel with new ideas. The black power controversy simply represented another example of SNCC's ability to remain in the forefront of social struggle. Yet, SNCC's problems in 1966 were more serious than ever before, because it no longer served as a catalyst for sustained local struggles. Rather than encouraging local leaders to develop their own ideas, SNCC was becoming merely one of many organizations seeking to speak on behalf of black communities. Instead of immersing themselves in protest activity and deriving their insights from an ongoing mass struggle, SNCC workers in 1966 stressed the need to inculcate among urban blacks a new racial consciousness as a foundation for future struggles. Those who joined SNCC's staff during 1966 generally were urban blacks attracted more by SNCC's militant image than by its rural southern projects. Most were dedicated activists, willing to take risks to achieve their ideals, but few wanted to engage in the difficult work of gaining the trust and support of southern black people who were older than themselves and less aware of the new currents of black nationalist thought. SNCC's rhetoric reflected the angry mood of many urban blacks, but its projects were unable to transform racial anger into local movements that could be sustained. . . .

The issue of white participation superseded all others as an illustration of SNCC's inability to resolve internal differences over policy on the basis of coherent political principles rather than emotions and fervent adherence to racial ideals. This issue, a source of internal conflict since 1964, was considered resolved for most staff members when SNCC decided to discourage the use of whites as organizers in black communities and made explicit the notion that black people should determine the direction of their struggle. By fall 1966 only a handful of white activists remained on SNCC's staff, and of these only Jack Minnis still exercised much influence in the organization. Nonetheless, SNCC was unable to leave behind the issue of white involvement, because the presence of whites brought to the surface differences among black staff members. For a significant number of black separatists, this issue symbolized SNCC's general inability to break with its past. Members of the Atlanta Project had indicated in their position paper that black people required all-black organizations to develop the racial confidence and militancy needed for future struggles. The separatists failed in their initial challenge to SNCC's leadership, but after Carmichael's election they continued to use the issue of white participation as a means of undermining SNCC's leadership. In the process, they demonstrated how the rhetoric of black power could be used as a weapon in the black leadership battles that would take place in SNCC and in black communities during the late 1960s.

The Atlanta Project separatists reflected and contributed to a mood of racial bitterness that was perceptively analyzed by black psychiatrist Alvin Poussaint, who worked closely with SNCC during the mid-1960s. Poussaint suggested that the southern struggle was an outlet for the resentments of black activists but many felt restrained by their friendly relations with white civil rights workers and by their desire to retain northern white support. Poussaint may have exaggerated somewhat when he wrote that many of the civil rights workers who shouted the black power slogan loudest after June 1966 had once been "exemplars of nonviolent, loving passive resistance in their struggle against white supremacy." But he was on firmer grounds in arguing that the advocates of black power "appeared to be seeking a sense of psychological emancipation from racism through self assertion and release of aggressive angry feelings."

Such feelings were released through public black power speeches that hinted of racial violence, and through verbal and sometimes physical attacks on other SNCC workers. Forman's description of SNCC as "a band of brothers, a circle of trust" became only a memory as the staff argued about the means of achieving black power. Ironically the bonds that held the staff together loosened while SNCC became more racially homogeneous. Eager to achieve more radical goals, SNCC workers sometimes deprecated SNCC's earlier accomplishments and lost sight of the organizing techniques responsible for those accomplishments.

Julius Lester, who joined SNCC's staff shortly after Carmichael's election, expressed the changing mood inside SNCC in an essay on "the angry children of Malcolm X." Naive and idealistic SNCC workers of the early 1960s—who had "honestly believed that once white people knew what segregation did, it would be abolished"—had given way to a new generation who believed that nonviolence did not work.

> Now it is over. The days of singing freedom songs and the days of combating bullets and billy clubs with Love . . . Love is fragile and gentle and seeks a like response. They used to sing "I Love Everybody" as they ducked bricks and bottles. Now they sing
>
> > Too much love,
> > Too much love,
> > Nothing kills a nigger like
> > Too much love.

In his popular tract *Look Out, Whitey! Black Power's Gon' Get Your Mama!* Lester went further, suggesting that a race war might be on the horizon. "You can't do what has been done to blacks and not expect retribution. The very act of retribution is liberating."

Rejecting the kind of moralistic struggle once waged by Sherrod, Lewis, Moses, and other SNCC workers, he asserted, "It is clearly written that the victim must become the executioner." SNCC workers in Chicago expressed a similar thought even more bluntly: "We must fill ourselves with hate for all white things." . . .

Less subject to feelings of racial ambivalence and eager to question the racial loyalties of others, the Atlanta Project separatists placed other SNCC staff members on the defensive during the summer and fall of 1966. They achieved only modest success in organizing blacks in the Vine City ghetto, in part because they failed to acquire the support of strong, indigenous, adult leaders who had traditionally provided entree for SNCC field secretaries, but they diverted attention from their failures by blaming them on the continued presence of whites in SNCC. . . .

The separatist orientation of the Atlanta Project came to public attention during the summer of 1966 when staff members clashed with Hector Black, a white Harvard graduate who had received a federal anti-poverty grant to work in Vine City. "What we saw was that he was a perpetuation of the missionary mentality, of the so-called good white men that had us looking toward them for our solution rather than looking toward ourselves," [Bill] Ware recalled. The fact that Black had considerable support in the community and was a member of the Vine City Council, an unofficial community forum, simply strengthened the separatists' resentments. Early in the summer Black received an overwhelming vote of confidence from the council after SNCC workers drove through the community with a loudspeaker asking residents, "What has your White Jesus done for you today?" . . .

. . . Separatists hoped for a final resolution of the "white" question as the staff gathered on December 1 for a meeting held on the New York estate of black entertainer "Peg Leg" Bates.

SNCC's officers had planned the meeting at the secluded resort to allow the staff to confront the problems caused by the black power controversy. Discussion of the role of whites was placed on the agenda but was expected to occupy only part of the first day of the meeting. During succeeding days planners hoped that discussions in a relaxed atmosphere might reverse the decline in SNCC's effectiveness. Although they reflected the desire of most staff members to solve SNCC's many problems, they seriously underestimated the emotional force of the arguments that the Atlanta separatists and their allies would present.

The majority of the approximately one hundred staff members at the meeting initially believed that it was unnecessary to expel whites, preferring instead to encourage them to organize white communities. Carmichael stated this view in his talk at the outset of the meeting, arguing that SNCC needed white financial support and a "buffer zone" of white liberals to forestall repression. Carmichael and other blacks criticized the Atlanta separatists for refusing to allow the staff to address other important issues until whites were expelled. Yet, though nearly all of SNCC's veteran leaders agreed with this view, the separatist forces were determined to press the issue and repeatedly interrupted the meeting demanding "whites had to go."

Ware opened his prepared statement by asserting that he was "convinced that Black People and [SNCC] do not understand the concept of Black Power," because if they did, "there would be no white people in the organization at this time." He explained that if SNCC's staff "understood that the cats on the corner do not dig having white people in the organization then of course they'd have to get . . . white people out." He repeated with greater force the arguments from the Atlanta project's Spring position paper, claiming that white participation was "the biggest obstacle" in the path of "Black folks getting liberation." He added that SNCC's taking time to debate the issue was in itself an argument for the expulsion of whites, since "sensitive white people" would recognize the problems caused by their presence and leave voluntarily. "Those who don't understand that ought to be expelled."

To the dismay of most SNCC officers, this debate continued for several days. The discussions were intensely emotional, particularly for the seven remaining white staff members. At one point Forman became so upset over the seemingly endless proceedings that he made a proposal to disband SNCC and send its remaining funds to the African liberation movements. He was particularly disturbed when a few black separatists ridiculed veteran staff member Fannie Lou Hamer, who opposed the expulsion of whites, by claiming that she was "no longer relevant" or not at their "level of development." The small group of white staff members at the meeting said little during the days of rancorous debate, and when Cordel Reagan finally moved the question, most did not participate in the vote. The staff passed a resolution excluding whites by a vote of nineteen for, eighteen against, with twenty-four abstaining. The remainder of the staff had either left the meeting or had gone to bed before the vote, which took place at about 2 A.M. Although only nineteen staff members voted against white participation, the separatist victory was made possible by the unwillingness of most staff members to resist an outcome that seemed inevitable. Jack Minnis recalled that he considered voting on the issue, but afterwards was relieved that he and other whites had abstained rather than providing the deciding votes against their own expulsion. Immediately after the vote white staff members walked out of the meeting. Some blacks who remained felt a mixture of relief and regret about the expulsion of white activists who had dedicated much of their adult lives to SNCC. Communications worker Ethel Minor supported the decision to expel whites, but recalled feeling guilty after the vote. Referring to Bob Zellner she said, "Here was someone who had been on the front lines long before I came into the organization. No one wanted to look at Bob afterwards."

Through their singleminded determination, the Atlanta Project staff dominated the December staff meeting, but ironically their effort to expel whites was followed soon afterward by their own expulsion. During subsequent months they continued to challenge the racial loyalty of SNCC's leaders and sought to undermine their authority. SNCC's officers finally took decisive action against the project when staff members refused to return a car belonging to SNCC. After repeated requests for the return of the car, Sellers and Carmichael reported the car to the police as missing. An enraged [Bill] Ware wrote a telegram to Forman protesting the action. "Your hand-picked Chairman, the alleged hope of Black America, has descended to the level of calling a racist henchman cop of the white master Allen of Atlanta to settle an internal dispute between the supposedly black people of SNCC." Ware [of the Atlanta Project] also menacingly alluded to Forman's marriage to a white ex-SNCC worker and added that he might release information damaging to Forman to the press.

When Carmichael heard from Forman about Ware's telegram, he acted immediately to end the insubordination by firing or suspending all members of the Atlanta Project staff. Because the Atlanta Project staff had considerable support within SNCC, Carmichael and Sellers wrote a letter listing the reasons for their action.

Most of the Atlanta separatists remained in the city after they had been expelled, hoping that they could garner enough backing to reverse the decision at the next general staff meeting. Ware accepted the finality of the decision, however, recalling that he dissuaded other project staff members from taking weapons to a central committee meeting at which the firing of all staff members except Donald Stone was ratified.

Even after the dismissal of the Atlanta separatists, SNCC was troubled by internal arguments. Indeed, the issue of white participation was not finally resolved until May 1967. Hoping that SNCC's staff would narrow the scope of the December decision on white participation, Zellner and his wife Dottie asked the Central Committee to approve their plan to organize whites in New Orleans and to be given full voting rights in SNCC. The Zellners' carefully worded statement argued that the committee should grant the request "not on the basis of our deep feelings about the years we have spent in SNCC, our length of service, what we feel to have been our contributions, and our emotional and personal ties." Instead they argued that SNCC should support the plan because a future coalition could not be achieved if white and black organizers were completely isolated from each other.

Forman, along with a few other SNCC veterans, initially argued for the proposal, but he feared that an attempt to overturn the December decision might prompt some staff members to question the motives of SNCC's officers in firing the Atlanta Project staff. Sellers recalled that he and other SNCC veterans were ambivalent about the Zellners' request, since Bob "was one of the few whites who commanded the unqualified respect of everyone in the organization," and that he was, like Moses, "a special SNCC person." Yet, despite these feelings, Sellers did not want to reopen the debate over the role of whites. The Central Committee unanimously denied the request, although it agreed to provide materials to aid the Zellners' work. The decision was an important one for SNCC, but Sellers recalled that the staff members were "so harried . . . that most of us hardly had time to do more than shake our heads and wish that things had turned out differently."

The internal conflicts and the continuous decline in SNCC's effectiveness did not prevent the organization from greatly influencing

Afro-American political attitudes. Indeed, it was during the year of Carmichael's chairmanship that SNCC acquired unprecedented importance as a source of new political ideas. SNCC did not by itself change the direction of black politics, but it did reflect a decisive shift in the focus of black struggles from the rural South to the urban North and from civil rights reforms to complex, interrelated problems of poverty, powerlessness, and cultural subordination. Like the thousands of black students who were ready to join the sit-ins of 1960 even before the initial Greensboro protests, millions of black people were prepared to adopt the rhetoric of black power in order to express their accumulated anger and to assume new, more satisfying racial identities.

Nonetheless, SNCC's efforts to transform black discontent into programs for achieving black power were hampered by the controversy that Carmichael stimulated and by the increasingly obvious political and personal differences that existed within SNCC. As the organization entered a period in which racial violence would reach new levels of intensity, SNCC endured external attacks that exacerbated its internal conflicts. SNCC sought new sources of support both within the United States and abroad, but as it became more isolated from former white allies and more openly identified with uncontrollable urban black militancy, it encountered ruthless government repression. As staff members continued to build upon the insights contained in the 1966 black power rhetoric, the deadly attacks they faced in subsequent years ensured that their message would reach an ever-decreasing number of blacks.

SUGGESTIONS FOR FURTHER READING

The scholarship on the civil rights movement has been expanding considerably into new and interesting interpretations since the 1960s. Many books, however, are not written by academics. And many histories are written by social scientists. Still, the development of the field is a continuous process with extensive possibilities for further exploration and analysis.

Histories of the Civil Rights Movement

The most significant overviews of the movement are Manning Marable, *Race, Reform, and Rebellion: The Second Reconstruction in Black America, 1945–1990* (1991); Kevin Gaines, *Uplifting the Race: Black Leadership, Politics, and Culture in the Twentieth Century* (1996); Rhoda Lois Blumberg, *Civil Rights: The 1960s Freedom Struggle* (1984); Adam Fairclough, *Better Day Coming: Blacks and Equality, 1890–2000* (2001); Richard King, *Civil Rights and the Idea of Freedom* (1992); Doug McAdam, *Political Process and the Development of Black Insurgency 1930–1970* (1999); Harvard Sitkoff, *The Struggle for Black Equality, 1954–1992* (1993); Robert Weisbrot, *Freedom Bound, A History of America's Civil Rights Movement* (1990); Benjamin Muse, *The American Negro Revolution: From Nonviolence to Black Power, 1963–1967* (1968); Jack Bloom, *Class, Race and the Civil Rights Movement* (1987); Aldon Morris, *The Origins of the Civil Rights Movement* (1984); Steven F. Lawson, *Running for Freedom, Civil Rights Movement: 1940–1970* (1974); Herbert H. Haines, *Black Radicals and the Civil Rights Movement, 1954–1970* (1988); Pat Watters, *Down to Now: Reflections on the Southern Civil Rights Movement* (1993); Hugh Davis Graham, *The Civil Rights Era* (1990); Benjamin Muse, *The American Negro Revolution* (1969).

For a more limited scope of time but important books, see Taylor Branch, *Parting the Waters: America in the King Years, 1954–1963* (1988) and its equally brilliant follow-up, *Pillar of Fire: America in the King Years, 1963–65* (1998); Benjamin Muse, *Ten Years of Prelude: The Story of Integration Since the Supreme Court's 1954 Decision*

(1964); Numan V. Bartley, *The Rise of Massive Resistance: Race and Politics in the South During the 1950s* (1969). See also Anthony Lewis, *Portrait of a Decade: The Second American Revolution* (1964); Howell Raines, *My Soul Is Rested: Movement Days in the Deep South Remembered* (1977); Clayborne Carson, et al., *The Eyes on the Prize Civil Rights Reader* (1991); Henry Hampton and Steve Fayer, *Voices of Freedom: An Oral History of the Civil Rights Movement from the 1950s through the 1980s* (1990) for personal testimonies. There are some good anthologies, including, Armstead L. Robinson and Patricia Sullivan, *New Directions in Civil Rights Studies* (1991); John H. Bracey, Jr., August Meier, and Elliott Rudwick, eds., *Conflict and Competition: Studies in the Recent Black Protest Movement* (1971); Kenneth B. Clark, ed., *The Negro Protest* (1963); John Hope Franklin and Isidore Starr, eds., *The Negro in Twentieth Century America: A Reader on the Struggle for Civil Rights* (1967); Charles W. Eagles, ed., *The Civil Rights Movement in America* (1986), and Michael V. Namorato, ed., *Have We Overcome?* (1979).

Organizations

Good examinations of the major organizations include Clayborne Carson's formidable study, *In Struggle: SNCC and the Black Awakening of the 1960s* (1981) as well as August Meier, and Elliot Rudwick, *CORE: A Study in the Civil Rights Movement, 1942–1968* (1973); Cleveland Sellers and Robert Terrell, *The River of No Return: The Autobiography of a Black Militant and the Life and Death of SNCC* (1973); Howard Zinn, *SNCC: The New Abolitionists* (1965); Inge Powell Bell, *CORE and the Strategy of Nonviolence* (1968); Langston Hughes, *Fight for Freedom: The Story of the NAACP* (1962); B. Joyce Ross, *J. E. Spingarn and the Rise of the N.A.A.C.P.* (1972); Adam Fairclough, *To Redeem the Soul of America: The Southern Christian Leadership Conference and Martin Luther King, Jr.* (1987).

Participant Narratives

There are numerous books from participants, which include some degree of intimate knowledge but lack the critical distance from the subject. See James Farmer, *Lay Bare the Heart: An Autobiography of the Civil Rights Movement* (1985); Andrew Young, *An Easy Burden: The Civil Rights Movement and the Transformation of America.* (1996); Martin Luther King, Jr.'s books: *Stride Toward Freedom: The*

Montgomery Story (1958), *Strength to Love* (1963), *Why We Can't Wait* (1964), *Where Do We Go From Here: Chaos or Community?* (1968), all provide insight into important elements of overarching ideas and philosophies as well as tactics in the movement. Several autobiographies are important additions to the body of work on the civil rights movement, including Cleveland Sellers, *River of No Return: The Autobiography of a Black Militant and the Life and Death of SNCC* (1973); Charles Evers, *Have No Fear, The Charles Evers Story* (1997); James Farmer, *Freedom—When?* (1965); James Peck, *Freedom Ride* (1962); Roy Wilkins, with Tom Matthews, *Standing Fast* (1982); James Meredith, *Three Years in Mississippi* (1966); Ann Moody, *Coming of Age in Mississippi* (1968). The following books give personal insight into the tumultuous Freedom Summer of 1964: Sally Belfrage, *Freedom Summer* (1965); Len Holt, *The Summer That Didn't End* (1968); Tracy Sugarman, *Stranger at the Gates* (1966). Also see Nicholas Von Hoffman, *Mississippi Notebook* (1964) and Elizabeth Sutherland, ed., *Letters from Mississippi* (1965).

Race and Society

Good theoretical discussions of the movement, race, and society include: James Baldwin, *The Fire Next Time* (1963); Lerone Bennett, Jr., *The Negro Mood* (1965); Debbie Lewis, *And We Are Not Saved: A History of the Movement as People* (1970); Lewis Lomax, *To Kill a Black Man* (1968); Angus Campbell, *White Attitudes Toward Black People* (1971); Peter Goldman, *Report from Black America* (1970); Joseph S. Himes, *Racial Conflict in American Society* (1973); and James W. Vandar Zanden, *Race Relations in Transition: The Segregation Crises within the South* (1965). Also see the two compilations of poll data by William Brink and Louis Harris, *The Negro Revolution in America* (1964) and *Black and White* (1967). The following books reflect the varying perspectives found in African American communities in the 1960s: Pat Watters, *Down To Now: Reflections on the Southern Civil Rights Movement* (1971); Gary Marx, *Protest and Prejudice: A Study of Belief in the Black Community* (rev. ed., 1969); Lerone Bennett, Jr., *Confrontation: Black and White* (1965). As Robert H. Brisbane demonstrates in *Black Activism: Racial Revolution in the United States, 1954–1970* (1974), black opinions were never static or monolithic. For perspectives on the opinions of white and black Americans, see Louis E. Lomax, *The Negro Revolt* (1962);

Edward Peeks, *The Long Struggle for Black Power* (1971); Samuel Lubell, *White and Black: Test of a Nation* (1964); Richard Lemon, *The Troubled Americans* (1970); W. Heywood Burns, *The Violence of Negro Protest in America* (1963). Good scholarly articles include James H. Laue, "Power, Conflict and Social Change," in Louis Masotti and Don Bowen, eds., *Riots and Rebellion: Civil Violence in the Urban Community* (1968); Kenneth B. Clark, "The Civil Rights Movement: Momentum and Organization," *Daedalus* XCV (Sinter 1966); James A. Geschwender, "Social Structure of the Negro Revolt: An Examination of Some Hypotheses," *Social Forces* XLIII (Dec. 1964).

Federal Government and Civil Rights

There is a relatively sizable body of scholarship on the role of the federal government in the civil rights movement. Several books study the role of the president in civil rights issues, including Mark Stern, *Calculating Visions: Kennedy, Johnson, and Civil Rights* (1992); James Duram, *Moderate Among Extremists: Dwight D. Eisenhower and the School Desegregation Crisis* (1981); Ruth P. Morgan, *The President and Civil Rights-Policy Making by Executive Order* (1970); Carl Brauer, *John F. Kennedy and the Second Revolution* (1977). For two of the most critical examinations of the shortcomings of the presidency see Allan Wolk, *The Presidency and Black Civil Rights: Eisenhower to Nixon* (1971) and Hugh Davis Graham, *Civil Rights and the Presidency: Race and Gender in American Politics, 1960–1972* (1992). See also Robert F. Burk, *The Eisenhower Administration and Black Civil Rights* (1984); Chester J. Pach, Jr. and Elmo Richardson, *The Presidency of Dwight D. Eisenhower* (1991); Vaughn Bornet, *The Presidency of Lyndon B. Johnson* (1983); Leon E. Panetta and Peter Gall, *Bring Us Together—The Nixon Team and Civil Rights Retreat* (1971).

For civil rights and the Supreme Court, there are many impressive studies. Richard Kluger's *Simple Justice: The History of Brown v. Board of Education: Black America's Struggle for Equality* (1976) is a superb work on the landmark decision of 1954. See also Robert V. Harris, *The Quest for Equality: The Constitution, Congress and the Supreme Court* (1960); Daniel M. Berman, *It Is So Ordered: The Supreme Court Rules on School Desegregation* (1966); Albert P. Blaustein and Clarence C. Ferguson, Jr., *Desegregation and the*

Law: The Meaning and Effect of the School Segregation Cases (1962); Jack Greenberg, *Race Relations and American Law* (1959). For a look at the role that recalcitrant congressmen played in stifling civil rights laws, see the somewhat dated J. Anderson, *Eisenhower, Brownell and the Congress: The Tangled Origins of the Civil Rights Bill of 1956–1957* (1964). Also consider Daniel M. Berman, *A Bill Becomes Law: The Civil Rights Commission: 1957–1965* (1968).

Documents

Important documents include work by Albert P. Blaustein and Robert L. Zangrando, eds., *Civil Rights and the American Negro: A Documentary History* (1968); Richard A. Bardolph, ed., *The Civil Rights Record: Black Americans and the Law, 1849–1970* (1970); Joanne Grant, ed., *Black Protest: History, Documents and Analyses, 1619 to the Present* (1968); August Meier, Elliott Rudwick, and Francis L. Broderick, eds., *Black Protest Thought in the Twentieth Century* (rev. ed., 1971); Lester A. Sobel, ed., *Civil Rights, 1960–66* (1967); Leon Friedman, ed., *The Civil Rights Reader: The Basic Documents of the Civil Rights Movement* (1967). There are also important government documents, including the controversial *The Negro Family: The Case for National Action* (1965) also known as the "Moynihan Report" by Daniel Patrick Moynihan which blames much of black America's woes on a black "matriarchy." See the *Report of the National Advisory Commission on Civil Disorders* (1968) on various race riots across the country.

Pre-Brown v. Board

For examinations of civil rights struggles before the *Brown v. Board of Education* case, see Herbert Garfinkel, *When Negroes March: The March on Washington Movement in the Organization's Politics for FEPC* (1959); Richard M. Dalfiume, *Desegregation of the U.S. Armed Forces* (1969); Richard T. Ruetten, *Quest and Response: Minority Rights and the Truman Administration* (1973). Gunnar Mrydal's *An American Dilemma: The Negro Social Structure* (rev. 1964) is a classic look at the structure of white supremacy and white and black opinions in the 1940s. Though limited to one city, another classic work of 1940s sociology is St. Claire Drake and Horace Cayton's *Black Metropolis: A Study of Negro Life in a Northern City* (1945). This book provides keen observations and analysis of 1940s urban black life in Chicago and provides many references to migration to and from the South as well as involvement in civil rights organizations.

Regional Studies

The number of studies of local civil rights efforts has been growing rapidly in recent years. One of the most significant studies on the movement and one of the best local studies is William H. Chafe's *Civilities and Civil Rights: Greensboro, North Carolina, and the Black Struggle for Freedom* (1980). The following are essential works in gaining a fuller view of the dynamic world of civil rights activities in Mississippi, a hotbed of violence and terror against black people: John Dittmer, *Local People: The Struggle for Civil Rights in Mississippi* (1995); Doug McAdam, *Freedom Summer* (1988); James Silver, *Mississippi: The Closed Society* (1964); Philip Dray, *We are Not Afraid: The Story of Goodman, Schwerner, and Chaney and the Civil Rights Campaign for Mississippi* (1988); Mary Aickin Rothschild, *A Case for Black and White: Northern Volunteers and the Southern Freedom Summer* (1982). For Alabama, see David J. Garrow, ed., *The Montgomery Bus Boycott and the Woman Who Started It: The Memoir of Jo Ann Gibson Robinson* (1987); Stuart Burns, *Daybreak of Freedom: The Montgomery Bus Boycott* (1997); Preston Valien, "The Montgomery Bus Protest as a Social Movement," in Jitsuichi Masuoka and Preston Valien, eds., *Race Relations: Problems and Theory* (1961); Glenn T. Eskew, *But for Birmingham: The Local and National Movements in the Civil Rights Struggle* (1997); David J. Garrow, *Protest at Selma* (1978).

For insight on the political landscape of Alabama and its segregationist governor, George Wallace, see Marshall Frady, *Wallace* (1970). Sheyanne Webb and Rachel West Nelson offer a local perspective in *Selma, Lord, Selma* (1980). For Birmingham, see Charles Morgan, Jr., *A Time to Speak* (1964); Bayard Rustin, "The Meaning of Birmingham," *Liberation* VIII (June 1963); Michael Dorman, *We Shall Overcome* (1964). Although not limited to the modern civil rights movement, Robin D. G. Kelley's *Hammer and Hoe: Alabama Communists During the Great Depression* (1990) is a brilliant book on the intersection of race and class struggle in Alabama in the years leading up to the civil rights movement. Adam Fairclough's *Race & Democracy: The Civil Rights Struggle in Louisiana, 1915–1972* (1999) is a very impressive examination of the roles of class and provincialism in civil rights politics at the state level. For Little Rock,

Arkansas see Virgil T. Blossom, *It Has Happened Here* (1959), Brook Hays, *A Southern Moderate Speaks* (1959), and Wilson and Jane C. Record, eds., *Little Rock U.S.A.: Materials and Analysis* (1960). See also Anthony J. Blasi, *Segregationist Violence and Civil Rights Movements in Tuscaloosa* (1980).

Biographies

There have been several very well done biographies and autobiographies completed about and by civil rights activists. (Also see "Participant Narratives" section above.) Martin Luther King, Jr. is the most examined movement figure. The most celebrated and thorough works about King's life are Taylor Branch's two-volume works: *Parting the Waters* (1988) and *Pillar of Fire* (1998) and David J. Garrow's *Bearing the Cross: Martin Luther King, Jr., and the Southern Christian Leadership Conference* (1986). Clayborne Carson's *The Autobiography of Martin Luther King, Jr.* (2001) incorporates King's own writing in this work published over thirty years after his death. See also David Lewis, *King: A Biography* (1978); Lawrence D. Reddick, Jr., *Crusader Without Violence* (1959); William Robert Miller, *Martin Luther King, Jr.* (1968); Lerone Bennett, Jr., *What Manner of Man* (1968); John J. Ansbro, *Martin Luther King, Jr., The Making of a Mind* (1982). See also August Meier's "On the Role of Martin Luther King," *New Politics* IV (Winter 1965). Ralph D. Abernathy's *And the Walls Came Tumbling Down: An Autobiography* (1989) evoked uproar when Abernathy chose to discuss some of the more intimate details of movement leaders' lives. Constance Baker Motley's *Equal Justice Under Law: An Autobiography* (1999) reveals the intriguing life of a major legal figure in the fight for civil rights and the first black woman appointed to the federal bench. Jervis Anderson studies Bayard Rustin, perhaps the most underrated figure of the civil rights movement, in *Bayard Rustin: Troubles I've Seen, a Biography* (1997). Anderson's earlier biography, *A. Philip Randolph: A Biographical Portrait* (1973), studies the life of the head of the NAACP during its most visible years. Joanne Grant's *Ella Baker: Freedom Bound* (1999) is a good, well-developed biography of one of the most important and overlooked figures in the civil rights movement. Grant's biography of Baker also provides insight into the protracted activities of activists in the decades before the Montgomery Bus Boycott. Chana Kai Lee provides a great biography of a major grassroots activist in *For Freedom's Sake: The Life of Fannie Lou Hamer* (2000). Another biography on Hamer, Kay Mills' *This Little Light of Mine: The Life of Fannie Lou Hamer* (1994) is also a solid study. Mary Stanton, in *From Selma to Sorrow: The Life and Death of Viola Liuzzo* (2000) explores the life of a white Detroit housewife who was murdered by Klansmen for her participation in voting rights work in Alabama. The book offers good analysis on the intersection of race and gender in the movement. See also Nancy J. Weiss, *Whitney M. Young, Jr. and the Struggle for Civil Rights* (1989); Eric Bruner, *And Gently He Shall Lead Them: Robert Purvis Moses and Civil Rights in Mississippi* (1994). Timothy Tyson's *Radio Free Dixie: Robert F. Williams and the Roots of Black Power* (1999) is a very impressive look at an icon of black radicals whose political beginnings were with the NAACP. An earlier biography on Williams is Robert Carl Cohen's *Black Crusader: A Biography of Robert Franklin Williams* (1972). Although not a civil rights activist, Malcolm X emerged as an important figure in the public debates surrounding civil rights. Some biographies and edited volumes include Bruce Perry's *Malcolm X: The Life of a Man Who Changed Black America* (1991); Jan Carew, ed. *Ghosts in Our Blood: With Malcolm X in Africa, England and the Caribbean* (1994); John H. Clarke, ed. *Malcolm X: The Man and His Times* (1969); Michael Eric Dyson, *Making Malcolm: The Myth and Meaning of Malcolm X* (1995). James Cone does a great job in contrasting the lives of Malcolm X and Martin L. King in *Martin and Malcolm and America: A Dream or a Nightmare* (1991), demonstrating the profound similarities shared between them as well as their strengths, foibles, and ideological shifts.

Northern Ghettoes and Black Power

For the ordeal of race relations in the North and West, see William Van Deburg, *New Day in Babylon* (1992), an examination of the Black Power movement and American popular culture. Also see Rod Bush, *We Are Not What We Seem* (1999); Nat Hentoff's *The New Equality* (1964); James R. Ralph, Jr., *Northern Protest: Martin Luther King, Jr., Chicago, and the Civil Rights Movement* (1993); Komozi Woodard, *A Nation Within a Nation* (1999) provides a good biography of Amiri Baraka, a leader of the black arts movement, while also giving a look into the larger social and political world of the late 1960s and early 1970s. See Gerald Horne, *The Fire*

This Time: The Watts Uprising and the 1960s (1995), a solid examination of the Watts Rebellion of 1965. Other books on urban unrest are James Button, *Black Violence: Political Impact of the 1960s Race Riots* (1978); Kenneth B. Clark, *Dark Ghetto: Dilemmas of Social Power* (1965); Joe Feagin and Harlan Hahn, *Ghetto Revolts* (1973), Harold Cruse, *Rebellion or Revolution* (1968). For a definitive biography of the most important architect of black nationalism in the U.S. see Claude Clegg, III, *An Original Man: The Life and Times of Elijah Muhammad* (1997). For examinations of black nationalism and Black Power, see Stokely Carmichael and Charles Hamilton, *Black Power: The Politics of Liberation in America* (1967). James Forman, *The Making of Black Revolutionaries* (1985) is a good first-hand observation of Black Power. The three most comprehensive works on the Nation of Islam are Mattias Gardell's generally overlooked *In the Name of Eijah Muhammad: Louis Farrakhan and the Nation of Islam* (1997); E. U. Essien-Udom's, *Black Nationalism* (1962); and an important early book, C. Eric Lincoln's, *Black Muslims in America* (1961). Surprisingly, there has yet to be a scholarly monograph on the Black Panther Party. The best work yet is an edited volume by Charles E. Jones, *The Black Panther Party Reconsidered* (1998). See also Bobby Seale, *Seize the Time* (1992); Huey Newton, *To Die for the People* (1972) and *Revolutionary Suicide* (1973); Hugh Pearson, *The Shadow of the Panther* (1994). Other works on black radicalism include Eugene Wolfenstein, *The Victims of Democracy: Malcolm X and the Black Revolutionaries* (1981); Lerone Bennett, Jr., *Confrontation: Black and White* (1965); Ward Churchill and Jim Vander Wall, *Agents of Repression* (1990); Eldridge Cleaver, *Soul on Ice* (1968); Theodore Draper, *The Rediscovery of Black Nationalism* (1970).

Women

There is no scholarly monograph on women in the modern civil rights movement; however, these is a growing body of work on the role of women in the movement. There are also several very strong biographies on women in the movement, as seen in the above section on biographies and autobiographies. A number of recent books give considerable attention to the role of gender in the movement. Lynne Olson's *Freedom's Daughters: The Unsung Heroines of the Civil Rights Movement from 1830 to 1970* (2001) is the first major monograph on women in civil rights activity, although Olson's focus extends over a hundred years before the modern civil rights movement. There are also good edited volumes, including *Women in the Civil Rights Movement: Trailblazers and Torchbearers, 1941–1965* (1990), edited by Vikki Crawford, Jacqueline Anne Rouse, and Barbara Woods; *Sisters in the Struggle: African-American Women in the Civil Rights-Black Power Movement* (2001), edited by Bettye Collier-Thomas. *Deep in Our Hearts: Nine White Women in the Freedom Movement* (2000), edited by Constance Curry and Debra L. Schultz's *Going South: Jewish Women in the Civil Rights Movement* (2001) are restricted in scope to white women; however, both books provide a thorough look at white women in the movement. For general histories that include substantive discussions of women in the civil rights movement see Paula Giddings, *When and Where I Enter: The Impact of Black Women on Race and Sex in America* (1984) and Deborah Gray White, *Too Heavy a Load: Black Women in Defense of Themselves, 1894–1994* (1999). Gerda Lerner, ed., in *Black Women in White America* (1992) provides a superb anthology on black women from slavery through the civil rights movement. See also Michele Wallace, *Black Macho and the Myth of the Superwoman* (1990), which discusses black male sexism and it's role in muting black feminism; Willi Coleman, "Black Women and Segregated Public Transportation: Ninety Years of Resistance," in *Black Women in United States History,* edited by Darlene Clark Hine, vol. 5 295–302 (1989); Dolores Janiewski, *Sisterhood Denied: Race, Gender and Class in a New South Community* (1985).

DATE DUE
